PATERSON

BY WILLIAM CARLOS WILLIAMS

Asphodel and Other Love Poems
The Autobiography of William Carlos Williams
The Build-up
The Collected Poems, Volume I
The Collected Poems, Volume II
The Collected Stories of William Carlos Williams
The Doctor Stories
The Embodiment of Knowledge
Imaginations
In the American Grain
In the Money
I Wanted to Write a Poem
Many Loves and Other Plays
Paterson
Pictures from Brueghel and Other Poems
Selected Essays
Selected Letters
Selected Poems
Something to Say: WCW on Younger Poets
A Voyage to Pagany
White Mule
The William Carlos Williams Reader
Yes, Mrs. Williams

William Carlos Williams on Garret Mountain with the city of Paterson behind him. *Photograph used courtesy of Magnum Photos, Inc.*

PATERSON

WILLIAM CARLOS WILLIAMS

Revised edition prepared by Christopher MacGowan

A NEW DIRECTIONS BOOK

Manufactured in the United States of America
New Directions books are printed on acid-free paper.
This revised edition first published clothbound in 1992; published as New Directions Paperbook 806 in 1995
Published simultaneously in Canada by Penguin Books Canada Limited

Acknowledgments can be found beginning p. 309. See additional acknowledgments, p. 311, for changes made with paperbook printing, 1995.

Library of Congress Cataloging-in-Publication Data

Williams, William Carlos, 1883–1963.
    Paterson / William Carlos Williams. —Rev. ed. / prepared by Christopher MacGowan.
        p.   cm.

    ISBN 978-0-8112-1298-4

    1. Paterson (N.J.)—Poetry.   I. MacGowan, Christopher J. (Christopher John) II. Title.
PS3545.I544P3   1992
811'.52—dc20   92–22956
                                                                CIP

New Directions Books are published for James Laughlin
by New Directions Publishing Corporation,
80 Eighth Avenue, New York 10011

TENTH PRINTING

Contents

Preface

This volume completes the new editions of William Carlos Williams' poetry begun with the *Collected Poems: Volume I*, 1909–1939 (1986), and *Collected Poems: Volume II*, 1939–1962 (1988).

When Williams' plans for *Paterson* began to take final shape in the early 1940s, he conceived of the poem as having four books, although he eventually published five, and in the last years of his life even started preliminary work on a sixth. The five books of *Paterson* were originally published in separate volumes, in limited editions, in 1946, 1948, 1949, 1951 and 1958, and as they sold out they were reprinted, starting with Books I and II in 1949, in the publisher's popularly priced New Classics series. For this reprint the text was entirely reset. Book III was added in 1950 and Book IV in 1951. The five books of *Paterson* were first published together, with the fragments of the sixth, in 1963, and this edition was itself rearranged with the fifth printing in 1969 for a reprint that reduced the total pagination by forty pages.

Throughout the printing history of the reprints, changes were made to various parts of the text, sometimes through error, sometimes apparently in response to directions by the poet, and in the case of the fifth book—for which the reprint appeared posthumously—in response to the large number of differences noticed between the poem's transcription of its prose sources and the language of those sources themselves, many of which had become available in research collections.

In preparing this edition I have studied the known manuscripts, galleys, and page proofs of the poem, as well as its various printings, and detail the general editorial procedures guiding my decisions in Appendix B, "A Note on the Text." I outline the principles governing the annotations at the head of Appendix C. I have provided information on the sources of the prose and some

of the other allusions in the poem, where these are known to me, and my in-
debtedness to earlier scholars and annotators of the poem is recorded in the
acknowledgments.

In general, I have avoided citing Williams' comments on particular
lines and passages in the poem since, unlike his observations on the shorter
poems, these remarks were numerous and many have been widely published
in interviews with the poet and in other sources. John Thirlwall, the assiduous
recorder of many of Williams' comments on his work in the 1950s, published
an extended essay on *Paterson* reproducing material from his meetings with
the poet, in *New Directions 17* (1961): 252–310. However, I have in-
cluded some of Williams' comments on his sources where these seemed par-
ticularly helpful, contributed to the background information on the poem's
composition, or had not previously, to my knowledge, been published. I have
included the introductory material on the poem that Williams published
with the first editions. In addition, at the conclusion of this Preface I repro-
duce some extended comments by the poet on Books I–IV, and some subse-
quent remarks he made concerning Book V.

My hope for the annotations and textual notes is that they illustrate the
relationship of the poem to its sources, provide a sense of the later stages of
the poem's evolution, and demonstrate the ways in which its text reflects the
intentions, the circumstances, and the mechanics of its composition. The reader
interested in the evolution of *Paterson* as recorded in the poems that Williams
published outside of his long poem needs to consult the *Collected* volumes. In
a number of his comments on *Paterson* Williams noted as some of its ante-
cedents his early poem "The Wanderer" (*Collected Poems: Volume I*, 27–
36 and 108–117), which contains a section on Paterson, and his 1927 prose/
poetry sequence "A Folded Skyscraper" (pp. 273–277). In 1927 Williams
published in *The Dial* an 85-line poem titled "Paterson" (pp. 263–266),
parts of which were subsequently reworked into the published Book I. In
the *New Directions 2* anthology of 1937 Williams published "Patterson
[*sic*]: Episode 17" (pp. 439–443), which contains many lines incorporated
into the finished Book III, and includes the oppressed but vital negro wom-
an, the gang rape, and the "beautiful thing" refrain that are three central
features of that book.

But much of Williams' work on *Paterson* in the late 1930s and early
1940s went into a concept of the poem that he eventually rejected, a long

series of short lyrics many of which were gathered into the manuscript "Detail & Parody for the poem Paterson" that Williams sent to his friend and publisher James Laughlin in March 1939. A version of this arrangement is now in the SUNY Buffalo collection (D4). During these years Williams published some of the poems arising from this conception of *Paterson* in magazines, and did not subsequently reprint some of them. These poems can be found among the first ninety-five pages of the *Collected Poems, Volume II*. In 1941 Williams published a fifteen-poem sequence titled "For the poem *Paterson*" in his pamphlet *The Broken Span* (see Volume II, pp. 14–22), but only the three lines serving as a headnote to the poems, beginning "A man like a city and a woman like a flower," appeared in *Paterson* as he finally conceived it.

Despite his struggles, Williams seems to have always felt close to the point of solving his formal difficulties. He told James Laughlin in 1942 that he would have the poem ready for the Spring 1943 list, but the book that he then did offer Laughlin was *The Wedge* (1944), which contains many poems pulled from the now-abandoned "Detail & Parody" concept. In April 1943 Williams published a short poem titled "Paterson: The Falls" (Volume II, 57–58), which outlined a work in "4 sections" and detailed a number of the central themes and features that subsequently appeared in the poem. But he wrote to Laughlin on December 27, 1943, "That God damned and I mean God damned poem *Paterson* has me down. I am burned up to do it but don't quite know how. I write and destroy, write and destroy. It's all shaped up in outline and intent, the body of the thinking is finished but the technique, the manner and the method are unresolvable to date. I flounder and flunk." In April 1944 he told Laughlin the poem was "near finished," and nine months later that it was "nearing completion." By May 1945 Book I was at the printer, but in September, on receiving the galleys, Williams was so dissatisfied he felt he must "slash it unmercifully . . . I wish I had the guts to say to burn the whole *Paterson* script." Book I, delayed by the extensive galley revisions, finally appeared the following June.

Even while working on Book IV Williams began to consider a fifth book, noting to himself on a typescript now filed at the Beinecke Library (Za 189) "maybe even a 5th Book of facts—Recollections." In October 1952, just over a year after the publication of Book IV, he published a twenty-four-line poem "Paterson, Book V: The River of Heaven," but reported to Laughlin in 1954 that the poem had "got side-tracked. It turned into something else"—that "something else" being his well-known poem "Asphodel, That Greeny Flower." *Paterson V* eventually appeared in 1958, on Williams' seventy-fifth birthday. Writing to Laughlin within the week to thank him for the publication party, Williams hinted at a possible *Paterson VI*, but the increasing handicaps produced by his periodic strokes left the four sheets Williams typed out in late 1960 and early 1961 as all there was to be of a sixth book.

With the fourth (1968) and subsequent printings of the collected *Paterson* New Directions printed the first three pages of Chapter 58 from Williams' *Autobiography* by way of an introduction to the first four books of the poem. The interested reader will find in that chapter a helpful supplement to the comments by Williams following this Preface. I reproduce below a statement by the poet from a New Directions press release marking the publication of Book IV in June 1951 that appeared two weeks before the publication date. Following the statement is the "Author's Note" that introduced the poem in all the New Classics and subsequent printings of the collected *Paterson*. (For the substantially similar version that appeared with Book I in 1946 see page 253.) Williams' comment on Book V that follows the "Author's Note" is part of a letter he wrote to Robert MacGregor, vice-president of New Directions, on May 16, 1958 (New Directions archives), that was reprinted on the dust jacket of the first, 1958, edition of Book V. A shorter version was printed when Book V was reset and joined the collected *Paterson* in 1963. I reprint the version on the dust jacket of the first edition.

C. M.

A STATEMENT BY WILLIAM CARLOS WILLIAMS
ABOUT THE POEM PATERSON

May 31, 1951

I have no recollection when it was that I first began thinking of writing a long poem upon the resemblance between the mind of modern man and a city. From something Vivienne Koch discovered among my notes it may be that 1925 was the year when I first made any record of the notion. Certainly by 1927 when I was given *The Dial*'s award following their publication of the poem "Paterson" my thoughts on the general theme I wanted to treat were well along.

Having decided what I wanted to do I took my time deciding how I should go about the task. The thing was to use the multiple facets which a city presented as representatives for comparable facets of contemporary thought thus to be able to objectify the man himself as we know him and love him and hate him. This seemed to me to be what a poem was for, to speak for us in a language we can understand. But first before we can understand it the language must be recognizable. We must know it as our own, we must be satisfied that it speaks for us. And yet it must remain a language like all languages, a symbol of communication.

Thus the city I wanted as my object had to be one that I knew in its most intimate details. New York was too big, too much a congeries of the entire world's facets. I wanted something nearer home, something knowable. I deliberately selected Paterson as my reality. My own suburb was not distinguished or varied enough for my purpose. There were other possibilities but Paterson topped them.

Paterson has a definite history associated with the beginnings of the United States. It has besides a central feature, the Passaic Falls which as I began to think about it became more and more the lucky burden of what I wanted to say. I began to read all I could about the history of the Falls, the park on the little hill beyond it and the early inhabitants. From the beginning I decided there would be four books following the course of the river whose life seemed more and more to resemble my own life as I more and more thought of it: the river above the Falls, the catastrophe of the Falls itself, the river below the Falls and the entrance at the end into the great sea.

There were a hundred modifications of this general plan as, following the theme rather than the river itself, I allowed myself to be drawn on. The noise of the Falls seemed to me to be a language which we were and are seeking and my search, as I looked about, became to struggle to interpret and use this language. This is the substance of the poem. But the poem is also the search of the poet for his language, his own language which I, quite apart from the material theme had to use to write at all. I had to write in a certain way to gain a verisimilitude with the object I had in mind.

So the objective became complex. It fascinated me, it instructed me besides. I had to think and write, I had to invent the means to get said, in the pattern of the terms I employed, what appeared as called for. And I had to think hard as to how I was going to end the poem. It wouldn't do to have a grand and soul satisfying conclusion because I didn't see any in my subject. Nor was I going to be confused or depressed or evangelical about it. It didn't belong to the subject. It would have been easy to make a great smash up with a 'beautiful' sunset at sea, or a flight of pigeons, love's end and the welter of man's fate.

Instead, after the little girl gets herself mixed up at last in the pathetic sophisticate of the great city, no less defeated and understandable, even lovable, than she is herself, we come to the sea at last. Odysseus swims in as man must always do, he doesn't drown, he is too able but, accompanied by his dog, strikes inland again (toward Camden) to begin again.

------------------◆•◆------------------

AUTHOR'S NOTE

Paterson is a long poem in four parts—that a man in himself is a city, beginning, seeking, achieving and concluding his life in ways which the various aspects of a city may embody—if imaginatively conceived—any city, all the details of which may be made to voice his most intimate convictions. Part One introduces the elemental character of the place. The Second Part comprises the modern replicas. Three will seek a language to make them vocal, and Four, the river below the falls, will be reminiscent of episodes—all that any one man may achieve in a lifetime.

In a letter to New Directions, Dr. Williams, now 75, commented on the making of *Paterson, Five,* as follows: "Were I younger, needless to say, it would have been a different poem. But then it would not have been written at all. After *Paterson, Four* ten years have elapsed. In that period I have come to understand not only that many changes have occurred in me and the world, but I have been forced to recognize that there can be no end to such a story I have envisioned with the terms which I had laid down for myself. I had to take the world of Paterson into a new dimension if I wanted to give it imaginative validity. Yet I wanted to keep it whole, as it is to me. As I mulled the thing over in my mind the composition began to assume a form which you see in the present poem, keeping, I fondly hope, a unity directly continuous with the Paterson of *Pat.* 1 to 4. Let's hope I have succeeded in doing so."

BOOK ONE

(1 9 4 6)

: a local pride; spring, summer, fall and the sea; a confession; a basket; a column; a reply to Greek and Latin with the bare hands; a gathering up; a celebration;

in distinctive terms; by multiplication a reduction to one; daring; a fall; the clouds resolved into a sandy sluice; an enforced pause;

hard put to it; an identification and a plan for action to supplant a plan for action; a taking up of slack; a dispersal and a metamorphosis.

Paterson: Book I

―――――――●◦●――――――

PREFACE

"Rigor of beauty is the quest. But how will you find beauty when
it is locked in the mind past all remonstrance?"

>   To make a start,
>   out of particulars
>   and make them general, rolling
>   up the sum, by defective means—
>   Sniffing the trees,
>   just another dog
>   among a lot of dogs. What
>   else is there? And to do?
>   The rest have run out—
>   after the rabbits.
>   Only the lame stands—on
>   three legs. Scratch front and back.
>   Deceive and eat. Dig
>   a musty bone
>
>   For the beginning is assuredly
>   the end—since we know nothing, pure
>   and simple, beyond
>   our own complexities.

Yet there is
no return: rolling up out of chaos,
a nine months' wonder, the city
the man, an identity—it can't be
otherwise—an
interpenetration, both ways. Rolling
up! obverse, reverse;
the drunk the sober; the illustrious
the gross; one. In ignorance
a certain knowledge and knowledge,
undispersed, its own undoing.

                        (The multiple seed,
packed tight with detail, soured,
is lost in the flux and the mind,
distracted, floats off in the same
scum)

Rolling up, rolling up heavy with
numbers.

                        It is the ignorant sun
rising in the slot of
hollow suns risen, so that never in this
world will a man live well in his body
save dying—and not know himself
dying; yet that is
the design. Renews himself
thereby, in addition and subtraction,
walking up and down.

                and the craft,
subverted by thought, rolling up, let
him beware lest he turn to no more than
the writing of stale poems . . .

[4]

Minds like beds always made up,
                    (more stony than a shore)
unwilling or unable.

                    Rolling in, top up,
under, thrust and recoil, a great clatter:
lifted as air, boated, multicolored, a
wash of seas —
from mathematics to particulars—

                    divided as the dew,
floating mists, to be rained down and
regathered into a river that flows
and encircles:

                    shells and animalcules
generally and so to man,

                    to Paterson.

The Delineaments of the Giants

I.

Paterson lies in the valley under the Passaic Falls
its spent waters forming the outline of his back. He
lies on his right side, head near the thunder
of the waters filling his dreams! Eternally asleep,
his dreams walk about the city where he persists
incognito. Butterflies settle on his stone ear.
Immortal he neither moves nor rouses and is seldom
seen, though he breathes and the subtleties of his
                    machinations
drawing their substance from the noise of the pouring
                    river
animate a thousand automatons. Who because they
neither know their sources nor the sills of their
disappointments walk outside their bodies aimlessly
                    for the most part,
locked and forgot in their desires—unroused.

        —Say it, no ideas but in things—
        nothing but the blank faces of the houses
        and cylindrical trees

bent, forked by preconception and accident—
split, furrowed, creased, mottled, stained—
secret—into the body of the light!

From above, higher than the spires, higher
even than the office towers, from oozy fields
abandoned to grey beds of dead grass,
black sumac, withered weed-stalks,
mud and thickets cluttered with dead leaves—
the river comes pouring in above the city
and crashes from the edge of the gorge
in a recoil of spray and rainbow mists—

     (What common language to unravel?
      . . combed into straight lines
     from that rafter of a rock's
     lip.)

A man like a city and a woman like a flower
—who are in love. Two women. Three women.
Innumerable women, each like a flower.

                                  But

only one man—like a city.

    In regard to the poems I left with you; will you be so kind as to return them to me at my new address? And without bothering to comment upon them if you should find that embarrassing—for it was the human situation and not the literary one that motivated my phone call and visit.
    Besides, I know myself to be more the woman than the poet; and to concern myself less with the publishers of poetry than with . . . living . . .
    But they set up an investigation . . . and my doors are bolted forever (I hope forever) against all public welfare workers, professional do-gooders and the like.

       Jostled as are the waters approaching
       the brink, his thoughts
       interlace, repel and cut under,

[7]

rise rock-thwarted and turn aside
but forever strain forward—or strike
an eddy and whirl, marked by a
leaf or curdy spume, seeming
to forget   .

Retake later the advance and
are replaced by succeeding hordes
pushing forward—they coalesce now
glass-smooth with their swiftness,
quiet or seem to quiet as at the close
they leap to the conclusion and
fall, fall in air! as if
floating, relieved of their weight,
split apart, ribbons; dazed, drunk
with the catastrophe of the descent
floating unsupported
to hit the rocks: to a thunder,
as if lightning had struck

All lightness lost, weight regained in
the repulse, a fury of
escape driving them to rebound
upon those coming after—
keeping nevertheless to the stream, they
retake their course, the air full
of the tumult and of spray
connotative of the equal air, coeval,
filling the void

And there, against him, stretches the low mountain.
The Park's her head, carved, above the Falls, by the quiet
river; Colored crystals the secret of those rocks;
farms and ponds, laurel and the temperate wild cactus,
yellow flowered   .   .   facing him, his
arm supporting her, by the *Valley of the Rocks*, asleep.

[8]

Pearls at her ankles, her monstrous hair
spangled with apple-blossoms is scattered about into
the back country, waking their dreams—where the deer run
and the wood-duck nests protecting his gallant plumage.

In February 1857, David Hower, a poor shoemaker with a large family, out
of work and money, collected a lot of mussels from Notch Brook near the City
of Paterson. He found in eating them many hard substances. At first he threw
them away but at last submitted some of them to a jeweler who gave him twenty-five
to thirty dollars for the lot. Later he found others. One pearl of fine lustre was
sold to Tiffany for $900 and later to the Empress Eugenie for $2,000 to be
known thenceforth as the "Queen Pearl," the finest of its sort in the world today.

News of this sale created such excitement that search for the pearls was started
throughout the country. The Unios (mussels) at Notch Brook and elsewhere were
gathered by the millions and destroyed often with little or no result. A large round
pearl, weighing 400 grains which would have been the finest pearl of modern
times, was ruined by boiling open the shell.

Twice a month Paterson receives
communications from the Pope and Jacques
        Barzun
(Isocrates). His works
have been done into French
and Portuguese. And clerks in the post-
office ungum rare stamps from
his packages and steal them for their
childrens' albums   .

Say it! No ideas but in things. Mr.
Paterson has gone away
to rest and write. Inside the bus one sees
his thoughts sitting and standing. His
thoughts alight and scatter—

Who are these people (how complex
the mathematic) among whom I see myself
in the regularly ordered plateglass of
his thoughts, glimmering before shoes and bicycles?

[9]

They walk incommunicado, the
equation is beyond solution, yet
its sense is clear—that they may live
his thought is listed in the Telephone
Directory—

And derivatively, for the Great Falls,
PISS-AGH! the giant lets fly! good *Muncie*, too

They craved the miraculous!

A gentleman of the Revolutionary Army, after describing the Falls, thus de-
scribes another natural curiosity then existing in the community: In the afternoon
we were invited to visit another curiosity in the neighborhood. This is a monster
in human form, he is twenty-seven years of age, his face from the upper part of his
forehead to the end of his chin, measures *twenty-seven inches*, and around the
upper part of his head is twenty-one inches: his eyes and nose are remarkably large
and prominent, chin long and pointed. His features are coarse, irregular and dis-
gusting, his voice rough and sonorous. His body is twenty-seven inches in length,
his limbs are small and much deformed, and he has the use of one hand only. He
has never been able to sit up, as he cannot support the enormous weight of his head;
but he is constantly in a large cradle, with his head supported on pillows. He is
visited by great numbers of people, and is peculiarly fond of the company of clergy-
men, always inquiring for them among his visitors, and taking great pleasure in
receiving religious instruction. General Washington made him a visit, and asked
"whether he was a Whig or a Tory." He replied that he had never taken an *active*
part on either side.

A wonder! A wonder!

From the ten houses Hamilton saw when he looked (at the falls!) and kept his
counsel, by the middle of the century—the mills had drawn a heterogeneous popu-
lation. There were in 1870, native born 20,711, which would of course include
children of foreign parents; foreign 12,868 of whom 237 were French, 1,420
German, 3,343 English—(Mr. Lambert who later built the Castle among them),
5,124 Irish, 879 Scotch, 1,360 Hollanders and 170 Swiss—

Around the falling waters the Furies hurl!
Violence gathers, spins in their heads summoning
them:

The twaalft, or striped bass was also abundant, and even sturgeon, of a huge bigness, were frequently caught:— On Sunday, August 31, 1817, one seven feet six inches long, and weighing 126 pounds, was captured a short distance below the Falls basin. He was pelted with stones by boys until he was exhausted, whereupon one of them, John Winters, waded into the water and clambered on the back of the huge fish, while another seized him by the throat and gills, and brought him ashore. The *Bergen Express and Paterson Advertiser* of Wednesday, September 3, 1817, devoted half a column to an account of the incident, under the heading, "The Monster Taken."

They begin!
The perfections are sharpened
The flower spreads its colored petals
wide in the sun
But the tongue of the bee
misses them
They sink back into the loam
crying out
—you may call it a cry
that creeps over them, a shiver
as they wilt and disappear:
Marriage come to have a shuddering
implication

Crying out
or take a lesser satisfaction:
a few go
to the Coast without gain—
The language is missing them
they die also
incommunicado.

The language, the language
fails them
They do not know the words
or have not
the courage to use them   .

                        —girls from
        families that have decayed and
        taken to the hills: no words.
        They may look at the torrent in
                        their minds
        and it is foreign to them.   .

        They turn their backs
        and grow faint—but recover!
                        Life is sweet
        they say: the language!
                        —the language
        is divorced from their minds,
        the language   .   .   the language!

If there was not beauty, there was a strangeness and a bold association of wild
and cultured life grew up together in the Ramapos: two phases.

In the hills, where the brown trout slithered among the shallow stones, Ring-
wood—where the old Ryerson farm had been—among its velvet lawns, was ringed
with forest trees, the butternut, and the elm, the white oak, the chestnut and the
beech, the birches, the tupelo, the sweet-gum, the wild cherry and the hackleberry
with its red tumbling fruit.

While in the forest clustered the ironworkers' cabins, the charcoal burners, the
lime kiln workers—hidden from lovely Ringwood—where General Washington,
gracing any poem, up from Pompton for rest after the traitors' hangings could be
at ease—and the links were made for the great chain across the Hudson at West
Point.

Violence broke out in Tennessee, a massacre by the Indians, hangings and exile—
standing there on the scaffold waiting, sixty of them. The Tuscaroras, forced to
leave their country, were invited by the Six Nations to join them in Upper New
York. The bucks went on ahead but some of the women and the stragglers got no
further than the valley-cleft near Suffern. They took to the mountains there where
they were joined by Hessian deserters from the British Army, a number of albinos
among them, escaped negro slaves and a lot of women and their brats released in
New York City after the British had been forced to leave. They had them in a
pen there—picked up in Liverpool and elsewhere by a man named Jackson under
contract with the British Government to provide women for the soldiers in America.

The mixture ran in the woods and took the general name, Jackson's Whites.
(There had been some blacks also, mixed in, some West Indian negresses, a ship-
load, to replace the whites lost when their ship, one of six coming from England,
had foundered in a storm at sea. He had to make it up somehow and that was the
quickest and cheapest way.)

New Barbadoes Neck, the region was called.

Cromwell, in the middle of the seventeenth century, shipped some thousands of Irish women and children to the Barbadoes to be sold as slaves. Forced by their owners to mate with the others these unfortunates were succeeded by a few generations of Irish-speaking negroes and mulattos. And it is commonly asserted to this day the natives of Barbadoes speak with an Irish brogue.

I remember
a *Geographic* picture, the 9 women
of some African chief semi-naked
astraddle a log, an official log to
be presumed, heads left:

Foremost
froze the young and latest,
erect, a proud queen, conscious of her power,
mud-caked, her monumental hair
slanted above the brows—violently frowning.

Behind her, packed tight up
in a descending scale of freshness
stiffened the others

and then   .   .
the last, the first wife,
present! supporting all the rest growing
up from her—whose careworn eyes
serious, menacing—but unabashed; breasts
sagging from hard use   .   .

Whereas the uppointed breasts
of that other, tense, charged with
pressures unrelieved   .
and the rekindling they bespoke
was evident.

[13]

　　　　　Not that the lightnings
do not stab at the mystery of a man
from both ends—and the middle, no matter
how much a chief he may be, rather the more
because of it, to destroy him at home　.

　　.　　.　　Womanlike, a vague smile,
unattached, floating like a pigeon
after a long flight to his cote.

Mrs. Sarah Cumming, consort of the Rev. Hooper Cumming, of Newark, was
a daughter of the late Mr. John Emmons, of Portland, in the district of Maine. . . .
She had been married about two months, and was blessed with a flattering prospect
of no common share of Temporal felicity and usefulness in the sphere which
Providence had assigned her; but oh, how uncertain is the continuance of every
earthly joy.

On Saturday, the 20th of June, 1812, the Rev. Cumming rode with his wife
to Paterson, in order to supply, by presbyterial appointment, a destitute congre-
gation in that place, on the following day. . . . On Monday morning, he went with
his beloved companion to show her the falls of the Passaic, and the surrounding
beautiful, wild and romantic scenery,—little expecting the solemn event to ensue.

Having ascended the flight of stairs (the Hundred Steps) Mr. and Mrs. Cum-
ming walked over the solid ledge to the vicinity of the cataract, charmed with the
wonderful prospect, and making various remarks upon the stupendous works of
nature around them. At length they took their station on the brow of the solid
rock, which overhangs the basin, six or eight rods from the falling water, where
thousands have stood before, and where there is a fine view of the sublime curiosities
of the place. When they had enjoyed the luxury of the scene for a considerable
length of time, Mr. Cumming said, "My dear, I believe it is time for us to set our
face homeward"; and at the same moment, turned round in order to lead the way.
He instantly heard the voice of distress, looked back and his wife was gone!

Mr. Cumming's sensations on the distressing occasion may, in some measure, be
conceived, but they cannot be described. He was on the borders of distraction,
and, scarcely knowing what he did, would have plunged into the abyss, had it not
been kindly ordered in providence that a young man should be near, who instantly
flew to him, like a guardian angel, and held him from a step which his reason, at
the time, could not have prevented. This young man led him from the precipice,
and conducted him to the ground below the stairs. Mr. Cumming forced himself
out of the hands of his protector, and ran with violence, in order to leap into the
fatal flood. His young friend, however, caught him once more. . . . Immediate
search was made, and diligently continued throughout the day, for the body of
Mrs. Cumming; but to no purpose. On the following morning, her mortal part was
found in a depth of 42 feet, and, the same day, was conveyed to Newark.

A false language. A true. A false language pouring—a
language (misunderstood) pouring (misinterpreted) without
dignity, without minister, crashing upon a stone ear. At least
it settled it for her. Patch too, as a matter of fact. He
became a national hero in '28, '29 and toured the country
diving from cliffs and masts, rocks and bridges—to prove his
thesis: Some things can be done as well as others.

THE GRRRREAT HISTORY of that

old time Jersey Patriot

N. F. PATERSON!

(N for Noah; F for Faitoute; P for short)

"Jersey Lightning" to the boys.

So far everything had gone smoothly. The pulley and ropes were securely
fastened on each side of the chasm, and everything made in readiness to pull the
clumsy bridge into position. It was a wooden structure boarded up on both sides,
and a roof. It was about two o'clock in the afternoon and a large crowd had
gathered—a large crowd for that time, as the town only numbered about four
thousand—to watch the bridge placed in position.

That day was a great day for old Paterson. It being Saturday, the mills were
shut down, so to give the people a chance to celebrate. Among those who came in
for a good part of the celebration was Sam Patch, then a resident in Paterson, who
was a boss over cotton spinners in one of the mills. He was my boss, and many a
time he gave me a cuff over the ears.

Well, this day the constables were on the look for Patch, because they thought
he would be on a spree and cause trouble. Patch had declared so frequently that
he would jump from the rocks that he was placed under arrest at various times.
He had previously been locked up in the basement under the bank with a bad case
of delirium tremens, but on the day the bridge was pulled across the chasm he was
let out. Some thought he was crazy. They were not far wrong.

But the happiest man in the town that day was Timothy B. Crane, who had
charge of the bridge. Tim Crane was a hotel keeper and kept a tavern on the Man-
chester side of the Falls. His place was a great resort for circus men. Such famous
circus men of the long ago as Dan Rice and James Cooke, the great bareback rider,
visited him.

Tim Crane built the bridge because his rival, Fyfield, who kept the tavern on the other side of the falls, was getting the benefit of the "Jacob's Ladder," as it was sometimes called—the "hundred steps," a long, rustic, winding stairs in the gorge leading to the opposite side of the river—it making his place more easy to get to. . . . Crane was a very robust man over six feet tall. He wore side whiskers. He was well known to the other citizens as a man of much energy and no little ability. In his manner he resembled the large, rugged stature of Sam Patch.

When the word was given to haul the bridge across the chasm, the crowd rent the air with cheers. But they had only pulled it half way over when one of the rolling pins slid from the ropes into the water below.

While all were expecting to see the big, clumsy bridge topple over and land in the chasm, as quick as a flash a form leaped out from the highest point and struck with a splash in the dark water below, swam to the wooden pin and brought it ashore. This was the starting point of Sam Patch's career as a famous jumper. I saw that, said the old man with satisfaction, and I don't believe there is another person in the town today who was an eye-witness of that scene. These were the words that Sam Patch said: "Now, old Tim Crane thinks he has done something great; but I can beat him." As he spoke he jumped.

There's no mistake in Sam Patch!

The water pouring still
from the edge of the rocks, filling
his ears with its sound, hard to interpret.
A wonder!

After this start he toured the West, his only companions a fox and a bear which he picked up in his travels.

He jumped from a rocky ledge at Goat Island into the Niagara River. Then he announced that before returning to the Jerseys he was going to show the West one final marvel. He would leap 125 feet from the falls of the Genesee River on November 13, 1829. Excursions came from great distances in the United States and even from Canada to see the wonder.

A platform was built at the edge of the falls. He went to great trouble to ascertain the depth of the water below. He even successfully performed one practice leap.

On the day the crowds were gathered on all sides. He appeared and made a short speech as he was wont to do. A speech! What could he say that he must leap so desperately to complete it? And plunged toward the stream below. But instead of descending with a plummet-like fall his body wavered in the air— Speech had failed him. He was confused. The word had been drained of its meaning. There's no mistake in Sam Patch. He struck the water on his side and disappeared.

A great silence followed as the crowd stood spellbound.

Not until the following spring was the body found frozen in an ice-cake.

He threw his pet bear once from the cliff overlooking the Niagara rapids and rescued it after, down stream.

II.

There is no direction. Whither? I
cannot say. I cannot say
more than how. The how (the howl) only
is at my disposal (proposal) : watching—
colder than stone   .

                    a bud forever green,
tight-curled, upon the pavement, perfect
in juice and substance but divorced, divorced
from its fellows, fallen low—

                        Divorce is
the sign of knowledge in our time,
divorce! divorce!

                 with the roar of the river
forever in our ears (arrears)
inducing sleep and silence, the roar
of eternal sleep   .   .   challenging
our waking—

—unfledged desire, irresponsible, green,
colder to the hand than stone,
unready—challenging our waking:

Two halfgrown girls hailing hallowed Easter,
(an inversion of all out-of-doors) weaving

about themselves, from under
the heavy air, whorls of thick translucencies
poured down, cleaving them away,
shut from the light: bare-
headed, their clear hair dangling—

Two—
          disparate among the pouring
waters of their hair in which nothing is
molten—

two, bound by an instinct to be the same:
ribbons, cut from a piece,
cerise pink, binding their hair: one—
a willow twig pulled from a low
leafless bush in full bud in her hand,
(or eels or a moon!)
holds it, the gathered spray,
upright in the air, the pouring air,
strokes the soft fur—

          Ain't they beautiful!

     Certainly I am not a robin nor erudite,
     no Erasmus nor bird that returns to the same
     ground year by year. Or if I am .   .
     the ground has undergone
     a subtle transformation, its identity altered.

     Indians!

     Why even speak of "I," he dreams, which
     interests me almost not at all?

                    The theme
     is as it may prove: asleep, unrecognized—

all of a piece, alone
in a wind that does not move the others—
in that way: a way to spend
a Sunday afternoon while the green bush shakes.

.   .   a mass of detail
to interrelate on a new ground, difficultly;
an assonance, a homologue
                              triple piled
pulling the disparate together to clarify
and compress

The river, curling, full—as a bush shakes
and a white crane will fly
and settle later! White, in
the shallows among the blue-flowered
pickerel-weed, in summer, summer! if it should
ever come, in the shallow water!

                    On the embankment a short,
compact cone (juniper)
that trembles frantically
in the indifferent gale: male—stands
rooted there   .

The thought returns: Why have I not
but for imagined beauty where there is none
or none available, long since
put myself deliberately in the way of death?

                    Stale as a whale's breath: breath!
Breath!

Patch leaped but Mrs. Cumming shrieked
and fell—unseen (though
she had been standing there beside her husband half
an hour or more twenty feet from the edge).

: a body found next spring
frozen in an ice-cake; or a body
fished next day from the muddy swirl—

both silent, uncommunicative

Only of late, late! begun to know, to
know clearly (as through clear ice) whence
I draw my breath or how to employ it
clearly—if not well:

                    Clearly!
speaks the red-breast his behest. Clearly!
clearly!

—and watch, wrapt! one branch
of the tree at the fall's edge, one
mottled branch, withheld,
among the gyrate branches
of the waist-thick sycamore,
sway less, among the rest, separate, slowly
with giraffish awkwardness, slightly
on a long axis, so slightly
as hardly to be noticed, in itself the tempest:

Thus

the first wife, with giraffish awkwardness
among thick lightnings that stab at
the mystery of a man: in sum, a sleep, a
source, a scourge   .

on a log, her varnished hair
trussed up like a termite's nest (forming
the lines) and, her old thighs
gripping the log reverently, that,
all of a piece, holds up the others—
alert: begin to know the mottled branch
that sings   .

                certainly NOT the university,
a green bud fallen upon the pavement its
sweet breath suppressed: Divorce (the
language stutters)

                        unfledged:

two sisters from whose open mouths
Easter is born—crying aloud,

                        Divorce!

                                    While
the green bush sways: is whence
I draw my breath, swaying, all of a piece,
separate, livens briefly, for the moment
unafraid   .   .

        Which is to say, though it be poorly
        said, there is a first wife
        and a first beauty, complex, ovate—
        the woody sepals standing back under
        the stress to hold it there, innate

a flower within a flower whose history
(within the mind) crouching
among the ferny rocks, laughs at the names
by which they think to trap it. Escapes!
Never by running but by lying still—

A history that has, by its den in the
rocks, bole and fangs, its own cane-brake
whence, half hid, canes and stripes
blending, it grins (beauty defied)
not for the sake of the encyclopedia.

Were we near enough its stinking breath
would fell us. The temple upon
the rock is its brother, whose majesty
lies in jungles—made to spring,
at the rifle-shot of learning: to kill

and grind those bones:

These terrible things they reflect:
the snow falling into the water,
part upon the rock, part in the dry weeds
and part into the water where it
vanishes—its form no longer what it was:

the bird alighting, that pushes
its feet forward to take up the impetus
and falls forward nevertheless
among the twigs. The weak-necked daisy
bending to the wind   .   .   .

                                    The sun
winding the yellow bindweed about a
bush; worms and gnats, life under a stone.

The pitiful snake with its mosaic skin
and frantic tongue. The horse, the bull
the whole din of fracturing thought
as it falls tinnily to nothing upon the streets
and the absurd dignity of a locomotive
hauling freight—

              Pithy philosophies of
daily exits and entrances, with books
propping up one end of the shaky table—
The vague accuracies of events dancing two
and two with language which they
forever surpass—and dawns
tangled in darkness—

      The giant in whose apertures we
      cohabit, unaware of what air supports
      us—the vague, the particular
      no less vague

              his thoughts, the stream
      and we, we two, isolated in the stream,
      we also: three alike—

            we sit and talk
      I wish to be with you abed, we two
      as if the bed were the bed of a stream
      —I have much to say to you

            We sit and talk,
      quietly, with long lapses of silence
      and I am aware of the stream
      that has no language, coursing
      beneath the quiet heaven of
      your eyes

which has no speech; to
go to bed with you, to pass beyond
the moment of meeting, while the
currents float still in mid-air, to
fall—
with you from the brink, before
the crash—

to seize the moment.

We sit and talk, sensing a little
the rushing impact of the giants'
violent torrent rolling over us, a
few moments.

If I should demand it, as
it has been demanded of others
and given too swiftly, and you should
consent. If you would consent

We sit and talk and the
silence speaks of the giants
who have died in the past and have
returned to those scenes unsatisfied
and who is not unsatisfied, the
silent, Singac the rock-shoulder
emerging from the rocks—and the giants
live again in your silence and
unacknowledged desire—

And the air lying over the water
lifts the ripples, brother
to brother, touching as the mind touches,
counter-current, upstream

[24]

brings in the fields, hot and cold
parallel but never mingling, one that whirls
backward at the brink and curls invisibly
upward, fills the hollow, whirling,
an accompaniment—but apart, observant of
the distress, sweeps down or up clearing
the spray—

           brings in the rumors of separate
worlds, the birds as against the fish, the grape
to the green weed that streams out undulant
with the current at low tide beside the
bramble in blossom, the storm by the flood—
song and wings—

           one unlike the other, twin
of the other, conversant with eccentricities
side by side, bearing the water-drops
and snow, vergent, the water soothing the air when
it drives in among the rocks fitfully—

While at 10,000 feet, coming in over
the sombre mountains of Haiti, the land-locked
bay back of Port au Prince, blue vitreol
streaked with paler streams, shabby as loose
hair, badly dyed—like chemical waste
mixed in, eating out the shores . .

He pointed it down and struck the rough
waters of the bay, hard; but lifted it again and
coming down gradually, hit again hard but
remained down to taxi to the pier where
they were waiting—

(Thence Carlos had fled in the 70's
leaving the portraits of my grandparents,
the furniture, the silver, even the meal
hot upon the table before the Revolutionists
coming in at the far end of the street.)

I was over to see my mother today. My sister, "Billy," was at the schoolhouse.
I never go when she is there. My mother had a sour stomach, yesterday. I found
her in bed. However, she had helped "Billy" do up the work. My mother has
always tried to do her part, and she is always trying to do something for her
children. A few days before I left I found her starting to mend my trousers. I
took them away from her and said, "Mother, you can't do that for me, with your
crippled head. You know, I always get Louisa or Mrs. Tony to do that work for
me." "Billy" looked up and said, "It's too bad about you."

I have already told you I helped with the work, did dishes, three times daily,
swept and mopped floors, porches and cleaned yards, mowed the lawn, tarred the
roofs, did repair work and helped wash, brought in the groceries and carried out
the pots and washed them each morning, even "Billy's" with dung in it, some-
times, and did other jobs and then it was not uncommon for "Billy" to say: "You
don't do anything here." Once she even said, "I saw you out there the other morn-
ing sweeping porches, pretending you were doing something."

Of course, "Billy" has been chopped on by the surgical chopper and has gone
through the menopause and she had a stroke of facial paralysis, but she has always
been eccentric and wanted to boss. My Hartford sister said she used to run over
her until she became big enough to throsh her. I have seen her slap her husband
square in the face. I would have knocked her so far she would not have got back
in a week. She has run at me with a poker, etc., but I always told her not to strike,
"Don't make that mistake," I would always caution.

"Billy" is a good worker and thorough going but she wants to lay blame—
always on the other fellow. I told my buddie, in Hartford, she was just like our
landlady, THE PISTOL. He said he had a sister just like that.

As to my mother, she is obsessed with fire. That's why she doesn't want me to
stay there, alone, when she is dead. The children have all said for years, she thinks
more of me than any child she has.

T.

They fail, they limp with corns. I
think he means to kill me, I don't know
what to do. He comes in after midnight,
I pretend to be asleep. He stands there,
I feel him looking down at me, I
am afraid!

        Who? Who? Who? What?
A summer evening?

A quart of potatoes, half a dozen oranges,
a bunch of beets and some soup greens.
Look, I have a new set of teeth. Why you
look ten years younger   .

But never, in despair and anxiety,
forget to drive wit in, in till it discover
his thoughts, decorous and simple,
and never forget that though his thoughts
are decorous and simple, the despair
and anxiety: the grace and detail of
a dynamo—

So in his high decorum he is wise.

A delirium of solutions, forthwith, forces
him into back streets, to begin again:
up hollow stairs among acrid smells
to obscene rendezvous. And there he finds
a festering sweetness of red lollipops—
and a yelping dog:
Come YEAH, Chichi! Or a great belly
that no longer laughs but mourns
with its expressionless black navel love's
deceit   .   .

They are the divisions and imbalances
of his whole concept, made weak by pity,
flouting desire; they are—No ideas but
in the facts   .   .

I positively feel no rancour against you, but will urge you toward those vapory ends, and implore you to submit to your own myths, and that any postponement in doing so is a lie for you. Delay makes us villainous and cheap: All that I can say of myself and of others is that it matters not so much how a man lies or fornicates or even loves money, provided that he has not a Pontius Pilate but an hungered Lazarus in his intestines. Once Plotinus asked, "What is philosophy?" and he replied, "What is most important." The late Miguel de Unamuno also cried out, not "More light, more light!" as Goethe did when he was dying, but "More warmth, more warmth!" I hate more than anything else the mocking stone bowels of Pilate; I abhor that more than cozening and falsehoods and the little asps of malice that are on all carnal tongues. That is why I am attacking you, as you put it, not because I think you cheat or lie for pelf, but because you lie and chafe and gull whenever you see a jot of the torn Galilean in a man's intestines. You hate it; it makes you writhe; that's why all the Americans so dote upon that canaille word, extrovert. Of course, nature in you knows better as some very lovely passages that you have written show.

But to conclude, you and I can do without each other, in the usual way of the sloughy habits and manners of people. I can continue with my monologue of life and death until inevitable annihilation. But it's wrong. And as I have said, whatever snares I make for myself, I won't weep over Poe, or Rilke, or Dickinson, or Gogol, while I turn away the few waifs and Ishmaels of the spirit in this country. I have said that the artist is an Ishmael; Call me Ishmael, says Melville in the very first line of Moby Dick; he is the wild ass of a man;—Ishmael means affliction. You see, I am always concerned with the present when I read the plaintive epitaphs in the American graveyard of literature and poetry, and in weighing the head and the heart that ached in the land, that you are not. With you the book is one thing, and the man who wrote it another. The conception of time in literature and in chronicles makes it easy for men to make such hoax cleavages. But I am getting garrulous:—

E. D.

III.

How strange you are, you idiot!
So you think because the rose
is red that you shall have the mastery?
The rose is green and will bloom,
overtopping you, green, livid
green when you shall no more speak, or
taste, or even be. My whole life
has hung too long upon a partial victory.

But, creature of the weather, I
don't want to go any faster than
I have to go to win.
                              Music it for yourself.

He picked a hairpin from the floor
and stuck it in his ear, probing
around inside—

The melting snow
dripped from the cornice by his window
90 strokes a minute—

He descried
in the linoleum at his feet a woman's
face, smelled his hands,

strong of a lotion he had used
not long since, lavender,
rolled his thumb

about the tip of his left index finger
and watched it dip each time,
like the head

of a cat licking its paw, heard the
faint filing sound it made: of
earth his ears are full, there is no sound

: And his thoughts soared
to the magnificence of imagined delights
where he would probe

as into the pupil of an eye
as through a hoople of fire, and emerge
sheathed in a robe

streaming with light. What heroic
dawn of desire
is denied to his thoughts?

They are trees
from whose leaves streaming with rain
his mind drinks of desire :

Who is younger than I?
   The contemptible twig?
that I was? stale in mind
   whom the dirt

[30]

recently gave up? Weak
    to the wind.
Gracile? Taking up no place,
too narrow to be engraved
    with the maps

of a world it never knew,
    the green and
dovegrey countries of
    the mind.

A mere stick that has
    twenty leaves
against my convolutions.
    What shall it become,

Snot nose, that I have
    not been?
I enclose it and
    persist, go on.

Let it rot, at my center.
    Whose center?
I stand and surpass
    youth's leanness.

My surface is myself.
    Under which
to witness, youth is
    buried. Roots?

Everybody has roots.

We go on living, we permit ourselves
to continue—but certainly
not for the university, what they publish

[31]

severally or as a group: clerks
got out of hand forgetting for the most part
to whom they are beholden.

spitted on fixed concepts like
roasting hogs, sputtering, their drip sizzling
in the fire

Something else, something else the same.

He was more concerned, much more concerned with detaching the label from
a discarded mayonnaise jar, the glass jar in which some patient had brought a
specimen for examination, than to examine and treat the twenty and more infants
taking their turn from the outer office, their mothers tormented and jabbering.
He'd stand in the alcove pretending to wash, the jar at the bottom of the sink
well out of sight and, as the rod of water came down, work with his fingernail in
the splash at the edge of the colored label striving to loose the tightly glued paper.
It must have been varnished over, he argued, to have it stick that way. One corner
of it he'd got loose in spite of all and would get the rest presently: talking pleasantly
the while and with great skill to the anxious parent.

Will you give me a baby? asked the young colored woman
in a small voice standing naked by the bed. Refused
she shrank within herself. She too refused. It makes me
too nervous, she said, and pulled the covers round her.

Instead, this:

In time of general privation
a private herd, 20 quarts of milk
to the main house and 8 of cream,
all the fresh vegetables, sweet corn,
a swimming pool, (empty!) a building

covering an acre kept heated
winter long (to conserve the plumbing)
Grapes in April, orchids
like weeds, uncut, at tropic
heat while the snow flies, left
to droop on the stem, not even
exhibited at the city show. To every
employee from the top down
the same in proportion—as many as
there are: butter daily by
the pound lot, fresh greens—even to
the gate-keeper. A special French maid,
her sole duty to groom
the pet Pomeranians—who sleep.

Cornelius Doremus, who was baptized at Acquackanonk in 1714, and died near
Montville in 1803, was possessed of goods and chattels appraised at $419.58½.
He was 89 years old when he died, and doubtless had turned his farm over to his
children, so that he retained only what he needed for his personal comfort:
24 shirts at .82½ cents, $19.88: 5 sheets, $7.00: 4 pillow cases, $2.12: 4 pair
trousers, $2.00: 1 sheet, $1.37½: a handkerchief, $1.75: 8 caps, .75 cents: 2 pairs
shoebuckles and knife, .25 cents: 14 pairs stockings, $5.25: 2 pairs "Mittins" .63
cents: 1 linen jacket, .50 cents: 4 pairs breeches, $2.63: 4 waist coats, $3.50:
5 coats, $4.75: 1 yellow coat, $5.00: 2 hats, .25 cents: 1 pair shoes, .12½ cents:
1 chest, .75 cents: 1 large chair, $1.50: 1 chest, .12½ cents: 1 pair andirons, $2.00:
1 bed and bedding, $18.00: 2 pocketbooks, .37½ cents: 1 small trunk, .19½ cents:
castor hat, .87½ cents: 3 reeds, $1.66: 1 "Quill wheal," .50 cents.

Who restricts knowledge? Some say
it is the decay of the middle class
making an impossible moat between the high
and the low where
the life once flourished   .   .   knowledge
of the avenues of information—

So that we do not know (in time)
where the stasis lodges. And if it is not
the knowledgeable idiots, the university,
they at least are the non-purveyors
should be devising means
to leap the gap. Inlets? The outward
masks of the special interests
that perpetuate the stasis and make it
profitable.

They block the release
that should cleanse and assume
prerogatives as a private recompense.
Others are also at fault because
they do nothing.

By nightfall of the 29th, acres of mud were exposed and the water mostly had
been drawn off. The fish did not run into the nets. But a black crowd of people
could be seen from the cars, standing about under the willows, watching the men
and boys on the drained lake bottom . . . some hundred yards in front of the dam.

The whole bottom was covered with people, and the big eels, weighing from
three to four pounds each, would approach the edge and then the boys would strike
at them. From this time everybody got all they wanted in a few moments.

On the morning of the 30th, the boys and men were still there. There seemed
to be no end to the stock of eels especially. All through the year fine messes of fish
have been taken from the lake; but nobody dreamt of the quantity that were living
in it. Singularly to say not a snake had been seen. The fish and eels seemed to have
monopolized the lake entirely. Boys in bathing had often reported the bottom as
full of big snakes that had touched their feet and limbs but they were without
doubt the eels.

Those who prepared the nets were not the ones who got the most fish. It was
the hoodlums and men who leaped into the mud and water where the nets could
not work that rescued from the mud and water the finest load of fish.

A man going to the depot with a peach basket gave the basket to a boy and he
filled it in five minutes, deftly snapping the vertebrae back of the heads to make
them stay in, and he charged the modest sum of .25 cents for the basket full of
eels. The crowd increased. There were millions of fish. Wagons were sent for to
carry away the heaps that lined both sides of the roadway. Little boys were dragging
behind them all they could carry home, strung on sticks and in bags and baskets.
There were heaps of catfish all along the walk, bunches of suckers and pike, and
there were three black bass on one stick, a silk weaver had caught them. At a quarter

past seven a wagon body was filled with fish and eels . . . four wagon loads had been carried away.

At least fifty men in the lake were hard at work and had sticks with which they struck the big eels and benumbed them as they glided along the top of the mud in shoal water, and so were able to hold them until they could carry them out: the men and boys splashed about in the mud. . . . Night did not put an end to the scene. All night long with lights on shore and lanterns over the mud, the work went on.

<blockquote>

Moveless
he envies the men that ran
and could run off
toward the peripheries—
to other centers, direct —
for clarity (if
they found it)
           loveliness and
authority in the world—

a sort of springtime
toward which their minds aspired
but which he saw,
within himself—ice bound

and leaped, "the body, not until
the following spring, frozen in
an ice cake"
</blockquote>

Shortly before two o'clock August 16, 1875, Mr. Leonard Sandford, of the firm of Post and Sandford, while at work on the improvements for the water company, at the Falls, was looking into the chasm near the wheel house of the water works. He saw what looked like a mass of clothing, and on peering intently at times as the torrent sank and rose, he could distinctly see the legs of a man, the body being lodged between two logs, in a very extraordinary manner. It was in the "crotch" of these logs that the body was caught.

The sight of a human body hanging over the precipice was indeed one which was as novel as it was awful in appearance. The news of its finding attracted a very large number of visitors all that day.

[35]

What more, to carry the thing through?

Half the river red, half steaming purple
from the factory vents, spewed out hot,
swirling, bubbling. The dead bank,
shining mud   .

What can he think else—along
the gravel of the ravished park, torn by
the wild workers' children tearing up the grass,
kicking, screaming? A chemistry, corollary
to academic misuse, which the theorem
with accuracy, accurately misses   .   .

He thinks: their mouths eating and kissing,
spitting and sucking, speaking; a
partitype of five   .

He thinks: two eyes; nothing escapes them,
neither the convolutions of the sexual orchid
hedged by fern and honey-smells, to
the last hair of the consent of the dying.

And silk spins from the hot drums to a music
of pathetic souvenirs, a comb and nail-file
in an imitation leather case—to
remind him, to remind him! and
a photograph-holder with pictures of himself
between the two children, all returned
weeping, weeping—in the back room
of the widow who married again, a vile tongue
but laborious ways, driving a drunken
husband   .   .

What do I care for the flies, shit with them.
I'm out of the house all day.

Into the sewer they threw the dead horse.
What birth does this foretell? I think
he'll write a novel bye and bye   .

P.   Your interest is in the bloody loam but what
     I'm after is the finished product.

I.   Leadership passes into empire; empire begets in-
      solence; insolence brings ruin.

Such is the mystery of his one two, one two.
And so among the rest he drives
in his new car out to the suburbs, out
by the rhubarb farm—a simple thought—
where the convent of the Little Sisters of
St. Ann pretends a mystery

                              What
irritation of offensively red brick is this,
red as poor-man's flesh? Anachronistic?
                              The mystery
of streets and back rooms—
wiping the nose on sleeves, come here
to dream   .   .

Tenement windows, sharp edged, in which
no face is seen—though curtainless, into
which no more than birds and insects look or
the moon stares, concerning which they dare
look back, by times.

[37]

It is the complement exact of vulgar streets,
a mathematic calm, controlled, the architecture
mete, sinks there, lifts here   .
the same blank and staring eyes.

                                        An incredible
clumsiness of address,
senseless rapes—caught on hands and knees
scrubbing a greasy corridor; the blood
boiling as though in a vat, where they soak—

Plaster saints, glass jewels
and those apt paper flowers, bafflingly
complex—have here
their forthright beauty, beside:

Things, things unmentionable,
the sink with the waste farina in it and
lumps of rancid meat, milk-bottle-tops: have
here a tranquility and loveliness
Have here (in his thoughts)
a complement tranquil and chaste.

            He shifts his change:

   "The 7th December, this year, (1737) at night, was a large shock of an earth-
quake, accompanied with a remarkable rumbling noise; people waked in their beds,
the doors flew open, bricks fell from the chimneys; the consternation was serious,
but happily no great damage ensued."

                  Thought clambers up,
      snail like, upon the wet rocks
      hidden from sun and sight—

         hedged in by the pouring torrent—
and has its birth and death there
in that moist chamber, shut from
the world—and unknown to the world,
cloaks itself in mystery—

               And the myth
that holds up the rock,
that holds up the water thrives there—
in that cavern, that profound cleft,
             a flickering green
inspiring terror, watching   .   .

And standing, shrouded there, in that din,
Earth, the chatterer, father of all
speech   .   .   .   .

N.B. "In order apparently to bring the meter still more within the sphere of prose and common speech, Hipponax ended his iambics with a spondee or a trochee instead of an iambus, doing thus the utmost violence to the rhythmical structure. These deformed and mutilated verses were called χωλίαμβοι or ἴαμβοι σκάζοντες (lame or limping iambics). They communicated a curious crustiness to the style. The choliambi are in poetry what the dwarf or cripple is in human nature. Here again, by their acceptance of this halting meter, the Greeks displayed their acute aesthetic sense of propriety, recognizing the harmony which subsists between crabbed verses and the distorted subjects with which they dealt—the vices and perversions of humanity—as well as their agreement with the snarling spirit of the satirist. Deformed verse was suited to deformed morality."

—*Studies of the Greek Poets*, John Addington Symonds
Vol. I, p. 284

BOOK TWO

(1948)

Sunday in the Park

I.

Outside

                outside myself

                              there is a world,

he rumbled, subject to my incursions
—a world

                (to me) at rest,

                        which I approach

concretely—

               The scene's the Park
               upon the rock,
               female to the city

—upon whose body Paterson instructs his thoughts
(concretely)

                  —late spring,
              a Sunday afternoon!

—and goes by the footpath to the cliff (counting:
the proof)

[43]

                    himself among the others,
—treads there the same stones
on which their feet slip as they climb,
paced by their dogs!

laughing, calling to each other—

                        Wait for me!

.   .   the ugly legs of the young girls,
pistons too powerful for delicacy!   .
the men's arms, red, used to heat and cold,
to toss quartered beeves and   .

                        Yah! Yah! Yah! Yah!

—over-riding
                    the risks:
                            pouring down!
For the flower of a day!

Arrived breathless, after a hard climb he,
looks back (beautiful but expensive!) to
the pearl-grey towers! Re-turns
and starts, possessive, through the trees,

                        —   that love,
that is not, is not in those terms
to which I'm still the positive
in spite of all;
the ground dry, — passive-possessive

Walking   —

            Thickets gather about groups of squat sand-pine,
            all but from bare rock   .   .

                        [44]

—a scattering of man-high cedars (sharp cones),
antlered sumac   .

—roots, for the most part, writhing
upon the surface
                    (so close are we to ruin every
day!)
            searching the punk-dry rot

Walking —

The body is tilted slightly forward from the basic standing
position and the weight thrown on the ball of the foot,
while the other thigh is lifted and the leg and opposite
arm are swung forward (fig. 6B). Various muscles, aided   .

Despite my having said that I'd never write to you again, I do so now because I
find, with the passing of time, that the outcome of my failure with you has been
the complete damming up of all my creative capacities in a particularly disastrous
manner such as I have never before experienced.

For a great many weeks now (whenever I've tried to write poetry) every thought
I've had, even every feeling, has been struck off some surface crust of myself
which began gathering when I first sensed that you were ignoring the real contents
of my last letters to you, and which finally congealed into some impenetrable sub-
stance when you asked me to quit corresponding with you altogether without even
an explanation.

That kind of blockage, exiling one's self from one's self—have you ever ex-
perienced it? I dare say you have, at moments; and if so, you can well understand
what a serious psychological injury it amounts to when turned into a permanent
day-to-day condition.

How do I love you? These!

(He hears! Voices   . indeterminate! Sees them
moving, in groups, by twos and fours — filtering
off by way of the many bypaths.)

[45]

I asked him, What do you do?

*He smiled patiently, The typical American question.
In Europe they would ask, What are you doing? Or,
What are you doing now?*

*What do I do? I listen, to the water falling. (No
sound of it here but with the wind!) This is my entire
occupation.*

No fairer day ever dawned anywhere than May 2, 1880, when the German
Singing Societies of Paterson met on Garret Mountain, as they did many years
before on the first Sunday in May.

However the meeting of 1880 proved a fatal day, when William Dalzell, who
owned a piece of property near the scene of the festivities, shot John Joseph Van
Houten. Dalzell claimed that the visitors had in previous years walked over his
garden and was determined that this year he would stop them from crossing any
part of his grounds.

Immediately after the shot the quiet group of singers was turned into an in-
furiated mob who would take Dalzell into their own hands. The mob then
proceeded to burn the barn into which Dalzell had retreated from the angry group.

Dalzell fired at the approaching mob from a window in the barn and one of
the bullets struck a little girl in the cheek. . . . Some of the Paterson Police rushed
Dalzell out of the barn [to] the house of John Ferguson some half furlong away.

The crowd now numbered some ten thousand,
                              "a great beast!"
                                                for many had come from the city to join the con-
flict. The case looked serious, for the Police were greatly outnumbered. The crowd
then tried to burn the Ferguson house and Dalzell went to the house of John
McGuckin. While in this house it was that Sergeant John McBride suggested
that it might be well to send for William McNulty, Dean of Saint Joseph's Catholic
Church.

In a moment the Dean set on a plan. He proceeded to the scene in a hack.
Taking Dalzell by the arm, in full view of the infuriated mob, he led the man
to the hack and seating himself by his side, ordered the driver to proceed. The
crowd hesitated, bewildered between the bravery of the Dean and   .

> Signs everywhere of birds nesting, while
> in the air, slow, a crow zigzags
> with heavy wings before the wasp-thrusts
> of smaller birds circling about him
> that dive from above stabbing for his eyes

[46]

Walking —

       he leaves the path, finds hard going
       across-field, stubble and matted brambles
       seeming a pasture—but no pasture   .
       —old furrows, to say labor sweated or
       had sweated here   .

                                         a flame,
     spent.

             The file-sharp grass   .

       When! from before his feet, half tripping,
       picking a way, there starts   .
                   a flight of empurpled wings!
       —invisibly created (their
       jackets dust-grey) from the dust kindled
       to sudden ardor!

               They fly away, churring! until
       their strength spent they plunge
       to the coarse cover again and disappear
       —but leave, livening the mind, a flashing
       of wings and a churring song   .

       AND a grasshopper of red basalt, boot-long,
       tumbles from the core of his mind,
       a rubble-bank disintegrating beneath a
       tropic downpour

       Chapultepec! grasshopper hill!

       —a matt stone solicitously instructed
       to bear away some rumor
       of the living presence that has preceded
       it, out-precedented its breath   .

[47]

These wings do not unfold for flight—
no need!
the weight (to the hand) finding
a counter-weight or counter buoyancy
by the mind's wings

He is afraid! What then?

Before his feet, at each step, the flight
is renewed. A burst of wings, a quick
churring sound   :

       couriers to the ceremonial of love!

—aflame in flight!
       —aflame only in flight!

          No flesh but the caress!

He is led forward by their announcing wings.

If that situation with you (your ignoring those particular letters and then your
final note) had belonged to the inevitable lacrimae rerum (as did, for instance, my
experience with Z.) its result could not have been (as it *has* been) to destroy the
validity for me myself *of* myself, because in that case nothing to do with my sense
of personal identity would have been maimed—the cause of one's frustrations in
such instances being not *in* one's self nor in the other person but merely in the
sorry scheme of things. But since your ignoring those letters was not "natural" in
that sense (or rather since to regard it as unnatural I am forced, psychologically, to
feel that what I wrote you about, was sufficiently trivial and unimportant and
absurd to merit your evasion) it could not but follow that that whole side of life
connected with those letters should in consequence take on for my own self that
same kind of unreality and inaccessibility which the inner lives of other people
often have for us.

      —his mind a red stone carved to be
      endless flight
      Love that is a stone endlessly in flight,

so long as stone shall last bearing
the chisel's stroke

.   .   and is lost and covered
with ash, falls from an undermined bank
and — begins churring!
AND DOES, the stone after the life!

The stone lives, the flesh dies
—we know nothing of death.

—boot long
window-eyes that front the whole head,
Red stone! as if
a light still clung in them   .

Love

combating sleep
_____

the sleep
piecemeal

Shortly after midnight, August 20, 1878, special officer Goodridge, when in front of the Franklin House, heard a strange squealing noise down towards Ellison Street. Running to see what was the matter, he found a cat at bay under the water table at Clark's hardware store on the corner, confronting a strange black animal too small to be a cat and entirely too large for a rat. The officer ran up to the spot and the animal got in under the grating of the cellar window, from which it frequently poked its head with a lightning rapidity. Mr. Goodridge made several strikes at it with his club but was unable to hit it. Then officer Keyes came along and as soon as he saw it, he said it was a mink, which confirmed the theory that Mr. Goodridge had already formed. Both tried for a while to hit it with their clubs but were unable to do so, when finally officer Goodridge drew his pistol and fired a shot at the animal. The shot evidently missed its mark, but the noise and powder so frightened the little joker that it jumped out into the street, and made down into Ellison Street at a wonderful gait, closely followed by the two officers. The mink finally disappeared down a cellar window under the grocery store below Spangermacher's lager beer saloon, and that was the last seen of it. The cellar was examined again in the morning, but nothing further could be discovered of the little critter that had caused so much fun.

Without invention nothing is well spaced,
unless the mind change, unless
the stars are new measured, according
to their relative positions, the
line will not change, the necessity
will not matriculate: unless there is
a new mind there cannot be a new
line, the old will go on
repeating itself with recurring
deadliness: without invention
nothing lies under the witch-hazel
bush, the alder does not grow from among
the hummocks margining the all
but spent channel of the old swale,
the small foot-prints
of the mice under the overhanging
tufts of the bunch-grass will not
appear: without invention the line
will never again take on its ancient
divisions when the word, a supple word,
lived in it, crumbled now to chalk.

Under the bush they lie protected
from the offending sun—
11 o'clock
                    They seem to talk

—a park, devoted to pleasure : devoted to   .   grasshoppers!

3 colored girls, of age! stroll by
—their color flagrant,
                    their voices vagrant
their laughter wild, flagellant, dissociated
from the fixed scene   .

[50]

But the white girl, her head
upon an arm, a butt between her fingers
lies under the bush   .   .

Semi-naked, facing her, a sunshade
over his eyes,
he talks with her

—the jalopy half hid
behind them in the trees—
I bought a new bathing suit, just

pants and a brassiere   :
the breasts and
the pudenda covered—beneath

the sun in frank vulgarity.
Minds beaten thin
by waste—among

the working classes SOME sort
of breakdown
has occurred. Semi-roused

they lie upon their blanket
face to face,
mottled by the shadows of the leaves

upon them, unannoyed,
at least here unchallenged.
Not undignified.   .   .

talking, flagrant beyond all talk
in perfect domesticity—
And having bathed

and having eaten (a few
sandwiches)
their pitiful thoughts do meet

in the flesh—surrounded
by churring loves! Gay wings
to bear them (in sleep)

—their thoughts alight,
away
    .   .   among the grass

Walking —

across the old swale—a dry wave in the ground
tho' marked still by the line of Indian alders

   .   .   they (the Indians) would weave
in and out, unseen, among them along the stream

   .   come out whooping between the log
house and men working the field, cut them
off! they having left their arms in the block-
house, and—without defense—carry them away
into captivity. One old man   .

Forget it! for God's sake, Cut
out that stuff   .

Walking —

he rejoins the path and sees, on a treeless
knoll—the red path choking it—
a stone wall, a sort of circular
redoubt against the sky, barren and
unoccupied. Mount. Why not?

                                      A chipmunk,
              with tail erect, scampers among the stones.

              (Thus the mind grows, up flinty pinnacles)

              .   but as he leans, in his stride,
              at sight of a flint arrow-head
                                      (it is not)
                                                —there
              in the distance, to the north, appear
              to him the chronic hills   .

                              Well, so they are.

                                      He stops short:
              Who's here?

                      To a stone bench, to which she's leashed,
              within the wall a man in tweeds—a pipe hooked in his jaw—is
              combing out a new-washed Collie bitch. The deliberate comb-
              strokes part the long hair—even her face he combs though her
              legs tremble slightly—until it lies, as he designs, like ripples in
              white sand giving off its clean-dog odor. The floor, stone slabs,
              she stands patiently before his caresses in that bare "sea chamber"

                      .   to the right
              from this vantage, the observation tower
              in the middle distance stands up prominently
              from its pubic grove

Dear B.   Please excuse me for not having told you this when I was over to your
house. I had no courage to answer your questions so I'll write it. Your dog *is* going
to have puppies although I prayed she would be okey. It wasn't that she was left
alone as she never was but I used to let her out at dinner time while I hung up my
clothes. At the time, it was on a Thursday, my mother-in-law had some sheets and
table cloths out on the end of the line. I figured the dogs wouldn't come as long
as I was there and none came thru my yard or near the apartment. He must have

                              [53]

come between your hedge and the house. *Every few* seconds I would run to the end of the line or peek under the sheets to see if Musty was alright. She was until I looked a minute too late. I took sticks and stones after the dog but he wouldn't beat it. George gave me plenty of hell and I started praying that I had frightened the other dog so much that nothing had happened. I know you'll be cursing like a son-of-a-gun and probably won't ever speak to me again for not having told you. Don't think I haven't been worrying about Musty. She's occupied my mind every day since that awful event. You won't think so highly of me now and feel like protecting me. Instead I'll bet you could kill . . .

> And still the picnickers come on, now
> early afternoon, and scatter through the
> trees over the fenced-in acres   .

>   Voices!
> multiple and inarticulate   .   voices
> clattering loudly to the sun, to
> the clouds. Voices!
> assaulting the air gaily from all sides.

> —among which the ear strains to catch
> the movement of one voice among the rest
> —a reed-like voice
>   of peculiar accent

> Thus she finds what peace there is, reclines,
> before his approach, stroked
> by their clambering feet—for pleasure

>   It is all for
> pleasure   .   their feet   .   aimlessly
>   wandering

> The "great beast" come to sun himself
>   as he may
> .   ·   .   their dreams mingling,
> aloof

Let us be reasonable!

                              Sunday in the park,
limited by the escarpment, eastward; to
the west abutting on the old road: recreation
with a view! the binoculars chained
to anchored stanchions along the east wall—
              beyond which, a hawk

                                        soars!

—a trumpet sounds fitfully.

Stand at the rampart (use a metronome
if your ear is deficient, one made in Hungary
if you prefer)
and look away north by east where the church
spires still spend their wits against
the sky   .   to the ball-park
in the hollow with its minute figures running
—beyond the gap where the river
plunges into the narrow gorge, unseen

—and the imagination soars, as a voice
beckons, a thundrous voice, endless
—as sleep: the voice
that has ineluctably called them—
                            that unmoving roar!
churches and factories
                        (at a price)
together, summoned them from the pit   .

—his voice, one among many (unheard)
moving under all.

                    The mountain quivers.

[55]

Time!   Count!   Sever and mark time!

So during the early afternoon, from place
to place he moves,
his voice mingling with other voices
—the voice in his voice
opening his old throat, blowing out his lips,
kindling his mind (more
than his mind will kindle)

                    —following the hikers.

At last he comes to the idlers' favorite
haunts, the picturesque summit, where
the blue-stone (rust-red where exposed)
has been faulted at various levels
                    (ferns rife among the stones)
into rough terraces and partly closed in
dens of sweet grass, the ground gently sloping.

Loiterers in groups straggle
over the bare rock-table—scratched by their
boot-nails more than the glacier scratched
them—walking indifferent through
each other's privacy   .

                    —in any case,
the center of movement, the core of gaiety.

Here a young man, perhaps sixteen,
is sitting with his back to the rock among
some ferns playing a guitar, dead pan   .

The rest are eating and drinking.

                    The big guy
in the black hat is too full to move   .

                              but Mary
is up!
              Come on! Wassa ma'? You got
broken leg?

              It is this air!
                        the air of the Midi
and the old cultures intoxicates them:
present!

              —lifts one arm holding the cymbals
of her thoughts, cocks her old head
and dances! raising her skirts:

                        La la la la!

What a bunch of bums! Afraid somebody see
you?
              Blah!
                   Excrementi!
                        —she spits.
Look a' me, Grandma! Everybody too damn
lazy.

This is the old, the very old, old upon old,
the undying: even to the minute gestures,
the hand holding the cup, the wine
spilling, the arm stained by it:

                              Remember

              the peon in the lost
              Eisenstein film drinking

              from a wine-skin with the abandon
              of a horse drinking

so that it slopped down his chin?
down his neck, dribbling

over his shirt-front and down
onto his pants—laughing, toothless?

                Heavenly man!

—the leg raised, verisimilitude   .
even to the coarse contours of the leg, the
bovine touch! The leer, the cave of it,
the female of it facing the male, the satyr—
    (Priapus!)
with that lonely implication, goatherd
and goat, fertility, the attack, drunk,
cleansed   .

            Rejected. Even the film
suppressed : but   .   persistent

The picnickers laugh on the rocks celebrating
the varied Sunday of their loves with
its declining light —

Walking —

    look down (from a ledge) into this grassy
den
       (somewhat removed from the traffic)
                 above whose brows
a moon! where she lies sweating at his side:

          She stirs, distraught,
against him—wounded (drunk), moves
against him (a lump) desiring,
against him, bored   .

[58]

flagrantly bored and sleeping, a
beer bottle still grasped spear-like
in his hand   .

while the small, sleepless boys, who
have climbed the columnar rocks
overhanging the pair (where they lie
overt upon the grass, besieged—

careless in their narrow cell under
the crowd's feet) stare down,
                              from history!
at them, puzzled and in the sexless
light (of childhood) bored equally,
go charging off   .

                    There where
the movement throbs openly
and you can hear the Evangelist shouting!

                    —moving nearer
         she—lean as a goat—leans
         her lean belly to the man's backside
         toying with the clips of his
         suspenders   .

—to which he adds his useless voice:
until there moves in his sleep
a music that is whole, unequivocal (in
his sleep, sweating in his sleep—laboring
against sleep, agasp!)
                    —and does not waken.

Sees, alive (asleep)
         —the fall's roar entering

his sleep (to be fulfilled)

        reborn
in his sleep—scattered over the mountain
severally   .

   —by which he woos her, severally.

And the amnesic crowd (the scattered),
called about — strains
to catch the movement of one voice   .

        hears,
   Pleasure! Pleasure!

         —feels,
half dismayed, the afternoon of complex
voices its own—
     and is relieved
      (relived)

   A cop is directing traffic
   across the main road up
   a little wooded slope toward
   the conveniences:

      oaks, choke-cherry,
dogwoods, white and green, iron-wood :
humped roots matted into the shallow soil
—mostly gone: rock out-croppings
polished by the feet of the picnickers:
sweetbarked sassafras   .

leaning from the rancid grease:
       deformity—

—to be deciphered (a horn, a trumpet!)
an elucidation by multiplicity,
a corrosion, a parasitic curd, a clarion
for belief, to be good dogs :

NO DOGS ALLOWED AT LARGE IN THIS PARK

II.

Blocked.
>   (Make a song out of that: concretely)
By whom?

    In its midst rose a massive church. . . And it all came to me then—that those poor souls had nothing else in the world, save that church, between them and the eternal stony, ungrateful and unpromising dirt they lived by . . . . .

>   Cash is mulct of them that others may live
>   secure
>   .   .   and knowledge restricted.

    An orchestral dullness overlays their world

I see they—the Senate, is trying to block Lilienthal and deliver "the bomb" over to a few industrialists. I don't think they will succeed but . . that is what I mean when I refuse to get excited over the cry, Communist! they use to blind us. It's terrifying to think how easily we can be destroyed, a few votes. Even though Communism is a threat, are Communists any *worse* than the guilty bastards trying in that way to undermine us?

>   We leap awake and what we see
>   fells us   .

>   Let terror twist the world!

Faitoute, sick of his diversions but proud of women,
his requites, standing with his back
to the lions' pit,
                    (where the drunken
lovers slept, now, both of them)
                                    indifferent,
started again wandering—foot pacing foot outward
into emptiness   .   .

        Up there.
                The cop points.
                        A sign nailed
        to a tree: Women.

                        You can see figures
            moving beyond the screen of the trees and, close
            at hand, music blurts out suddenly.

Walking —

                                            a
            cramped arena has been left clear at the base
            of the observation tower near the urinals. This
            is the Lord's line: Several broken benches
            drawn up in a curving row against the shrubbery
            face the flat ground, benches on which
            a few children have been propped by the others
            against their running off   .

            Three middle aged men with iron smiles
            stand behind the benches—backing (watching)
            the kids, the kids and several women—and
            holding,
                    a cornet, clarinet and trombone,
            severally, in their hands, at rest.
                            There is also,
            played by a woman, a portable organ   .   .

[63]

Before them an old man,
wearing a fringe of long white hair, bareheaded,
his glabrous skull reflecting the sun's
light and in shirtsleeves, is beginning to
speak—

calling to the birds and trees!

Jumping up and down in his ecstasy he beams
into the empty blue, eastward, over the parapet
toward the city   .   .

.   .   .   .

There are people—especially among women—who can speak only to one person.
And I am one of those women. I do not come easily to confidences (though it
cannot but seem otherwise to you). I could not possibly convey to any one of those
people who have crossed my path in these few months, those particular phases of
my life which I made the subject of my letters to you. I must let myself be en-
tirely misunderstood and misjudged in all my economic and social maladjustments,
rather than ever attempt to communicate to anyone else what I wrote to you about.
And so my having heaped these confidences upon you (however tiresome you may
have found them and however far I may yet need to go in the attainment of
complete self-honesty which is difficult for anyone) was enough in itself to have
caused my failure with you to have so disastrous an effect upon me.

Look, there lies the city!

—calling with his back
to the paltry congregation, calling the winds;
a voice calling, calling   .

Behind him the drawn children whom his suit
of holy proclamation so very badly fits,
winkless, under duress, must feel
their buttocks ache on the slats of the sodden
benches.

But as he rests, they sing—when
prodded—as he wipes his prismed brow.
                                    The light
fondles it as if inclined to form a halo—

Then he laughs:

                    One sees him first. Few listen.
Or, in fact, pay the least
attention, walking about, unless some Polock
with his mouth open tries to make it out,
as if it were some Devil (looks into the faces
of a young couple passing, laughing
together, for some hint) What kind of priest
is this? Alarmed, goes off scowling, looking
back.

        This is a Protestant! protesting—as
though the world were his own   .

                                    · —another,
twenty feet off, walks his dog absorbedly
along the wall top—thoughtful of the dog—
at the cliff's edge above a fifty foot drop   .

    .   .   alternately the harangue, followed
by horn blasts surmounting
what other sounds   .   they quit now
as the entranced figure of a man resumes—

But his decoys bring in no ducks—other than
the children with their dusty little minds
and happiest *non sequiturs.*

                    No figure
from the clouds seems brought hovering near

The detectives found a note on the kitchen table addressed to a soldier from Fort Bragg, N. C. The contents of the letter showed that she was in love with the soldier, the detective said.

This is what the preacher said: Don't think
about me. Call me a stupid old man, that's
right. Yes, call me an old bore who talks until
he is hoarse when nobody wants to listen. That's
the truth. I'm an old fool and I know it.

BUD   .   !
You can't ignore the words of Our Lord Jesus
Christ who died on the Cross for us that we
may have Eternal Life!   Amen.

Amen!   Amen!

shouted the disciples standing behind the
benches.   Amen!

—the spirit of our Lord that gives
the words of even such a plain, ignorant fellow
as I a touch of His Own blessed dignity and
and strength among you   .   .

I tell you—lifting up his arms—I bring
the riches of all the ages to you here today.

It was windless and hot in the sun
where he was standing bareheaded.

Great riches shall be yours!
I wasn't born here. I was born in what we call
over here the Old Country. But it's the same

[66]

people, the same kind of people there as here
and they're up to the same kind of tricks as over
here—only, there isn't as much money
over there—and that makes the difference.

My family were poor people. So I started to work
when I was pretty young.
　　　　　　　—Oh, it took me a long time! but
one day I said to myself, Klaus, that's my name,
Klaus, I said to myself, you're a success.
　　　You have worked hard but you have been
lucky.
　　　　　　　　　　　　You're
rich—and now we're going to enjoy ourselves.

Hamilton saw more clearly than anyone else with what urgency the new government must assume authority over the States if it was to survive. He never trusted the people, "a great beast," as he saw them and held Jefferson to be little better if not worse than any.

So I came to America!

Especially in the matter of finances a critical stage presented itself. The States were inclined to shrug off the debt incurred during the recent war—each state preferring to undertake its own private obligations separately. Hamilton saw that if this were allowed to ensue the effect would be fatal, to future credit. He came out with vigor and cunning for "Assumption," assumption by the Federal Government of the national debt, and the granting to it of powers of taxation without which it could not raise the funds necessary for this purpose. A storm followed in which he found himself opposed by Madison and Jefferson.

But when I got here I soon found out that I
was a pretty small frog in a mighty big pool. So
I went to work all over again. I suppose
I was born with a gift for that sort of thing.
I throve and I gloried in it. And I thought then
that I was happy. And I was — as happy
as money could make me.

[67]

But did it make me GOOD?

He stopped to laugh, healthily, and
his wan assistants followed him,
forcing it out—grinning against
the rocks with wry smiles   .

NO! he shouted, bending
at the knees and straightening himself up
violently with the force of his emphasis—like
Beethoven getting a crescendo out of an
orchestra—NO!

It did *not* make me good. (His clenched fists
were raised above his brows.) I kept on making
money, more and more of it, but it didn't make
me good.

America the golden!
with trick and money
        damned
like Altgeld sick
    and molden
we love thee bitter
    land

Like Altgeld on the
        corner
seeing the mourners
        pass
we bow our heads
    before thee
and take our hats
    in hand

[68]

                                          And so
one day I heard a voice . . . a voice—just
as I am talking to you here today.   .   .

   .   .   .   .

   .   .   .   .   .   .   And the voice said,
Klaus, what's the matter with you? You're not
happy. I am happy! I shouted back,
I've got everything I want. No, it said.
Klaus, that's a lie. You're not happy.
And I had to admit it was the truth. I wasn't
happy. That bothered me a lot. But I was pig-
headed and when I thought it over I said
to myself, Klaus, you must be getting old
to let things like that worry you.

   .   .   .   .   .   .   then one day
our blessed Lord came to me and put His hand
on my shoulder and said, Klaus, you old fool,
you've been working too hard. You look
tired and worried. Let me help you.

I am worried, I replied, but I don't know what to
do about it. I got everything that money can
buy but I'm not happy, that's the truth.

And the Lord said to me, Klaus, get rid of your
money. You'll never be happy until you do that.

   As a corollary to the famous struggle for assumption lay the realization among
many leading minds in the young republic that unless industry were set upon its
feet, unless manufactured goods could be produced income for taxation would be
a myth.
   The new world had been looked on as a producer of precious metals, pelts and
raw materials to be turned over to the mother country for manufactured articles
which the colonists had no choice but to buy at advanced prices. They were pre-
vented from making woolen, cotton or linen cloth for sale. Nor were they allowed
to build furnaces to convert the native iron into steel.

Even during the Revolution Hamilton had been impressed by the site of the Great Falls of the Passaic. His fertile imagination envisioned a great manufacturing center, a great Federal City, to supply the needs of the country. Here was water-power to turn the mill wheels and the navigable river to carry manufactured goods to the market centers: a national manufactory.

Give up my money!

                    —with monotonous insistence
the falls of his harangue hung featureless
upon the ear, yet with a certain strangeness
as if arrested in space

                    That would be a hard thing
for me to do. What would my rich friends say?
They'd say, That old fool Klaus Ehrens must
be getting pretty crazy, getting rid of his
cash. What! give up the thing I'd struggled all
my life to pile up—so I could say I was rich?
No! that I couldn't do. But I was troubled
in mind.

        He paused to wipe his brow while
the singers struck up a lively hymn tune.

                        I couldn't eat, I couldn't
sleep for thinking of my trouble so that
when the Lord came to me the third time I was
ready and I kneeled down before Him
and said, Lord, do what you will with me!

Give away your money, He said, and I
will make you the richest man in the world!

And I bowed my head and said to Him, Yea, Lord.
And His blessed truth descended upon me and filled
me with joy, such joy and such riches as I
had never in my life known to that day and I said
to Him, Master!
                    In the Name of the Father
and the Son and the Holy Ghost.
                                        Amen.

Amen! Amen! echoed the devout assistants.

                Is this the only beauty here?
                And is this beauty—
                torn to shreds by the
                lurking schismatists?

                Where is beauty among
                these trees?
                Is it the dogs the owners
                bring here to dry their coats?

                These women are not
                beautiful and reflect
                no beauty but gross   .   .
                Unless it is beauty

                to be, anywhere,
                so flagrant in desire   .
                The beauty of holiness,
                if this it be,

                is the only beauty
                visible in this place
                other than the view
                and a fresh budding tree.

So I started to get rid of my money. It didn't take
me long I can tell you! I threw it away with both
hands. And I began to feel better .   .   .   .

—and leaned on the parapet, thinking

From here, one could see him— that
tied man, that cold blooded
murderer   .   April! in the distance
being hanged. Groups at various
vantages along the cliff   .   having
gathered since before daybreak
to witness it.

                    One kills
for money but doesn't always get it.

Leans on the parapet thinking, while
the preacher, outnumbered, addresses
the leaves in the patient trees   :

            The gentle Christ
            child of Pericles
            and femina practa

            Split between
            Athens and
            the amphioxus

            The gentle Christ—
            weed and worth
            wistfully forthright

            Weeps and is
            remembered as of
            the open tomb

[72]

—threw it away with both hands.   .   until
it was gone

            —he made a wide motion with both
hands as of scattering money to the winds—

—but the riches that had been given me are
beyond all counting. You can throw them
carelessly about you on all sides—and still
you will have more. For God Almighty has
boundless resources and never fails. There is no
end to the treasures of our Blessed Lord who
died on the Cross for us that we may be saved.
Amen.

The Federal Reserve System is a private enterprise . . . a private monopoly . . .
(with power) . . . given to it by a spineless Congress . . . to issue and regulate all
our money.
    They create money from nothing and lend it to private business (the same
money over and over again at a high rate of interest), and also to the Government
whenever it needs money in war and peace; for which we, the people, representing
the Government (in this instance at any rate) must pay interest to the banks in the
form of high taxes.

            The bird, the eagle, made himself
            small—to creep into the hinged egg
            until therein he disappeared, all
            but one leg upon which a claw opened
            and closed wretchedly gripping
            the air, and would not—for all
            the effort of the struggle, remain
            inside   .

    Witnessing the Falls Hamilton was impressed by this show of what in those times
was overwhelming power . . . planned a stone aqueduct following a proposed
boulevard, as the crow flies, to Newark with outlets every mile or two along the
river for groups of factories: The Society for Useful Manufactures: SUM, they
called it.

The newspapers of the day spoke in enthusiastic terms of the fine prospects of the "National Manufactory" where they fondly believed would be produced all cotton, cassimeres, wall papers, books, felt and straw hats, shoes, carriages, pottery, bricks, pots, pans and buttons needed in the United States. But L'Enfant's plans were more magnificent than practical and Peter Colt, Treasurer of the State of Connecticut, was chosen in his place.

.   .   .   .   .   The prominent purpose of the
Society was the manufacture of cotton goods.

> Washington at his first inaugural
> .   .   .   .   .   .   wore
> a coat of Crow-black homespun woven
> in Paterson   .   .   .   .   .   .

In other words, the Federal Reserve Banks constitute a Legalized National Usury System, whose Customer No. 1 is our Government, the richest country in the world. Every one of us is paying tribute to the money racketeers on every dollar we earn through hard work.

.   .   .   .   In all our great bond issues the interest is always greater than the principle. All of the great public works cost more than twice the actual cost, on that account. Under the present system of doing business we SIMPLY ADD 120 to 150 per cent to the stated cost.

The people must pay anyway; why should they be compelled to pay twice? THE WHOLE NATIONAL DEBT IS MADE UP ON INTEREST CHARGES. If the people ever get to thinking of bonds and bills at the same time, the game is up.

> If there is subtlety,
> you are subtle. I beg your indulgence:
> no prayer should cause you anything
> but tears.   I had a friend   .   .   .
> let it pass. I remember when as a child
> I stopped praying and shook with fear
> until sleep—your sleep calmed me   —
>
> You also, I am sure, have read
> Frazer's Golden Bough. It does you
> justice—a prayer such as might be made
> by a lover who
> appraises every feature of his bride's
> comeliness, and terror—

terror to him such as one, a man
married, feels toward his bride—

You are the eternal bride and
father—quid pro quo,
a simple miracle that knows
the branching sea, to which the oak
is coral, the coral oak.
The Himalayas and prairies
of your features amaze and delight—

Why should I move from this place
where I was born? knowing
how futile would be the search
for you in the multiplicity
of your debacle. The world spreads
for me like a flower opening—and
will close for me as might a rose—

wither and fall to the ground
and rot and be drawn up
into a flower again. But you
never wither—but blossom
all about me. In that I forget
myself perpetually—in your
composition and decomposition
I find my   .   .
                              despair!

.   .   .   .

Whatever your reasons were for that note of yours and for your indifferent evasion of my letters just previous to that note—the one thing that I still wish more than any other is that I could see you. It's tied up with even more than I've said here. And more importantly, it is the *one* impulse I have that breaks through that film, that crust, which has gathered there so fatally between my true self and that which can make only mechanical gestures of living. But even if you should grant it, I wouldn't want to see you unless with some little warmth of friendliness and friendship on your part. . . . Nor should I want to see you at your office under any circumstances. That is not what I mean (because I have no specific matter to see you about now as I had when I first called upon you as a complete stranger, nor as I could have had, just before your last note when I wanted so badly to have you go over some of my most faulty poems with me), I have been feeling (with that feeling increasingly stronger) that I shall never again be able to recapture any sense of my own personal identity (without which I cannot write, of course—but in itself far more important than the writing) until I can recapture some faith in the reality of my own thoughts and ideas and problems which were turned into dry sand by your attitude toward those letters and by that note of yours later. That is why I cannot throw off my desire to see you—not impersonally, but in the most personal ways, since I could never have written you at all in a completely impersonal fashion.

III.

Look for the nul
defeats it all

the N of all
equations   .

that rock, the blank
that holds them up

which pulled away—
the rock's

their fall. Look
for that nul

that's past all
seeing

the death of all
that's past

all being   .

But Spring shall come and flowers will bloom
and man must chatter of his doom   .   .

[77]

The descent beckons
                    as the ascent beckoned
                            Memory is a kind
of accomplishment
                    a sort of renewal
                                even
an initiation, since the spaces it opens are new
places
                    inhabited by hordes
                            heretofore unrealized,
of new kinds—
                    since their movements
                                are towards new objectives
(even though formerly they were abandoned)

No defeat is made up entirely of defeat—since
the world it opens is always a place
                    formerly
                                unsuspected. A
world lost,
                    a world unsuspected
                            beckons to new places
and no whiteness (lost) is so white as the memory
of whiteness   .

With evening, love wakens
                    though its shadows
                            which are alive by reason
of the sun shining—
                    grow sleepy now and drop away
                                from desire   .

Love without shadows stirs now
                    beginning to waken
                                as night
advances.

[78]

The descent
          made up of despairs
                    and without accomplishment
realizes a new awakening   :
                    which is a reversal
of despair.

          For what we cannot accomplish, what
is denied to love,
          what we have lost in the anticipation—
                    a descent follows,
endless and indestructible   .

Listen!   —

          the pouring water!
                    The dogs and trees
          conspire to invent
          a world—gone!

          Bow, wow! A
          departing car scatters gravel as it
          picks up speed!

          Outworn! *le pauvre petit ministre*
          did his best, they cry,
          but though he sweat for all his worth
          no poet has come   .

          Bow, wow! Bow, wow!

          Variously the dogs barked, the trees
          stuck their fingers to their noses. No
          poet has come, no poet has come.

—soon no one in the park but
guilty lovers and stray dogs   .

                        Unleashed!

Alone, watching the May moon above the
trees   .

At nine o'clock the park closes. You
must be out of the lake, dressed, in
your cars and going: they change into
their street clothes in the back seats
and move out among the trees   .

The "great beast" all removed
before the plunging night, the crickets'
black wings and hylas wake   .

Missing was the thing Jim had found in Marx and Veblen and Adam Smith
and Darwin—the dignified sound of a great, calm bell tolling the morning of a
new age   .   .   instead, the slow complaining of a
door loose on its hinges.

                    Faitoute, conscious by moments,
          rouses by moments, rejects him finally
          and strolls off   .

                    That the poem,
          the most perfect rock and temple, the highest
          falls, in clouds of gauzy spray, should be
          so rivaled   .   that the poet,
          in disgrace, should borrow from erudition (to
          unslave the mind): railing at the vocabulary
          (borrowing from those he hates, to his own
          disfranchisement)   .

                    [80]

—discounting his failures   .
seeks to induce his bones to rise into a scene,
his dry bones, above the scene, (they will not)
illuminating it within itself, out of itself
to form the colors, in the terms of some
back street, so that the history may escape
the panders

.   .   accomplish the inevitable
poor, the invisible, thrashing, breeding
.   debased city

Love is no comforter, rather a nail in the
skull

.   reversed in the mirror of its
own squalor, debased by the divorce from learning,
its garbage on the curbs, its legislators
under the garbage, uninstructed, incapable of
self instruction   .

a thwarting, an avulsion   :

—flowers uprooted, columbine, yellow and red,
strewn upon the path; dogwoods in full flower,
the trees dismembered; its women
shallow, its men steadfastly refusing—at
the best   .

The language   .   words
without style! whose scholars (there are none)
.   or dangling, about whom
the water weaves its strands encasing them
in a sort of thick lacquer, lodged
under its flow   .

                    Caught (in mind)
          beside the water he looks down, listens!
          But discovers, still, no syllable in the confused
          uproar: missing the sense (though he tries)
          untaught but listening, shakes with the intensity
          of his listening   .

               Only the thought of the stream comforts him,
               its terrifying plunge, inviting marriage—and
               a wreath of fur   .

And She   —
               Stones invent nothing, only a man invents.
               What answer the waterfall? filling
               the basin by the snag-toothed stones?

And He   —
               Clearly, it is the new, uninterpreted, that
               remoulds the old, pouring down   .

And She   —
               It has not been enacted in our day!

                                                   Le
          pauvre petit ministre, swinging his arms, drowns
          under the indifferent fragrance of the bass-wood
          trees   .

My feelings about you now are those of anger and indignation; and they enable
me to tell you a lot of things straight from the shoulder, without my usual tongue
tied round-aboutness.
     You might as well take all your own literature and everyone else's and toss it
into one of those big garbage trucks of the Sanitation Department, so long as the
people with the top-cream minds and the "finer" sensibilities use those minds and
sensibilities not to make themselves more humane human beings than the average
person, but merely as means of ducking responsibility toward a better understanding
of their fellow men, except theoretically—which doesn't mean a God damned
thing.

                              [82]

                .   and there go the Evangels! (their organ
loaded into the rear of a light truck) scooting
down-hill   .   the children
are at least getting a kick out of *this!*

His anger mounts. He is chilled to the bone.
As there appears a dwarf, hideously deformed—
he sees squirming roots trampled
under the foliage of his mind by the holiday
crowds as by the feet of the straining
minister. From his eyes sparrows start and
sing. His ears are toadstools, his fingers have
begun to sprout leaves (his voice is drowned
under the falls)   .

Poet, poet! sing your song, quickly! or
not insects but pulpy weeds will blot out
your kind.
                    He all but falls   .   .

And She   —

Marry us! Marry us!
                    Or! be dragged down, dragged
under and lost

She was married with empty words:
                            better to
                            stumble at
                              the edge
                                to fall
                                  fall
                                and be

                        —divorced

[83]

from the insistence of place—
                        from knowledge,
from learning—the terms
foreign, conveying no immediacy, pouring down.

                        —divorced
from time (no invention more), bald as an
egg   .

        and leaped (or fell) without a
language, tongue-tied
                the language worn out   .

The dwarf lived there, close to the waterfall—
saved by his protective coloring.

Go home. Write. Compose   .

Ha!

Be reconciled, poet, with your world, it is
the only truth!

Ha!

—the language is worn out.

And She   —
                You have abandoned me!

                —at the magic sound of the stream
                she threw herself upon the bed—
                a pitiful gesture! lost among the words:

[84]

Invent (if you can) discover or
nothing is clear—will surmount
the drumming in your head. There will be
nothing clear, nothing clear   .

He fled pursued by the roar.

Seventy-five of the world's leading scholars, poets and philosophers gathered
at Princeton last week   .   .   .

                    Faitoute ground his heel
          hard down on the stone:

Sunny today, with the highest temperature near 80 degrees; moderate southerly
winds. Partly cloudy and continued warm tomorrow, with moderate southerly winds.

          Her belly   .   her belly is like
          a cloud   .   a cloud
                              at evening   .

          His mind would reawaken:

He   Me with my pants, coat and vest still on!

She   And me still in my galoshes!

          —the descent follows the ascent—to wisdom
          as to despair.
          A man is under the crassest necessity
          to break down the pinnacles of his moods
          fearlessly   —
          to the bases; base! to the screaming dregs,
          to have known the clean air   .

[85]

From that base, unabashed, to regain
the sun kissed summits of love!

                            —obscurely
in to scribble   .   and a war won!

—saying over to himself a song written
previously   .   inclines to believe
he sees, in the structure, something
                      of interest:

On this most voluptuous night of the year
the term of the moon is yellow with no light
the air's soft, the night bird has
only one note, the cherry tree in bloom

makes a blur on the woods, its perfume
no more than half guessed moves in the mind.
No insect is yet awake, leaves are few.
In the arching trees there is no sleep.

The blood is still and indifferent, the face
does not ache nor sweat soil nor the
mouth thirst. Now love might enjoy its play
and nothing disturb the full octave of its run.

Her belly   .   her belly is like a white cloud   .   a
white cloud at evening   .   before the shuddering night!

My attitude toward woman's wretched position in society and my ideas about all the changes necessary there, were interesting to you, weren't they, in so far as they made for *literature?* That my particular emotional orientation, in wrenching myself free from patterned standardized feminine feelings, enabled me to do some passably good work with *poetry*—all that was fine, wasn't it—something for you to sit up and take notice of! And you saw in one of my first letters to you (the one you had wanted to make use of, then, in the Introduction to your Paterson) an indication that my thoughts were to be taken seriously, because that too could be turned by you into literature, as something disconnected from life.

But when my actual personal life crept in, stamped all over with the *very same* attitudes and sensibilities and preoccupations that you found quite admirable as *literature*—that was an entirely different matter, wasn't it? No longer admirable, but, on the contrary, deplorable, annoying, stupid, or in some other way unpardonable; because those very ideas and feelings which make one a writer with some kind of new vision, are often the *very same ones* which, in living itself, make one clumsy, awkward, absurd, ungrateful, confidential where most people are reticent, and reticent where one should be confidential, and which cause one, all too often, to step on the toes of other people's sensitive egos as a result of one's stumbling earnestness or honesty carried too far. And that they *are* the very same ones—that's important, something to be remembered at all times, especially by writers like yourself who are so sheltered from life in the raw by the glass-walled conditions of their own safe lives.

Only my writing (when I write) is myself: only that is the real me in any essential way. Not because I bring to literature and to life two different inconsistent sets of values, as you do. No, *I* don't do that; and I feel that when anyone does do it, literature is turned into just so much intellectual excrement fit for the same stinking hole as any other kind.

But in writing (as in all forms of creative art) one derives one's unity of being and one's freedom to be one's self, from one's relationship to those particular externals (language, clay, paints, et cetera) over which one has complete control and the shaping of which lies entirely in one's own power; whereas in living, one's shaping of the externals involved there (of one's friendships, the structure of society, et cetera) is no longer entirely within one's own power but requires the cooperation and the understanding and the humanity of others in order to bring out what is best and most real in one's self.

That's why all that fine talk of yours about woman's need to "sail free in her own element" as a *poet*, becomes nothing but empty rhetoric in the light of your behavior towards me. No woman will ever be able to do that, completely, until she is able *first* to "sail free in her own element" in living itself—which means in her relationships with men even before she can do so in her relationships with other women. The members of any underprivileged class distrust and hate the "outsider" who is *one of them*, and women therefore—women in general—will never be content with their lot until the light seeps down to them, not from one of their own, but from the eyes of changed male attitudes toward them—so that in the mean time, the problems and the awareness of a woman like myself are looked upon even more unsympathetically by other women than by men.

And that, my dear doctor, is another reason why I needed of you a very different kind of friendship from the one you offered me.

I still don't know of course the specific thing that caused the cooling of your friendliness toward me. But I do know that if you were going to bother with me *at all*, there were only two things for you to have considered: (1) that I was, as I still am, a woman dying of loneliness—yes, really dying of it almost in the same way that people die slowly of cancer or consumption or any other such disease (and with all my efficiency in the practical world continually undermined by that loneliness); and (2) that I needed desperately, and still do, some ways and means of leading a *writer's* life, either by securing some sort of writer's job (or any other job having to do with my cultural interests) or else through some kind of literary journalism such as the book reviews—because only in work and jobs of that kind, can I turn into assets what are liabilities for me in jobs of a different kind.

Those were the two problems of mine that you continually and almost deliberately placed in the background of your attempts to help me. And yet they were, and remain, much greater than whether or not I get my poetry published. I didn't need the *publication* of my poetry with your name lent to it, in order to go on writing poetry, half as much as I needed your friendship in other ways (the very ways you ignored) in order to write it. I couldn't, for that reason, have brought the kind of responsiveness and appreciation that you expected of me (not with any real honesty) to the kind of help from you which I needed so much less than the kind you withheld.

Your whole relationship with me amounted to pretty much the same thing as your trying to come to the aid of a patient suffering from pneumonia by handing her a box of aspirin or Grove's cold pills and a glass of hot lemonade. I couldn't tell you that outright. And how were you, a man of letters, to have realized it when the imagination, so quick to assert itself most powerfully in the creation of a piece of literature, seems to have no power at all in enabling writers in your circumstances to fully understand the maladjustment and impotencies of a woman in my position?

When you wrote to me up in W. about that possible censor job, it seemed a very simple matter to you, didn't it, for me to make all the necessary inquiries about the job, arrange for the necessary interviews, start work (if I was hired) with all the necessary living conditions for holding down such a job, and thus find my life all straightened out in its practical aspects, at least—as if by magic?

But it's never so simple as that to get on one's feet even in the most ordinary practical ways, for anyone on *my* side of the railway tracks—which isn't your side, nor the side of your great admirer, Miss Fleming, nor even the side of those well cared for people like S. T. and S. S. who've spent most of their lives with some Clara or some Jeanne to look after them even when they themselves have been flat broke.

A completely down and out person with months of stripped, bare hardship behind him needs all kinds of things to even get himself in shape for looking for a respectable, important white-collar job. And then he needs ample funds for eating and sleeping and keeping up appearances (especially the latter) while going around for various interviews involved. And even if and when a job of that kind is obtained, he still needs the eating and the sleeping and the carfares and the keeping up of appearances and what not, waiting for his first pay check and even perhaps for the second pay check since the first one might have to go almost entirely for back rent or something else of that sort.

[88]

And all that takes a hell of a lot of money (especially for a woman)—a lot more than ten dollars or twenty five dollars. Or else it takes the kind of very close friends at whose apartment one is quite welcome to stay for a month or two, and whose typewriter one can use in getting off some of the required letters asking for interviews, and whose electric iron one can use in keeping one's clothes pressed, et cetera—the kind of close friends that I don't have and never have had, for reasons which you know.

Naturally, I couldn't turn to *you*, a stranger, for any such practical help on so large a scale; and it was stupid of me to have minimized the extent of help I needed when I asked you for that first money-order that got stolen and later for the second twenty five dollars—stupid because it was misleading. But the different kind of help I asked for, *finally* (and which you placed in the background) would have been an adequate substitute, because I could have carried out *those* plans which I mentioned to you in the late fall (the book reviews, supplemented by almost any kind of part-time job, and later some articles, and maybe a month at Yaddo this summer) *without* what it takes to get on one's feet in other very different ways. And then, eventually, the very fact that my name had appeared here and there in the book review sections of a few publications (I'd prefer not to *use* poetry that way) would have enabled me to obtain certain kinds of jobs (such as an O. W. I. job for instance) without all that red tape which affects only obscure, unknown people.

The anger and the indignation which I feel towards you now has served to pierce through the rough ice of that congealment which my creative faculties began to suffer from as a result of that last note from you. I find myself thinking and feeling in terms of poetry again. But over and against that is the fact that I'm even more lacking in anchorage of any kind than when I first got to know you. My loneliness is a million fathoms deeper, and my physical energies even more seriously sapped by it; and my economic situation is naturally worse, with living costs so terribly high now, and with my contact with your friend Miss X having come off so badly.

However, she may have had another reason for paying no attention to that note of mine—perhaps the reason of having found out that your friendliness toward me had cooled—which would have made a difference to her, I suppose, since she is such a great "admirer" of yours. But I don't know. That I'm in the dark about, too; and when I went up to the "Times" last week, to try, on my own, to get some of their fiction reviews (the "Times" publishes so many of those), nothing came of that either. And it's *writing* that I want to do—not operating a machine or a lathe, because with literature more and more tied up with the social problems and social progress (for me, in my way of thinking) any contribution I might be able to make to the welfare of humanity (in war-time or peace-time) would have to be as a writer, and not as a factory worker.

When I was very young, ridiculously young (of school-girl age) for a critical role, with my mind not at all developed and all my ideas in a state of first-week embryonic formlessness, I was able to obtain book-reviews from any number of magazines without any difficulty—and *all* of them books by writers of accepted importance (such as Cummings, Babette Deutsch, H. D.) whereas now when my ideas have matured, and when I really have something to say, I can get no work of that kind at all. And why is that? It's because in all those intervening years, I have been forced, as a woman not content with woman's position in the world, to do a lot of pioneer *living* which writers of your sex and with your particular social background do not have thrust upon them, and which the members of my own sex frown upon (for reasons I've already referred to)—so that at the very moment when I wanted to return to writing from living (with my ideas clarified and enriched by living) there I was (and still am)—because of that living—completely in exile socially.

I glossed over and treated very lightly (in my first conversation with you) those literary activities of my early girlhood, because the work in itself was not much better than that which any talented college freshman or precocious prep-school senior contributes to her school paper. But, after all, that work, instead of appearing in a school paper where it belonged, was taken so seriously by editors of the acceptably important literary publications of that time, that I was able to average as much as $15 a week, very easily, from it. And I go into that now and stress it here; because you can better imagine, in the light of that, just how I feel in realizing that on the basis of just a few superficials (such as possessing a lot of appealingly youthful sex-appeal and getting in with the right set) I was able to maintain my personal identity as a writer in my relationship to the world, whereas now I am cut off from doing so because it was necessary for me in my living, to strip myself of those superficials.

You've never had to live, Dr. P—not in any of the by-ways and dark underground passages where life so often has to be tested. The very circumstances of your birth and social background provided you with an escape from life in the raw; and you confuse that protection from life with an *inability* to live—and are thus able to regard literature as nothing more than a desperate last extremity resulting from that illusionary inability to live. (I've been looking at some of your autobiographical works, as this indicates.)

But living (unsafe living, I mean) isn't something one just sits back and decides about. It happens to one, in a small way, like measles; or in a big way, like a leaking boat or an earthquake. Or else it doesn't happen. And when it does, then one must bring, as I must, one's life to literature; and when it doesn't then one brings to life (as you do) purely literary sympathies and understandings, the insights and humanity of words on paper *only*—and also, alas, the ego of the literary man which most likely played an important part in the change of your attitude toward me. That literary man's ego wanted to help me in such a way, I think, that my own achievements might serve as a flower in his buttonhole, if that kind of help had been enough to make me bloom.

But I have no blossoms to bring to any man in the way of either love *or* friendship. That's one of the reasons why I didn't want that introduction to my poems. And I'm not wanting to be nasty or sarcastic in the last lines of this letter. On the contrary a feeling of profound sadness has replaced now the anger and the indignation with which I started to write all this. I wanted your friendship more than I ever wanted anything else (yes, *more*, and I've wanted other things badly) I wanted it desperately, not because I have a single thing with which to adorn any man's pride—but just because I haven't.

Yes, the anger which I imagined myself to feel on all the previous pages, was false. I am too unhappy and too lonely to be angry; and if some of the things to which I have called your attention here should cause any change of heart in you regarding me, that would be just about the only thing I can conceive of as occurring in my life right now.

La votre

C.

P. S.   That I'm back here at 21 Pine Street causes me to add that that mystery as to who forged the "Cress" on that money order and also took one of Brown's checks (though his was *not* cashed, and therefore replaced later) never did get cleared up. And the janitor who was here at the time, is dead now. I don't think it was he took any of the money. But still I was rather glad that the postoffice didn't follow it through because just in case Bob did have anything to do with it, he would have gotten into serious trouble—which I shouldn't have welcomed, because he was one of those miserably underpaid negroes and an awfully decent human being in lots of ways. But now I wish it *had* been followed through *after* he died (which was over two months ago) because the crooks may have been those low vile upstate farm people whose year-round exploitation of down and out farm help ought to be brought to light in some fashion, and because if they *did* steal the money order and were arrested for it, that in itself would have brought to the attention of the proper authorities all their other illegal activities as well : And yet that kind of justice doesn't interest me greatly. What's at the root of this or that crime or antisocial act, both psychologically and environmentally, always interests me more. But as I make that last statement, I'm reminded of how much I'd like to do a lot of things with *people* in some prose—some stories, maybe a novel. I can't tell you how much I want the living which I need in order to write. And I simply can't achieve them entirely alone. I don't even possess a typewriter now, nor have even a rented one—and I can't think properly except on a typewriter. I can do poetry (though only the first draft) in long-hand, and letters. But for any prose writing, other than letters, I can't do any work without a typewriter. But that of course is the least of my problems—the typewriter; at least the easiest to do something about.

C.

Dr. P.:

This is the simplest, most outright letter I've ever written to you; and you ought to read it all the way through, and carefully, because it's about you, as a writer, and about the ideas regarding women that you expressed in your article on A. N., and because in regard to myself, it contains certain information which I did not think it necessary to give you before, and which I do think now you ought to have. And if my anger in the beginning makes you too angry to go on from there—well, that anger of mine isn't there in the last part, now as I attach this post-script.

C.

And if you don't feel like reading it even for those reasons, will you then do so, *please*, merely out of fairness to me—much time and much thought and much unhappiness having gone into those pages.

[91]

BOOK THREE

(1949)

Cities, for Oliver, were not a part of nature. He could hardly feel, he could hardly admit even when it was pointed out to him, that cities are a second body for the human mind, a second organism, more rational, permanent and decorative than the animal organism of flesh and bone: a work of natural yet moral art, where the soul sets up her trophies of action and instruments of pleasure.

—*The Last Puritan*. SANTAYANA.

The Library

I.

I love the locust tree
the sweet white locust
    How much?
    How much?
How much does it cost
to love the locust tree
    in bloom?

A fortune bigger than
Avery could muster
    So much
    So much
the shelving green
    locust
whose bright small leaves
    in June
lean among flowers
sweet and white at
    heavy cost

                    A cool of books
will sometimes lead the mind to libraries
of a hot afternoon, if books can be found
cool to the sense to lead the mind away.

For there is a wind or ghost of a wind
in all books echoing the life
there, a high wind that fills the tubes
of the ear until we think we hear a wind,
actual   .

                    to lead the mind away.

Drawn from the streets we break off
our minds' seclusion and are taken up by
the books' winds, seeking, seeking
down the wind
until we are unaware which is the wind and
which the wind's power over us   .
                         to lead the mind away

and there grows in the mind
a scent, it may be, of locust blossoms
whose perfume is itself a wind moving
                         to lead the mind away

through which, below the cataract
soon to be dry
the river whirls and eddys
                         first recollected.

Spent from wandering the useless
streets these months, faces folded against
him like clover at nightfall, something
has brought him back to his own
                         mind   .

                              in which a falls unseen
        tumbles and rights itself
        and refalls—and does not cease, falling
        and refalling with a roar, a reverberation
        not of the falls but of its rumor
                                        unabated

                                  Beautiful thing,
        my dove, unable and all who are windblown,
        touched by the fire
                              and unable,
        a roar that (soundless) drowns the sense
        with its reiteration
                              unwilling to lie in its bed
        and sleep and sleep, sleep
                                  in its dark bed.

        Summer! it is summer   .
        —and still the roar in his mind is
        unabated

The last wolf was killed near the Weisse Huis in the year 1723

        Books will give rest sometimes against
        the uproar of water falling
        and righting itself to refall filling
        the mind with its reverberation
                                  shaking stone.

        Blow! So be it. Bring down! So be it. Consume
        and submerge! So be it. Cyclone, fire
        and flood. So be it. Hell, New Jersey, it said
        on the letter. Delivered without comment.
        So be it!
                  Run from it, if you will. So be it.

                              [97]

(Winds that enshroud us in their folds—
or no wind). So be it. Pull at the doors, of a hot
afternoon, doors that the wind holds, wrenches
from our arms — and hands. So be it. The Library
is sanctuary to our fears. So be it. So be it.
— the wind that has tripped us, pressed upon
us, prurient or upon the prurience of our fears
— laughter fading. So be it.

                    Sit breathless
or still breathless. So be it. Then, eased
turn to the task. So be it   :
                    Old newspaper files,
to find — a child burned in a field,
no language. Tried, aflame, to crawl under
a fence to go home. So be it. Two others,
boy and girl, clasped in each other's arms
(clasped also by the water) So be it. Drowned
wordless in the canal. So be it. The Paterson
Cricket Club, 1896. A woman lobbyist. So
be it. Two local millionaires — moved away.
So be it. Another Indian rock shelter
found — a bone awl. So be it. The
old Rogers Locomotive Works. So be it.
Shield us from loneliness. So be it. The mind
reels, starts back amazed from the reading   .
So be it.

      He turns: over his right shoulder
a vague outline, speaking   .

           Gently!   Gently!
           as in all things an opposite
               that awakes
           the fury, conceiving
             knowledge

by way of despair that has
     no place
to lay its glossy head—

Save only—not alone!
     Never, if possible
alone!   to escape the accepted
     chopping block
and a square hat !   .

The "Castle" too to be razed. So be it. For no
reason other than that it is *there*, in-
comprehensible;   of no USE! So be it. So be it.

          Lambert, the poor English boy,
the immigrant, who built it
          was the first
                         to oppose the unions:

This is MY shop. I reserve the right (and he did)
to walk down the row (between his looms) and
fire any son-of-a-bitch I choose without excuse
or reason more than that I don't like his face.

Rose and I didn't know each other when we both went to the Paterson strike
around the first war and worked in the Pagent. She went regularly to feed Jack
Reed in jail and I listened to Big Bill Haywood, Gurley Flynn and the rest of
the big hearts and helping hands in Union Hall. And look at the damned thing
now.

They broke him all right   .

               —the old boy himself, a Limey,
his head full of castles, the pivots of that
curt dialectic (while it lasted), built himself a
Balmoral on the alluvial silt, the rock-fall skirt-
ing the volcanic upthrust of the "Mountain"

　　　　　　　　　—some of the windows
of the main house illuminated by translucent
laminae of planed pebbles (his first wife
admired them) by far the most authentic detail
of the place; at least the best
to be had there and the best artifact　　.

　　The province of the poem is the world.
　　When the sun rises, it rises in the poem
　　and when it sets darkness comes down
　　and the poem is dark　　.

　　and lamps are lit, cats prowl and men
　　read, read—or mumble and stare
　　at that which their small lights distinguish
　　or obscure or their hands search out

　　in the dark. The poem moves them or
　　it does not move them.　　Faitoute, his ears
　　ringing　.　no sound　.　no great city,
　　as he seems to read —

　　　　　　　　　a roar of books
　　from the wadded library oppresses him
　　　　　　　　　　　　　　　until
　　his mind begins to drift　　.

　　　　　　　　Beautiful thing:

　　　　　　　　　　　—a dark flame,
　　a wind, a flood—counter to all staleness.

Dead men's dreams, confined by these walls, risen,
seek an outlet. The spirit languishes,
unable, unable not from lack of innate ability —

                              (barring alone sure death)

but from that which immures them pressed here
together with their fellows, for respite   .

Flown in from before the cold or nightbound
(the light attracted them)
                    they sought safety (in books)
but ended battering against glass
                    at the high windows

The Library is desolation, it has a smell of its own
of stagnation and death   .

                    Beautiful Thing!

—the cost of dreams.
            in which we search, after a surgery
of the wits and must translate, quickly
step by step or be destroyed—under a spell
to remain a castrate (a slowly descending veil
closing about the mind
                    cutting the mind away)   .

                    SILENCE!

            Awake, he dozes in a fever heat,
cheeks burning   .   .   loaning blood
to the past, amazed   .   risking life.

And as his mind fades, joining the others, he
seeks to bring it back—but it
eludes him, flutters again and flies off and
again away   .

                    [101]

O Thalassa, Thalassa!
the lash and hiss of water

The sea!

How near it was to them!

Soon!

Too soon   .

—and still he brings it back, battering
with the rest against the vents and high windows

(They do not yield but shriek
                              as furies,
shriek and execrate the imagination, the impotent,
a woman against a woman, seeking to destroy
it but cannot, the life will not out of it)   .

A library — of books! decrying all books
that enfeeble the mind's intent

Beautiful thing!

The Indians were accused of killing two or three pigs—this was untrue, as
afterward proved, because the pigs had been butchered by the white men them-
selves. The following incident is concerned with two of the Indians who had
been captured by Kieft's soldiers because of the accusations: The braves had been
turned over to the soldiers, by Kieft, to do with as they pleased.

The first of these savages, having received a frightful wound, desired them to
permit him to dance the Kinte Kaye, a religious use among them before death;
he received, however, so many wounds that he dropped dead. The soldiers then
cut strips down the other's body. . . . While this was going forward Director Kieft,
with his Councillor (the first trained physician in the colony) Jan de la Montagne,

a Frenchman, stood laughing heartily at the fun, and rubbing his right arm, so much delight he took in such scenes. He then ordered him (the brave) to be taken out of the fort, and the soldiers bringing him to the Beaver's Path, he dancing the Kinte Kaye all the time, mutilated him, and at last cut off his head.

There stood at the same time, 24 or 25 female savages, who had been taken prisoners, at the north-west corner of the fort: they held up their arms, and in their language exclaimed. "For shame! for shame! such unheard of cruelty was never known, or even thought of, among us."

They made money of sea-shells. Bird feathers. Beaver skins. When a priest died and was buried they encased him with such wealth as he possessed. The Dutch dug up the body, stole the furs and left the carcass to the wolves that roamed the woods.

> Doc, listen — fiftyish, a grimy hand
> pushing back the cap: In gold —
> Volunteers of America

>   I got
> a woman outside I want to marry, will
> you give her a blood test?

From 1869 to 1879 several crossed the falls on a tight rope (in the old pictures the crowd, below, on the dry rocks in their short sleeves and summer dresses look more like water-lilies or penguins than men and women staring up at them): De Lave, Harry Leslie and Geo. Dobbs—the last carrying a boy upon his shoulders. Fleetwood Miles, a semi-lunatic, announced that he too would perform the feat but could not be found when the crowd had assembled.

> The place sweats of staleness and of rot
> a back-house stench   .   a
> library stench

> It is summer! stinking summer

> Escape from it—but not by running
> away. Not by "composition." Embrace the
> foulness

                    —the being taut, balanced between
        eternities

A spectator on Morris Mountain, when Leslie had gone out with a cookstove
strapped to his back—tugged at one of the guy-ropes, either out of malice or
idleness, so that he almost fell off. Having carried the stove to the center of the
rope he kindled a fire in it, cooked an omelet and ate it. It rained that night so
that the later performance had to be postponed.

But on Monday he did the Washerwoman's Frolic, in female attire, staggering
drunkenly across the chasm, going backward, hopping on one foot and at the rope's
center lay down on his side. He retired after that having "busted" his tights—to the
cottage above for repairs.

The progress of the events was transmitted over the new telephone to the city
from the tower of the water works. The boy, Tommy Walker, was the real hero
of these adventures.

                And as reverie gains and
                    your joints loosen
                    the trick's done!
                Day is covered and we see you—
                    but not alone!
                drunk and bedraggled to release

                the strictness of beauty
                under a sky full of stars
                    Beautiful thing
                and a slow moon —
                                The car
                    had stopped long since
                    when the others
                came and dragged those out
                    who had you there
                    indifferent
                to whatever the anesthetic
                    Beautiful Thing
                might slum away the bars—

Reek of it!
        What does it matter?
        could set free
only the one thing—

But you!
—in your white lace dress

.   .   .

    Haunted by your beauty (I said),
exalted and not easily to be attained, the
whole scene is haunted:
                        Take off your clothes,
(I said)
    Haunted, the quietness of your face
is a quietness, real

                        out of no book.

Your clothes (I said) quickly, while
your beauty is attainable.

        Put them on the chair
(I said. Then in a fury, for which I am
ashamed)
        You smell as though you need
a bath. Take off your clothes and purify
yourself   .   .
And let me purify myself
                        —to look at you,
                to look at you (I said)

(Then, my anger rising)   TAKE OFF YOUR
CLOTHES! I didn't ask you

[105]

to take off your skin . I said your
clothes, your clothes. You smell
like a whore. I ask you to bathe in my
opinions, the astonishing virtue of your
lost body (I said)   .

                       —that you might
send me hurtling to the moon
     .   .   let me look at you (I
said, weeping)

Let's take a ride around, to see what the town looks like   .

          Indifferent, the indifference of certain death
          or incident upon certain death
          propounds a riddle (in the Joyceian mode —
                                        or otherwise,
          it is indifferent which)
                            A marriage riddle:

          So much talk of the language—when there are no
          ears.

          .   .   .   .

          What is there to say? save that
          beauty is unheeded   .   tho' for sale and
          bought glibly enough

                       But it is true, they fear
          it more than death, beauty is feared
          more than death, more than they fear death

                            Beautiful thing

—and marry only to destroy, in private, in
their privacy only to destroy, to hide
                              (in marriage)
that they may destroy and not be perceived
in it—the destroying

Death will be too late to bring us aid   .

What end but love, that stares death in the eye?
A city, a marriage — that stares death
in the eye

The riddle of a man and a woman

For what is there but love, that stares death
in the eye, love, begetting marriage —
not infamy, not death

                        tho' love seem to beget
only death in the old plays, only death, it is
as tho' they wished death rather than to face
infamy, the infamy of old cities   .

.   .   .   a world of corrupt cities,
nothing else, that death stares in the eye,
lacking love: no palaces, no secluded gardens,
no water among the stones; the stone rails
of the balustrades, scooped out, running with
clear water, no peace   .

                              The waters
are dry. It is summer, it is   .   ended

Sing me a song to make death tolerable, a song
of a man and a woman: the riddle of a man
and a woman.

What language could allay our thirsts,
what winds lift us, what floods bear us
                                    past defeats
but song but deathless song ?

                    The rock
                    married to the river
                    makes
                    no sound

                    And the river
                    passes—but I remain
                    clamant
                    calling out ceaselessly
                    to the birds
                    and clouds
(listening)
                    Who am I?

                                        —the voice!

            —the voice rises, neglected
            (with its new) the unfaltering
            language. Is there no release?

            Give it up. Quit it. Stop writing.
            "Saintlike" you will never
            separate that stain of sense,

                                an offense
            to love, the mind's worm eating
            out the core, unappeased

            —never separate that stain
            of sense from the inert mass. Never.

Never that radiance

                           quartered apart,
unapproached by symbols   .

Doctor, do you believe in
"the people," the Democracy? Do
you still believe — in this
swill-hole of corrupt cities?
Do you, Doctor?   Now?

                            Give up
the poem. Give up the shilly-
shally of art.

                         What can you, what
can YOU hope to conclude —
on a heap of dirty linen?

                               — you
a poet (ridded) from Paradise?

Is it a dirty book? I'll bet
it's a dirty book, she said.

               Death lies in wait,
a kindly brother —
full of the missing words,
the words that never get said—
a kindly brother to the poor.
The radiant gist that
resists the final crystallization

     .   in the pitch-blend
the radiant gist   .

There was an earlier day, of prismatic colors : whence
to New Barbadoes came the Englishman .

Thus it began .

Certainly there is no mystery to the fact
that Costs Spiral According to a Rebus—known
or unknown, plotted or automatic. The fact
of poverty is not a matter of argument. Language
is not a vague province. There is a poetry
of the movements of cost, known or unknown .

The cost. The cost

and dazzled half sleepy eyes
Beautiful thing
of some trusting animal
makes a temple
of its place of savage slaughter

.   .   .   .   .   .

Try another book. Break through
the dry air of the place

An insane god
—nights in a brothel .
And if I had .
What then?

—made brothels my home?
(Toulouse Lautrec
again. .)

[110]

Say I am the locus
   where two women meet

One from the backwoods
   a touch of the savage
   and of T.B.
   (a scar on the thigh)

The other — wanting,
   from an old culture .
—and offer the same dish
   different ways

Let the colors run   .

Toulouse Lautrec witnessed
it: limbs relaxed
—all religions
   have excluded it—
at ease, the tendons
untensed .

And so he recorded them

—a stone
thrust flint-blue
up through the sandstone
of which, broken,
   but unbreakable
we build our roads .

—we stammer and elect .

Quit it. Quit this place. Go where all
mouths are rinsed : to the river for
an answer

[111]

for relief from "meaning"

A tornado approaches (We don't have
tornados in these latitudes. What, at
Cherry Hill?)

                                   It pours
over the roofs of Paterson, ripping,
twisting, tortuous   :

a wooden shingle driven half its length
into an oak
                (the wind must have steeled
it, held it hard on both sides)

                            The church
moved 8 inches through an arc, on its
foundations —

            Hum, hum!

                —the wind
where it poured its heavy plaits (the face
unshowing) from the rock's edge —

            where in the updraft,
summer days, the red-shouldered hawks ride
and play
            (in the up-draft)

                    and the poor cotton-
spinner, over the roofs, preparing to dive
        .   looks down
Searching among books; the mind elsewhere
looking down   .

                    Seeking.

II.

Fire burns; that is the first law.
When a wind fans it the flames

are carried abroad. Talk
fans the flames. They have

manoeuvred it so that to write
is a fire and not only of the blood.

The writing is nothing, the being
in a position to write (that's

where they get you) is nine tenths
of the difficulty: seduction

. or strong arm stuff. The writing
should be a relief,

relief from the conditions
which as we advance become — a fire,

a destroying fire. For the writing
is also an attack and means must be

found to scotch it — at the root
if possible. So that

[113]

to write, nine tenths of the problem
is to live. They see

to it, not by intellection but
by sub-intellection (to want to be

blind as a pretext for
saying, We're so proud of you!

A wonderful gift! How *do*
you find the time for it in

your busy life? It must be a great
thing to have such a pastime.

But you were always a strange
boy. How's your mother?)

—the cyclonic fury, the fire,
the leaden flood and finally
the cost—

Your father was *such* a nice man.
I remember him well   .

Or, Geeze, Doc, I guess it's all right
but what the hell does it mean?

    With due ceremony a hut would be constructed consisting of twelve poles, each
of a different species of wood. These they run into the ground, tie them together
at the top, cover them entirely with bark, skins or blankets joined close together.
       .   Now here is where one sits who will address the Spirit of Fire, He-
Who-Lies-With-His-Eyes-Bulging-In-The-Smoke-Hole   .   Twelve *manit-
tos* attend him as subordinate deities, half representing animals and the others vege-
tables. A large oven is built in the house of sacrifice   .   heated with twelve
large red-hot stones.

Meanwhile an old man throws twelve pipefuls of tobacco upon the hot stones, and directly another follows and pours water on them, which occasions a smoke or vapor almost powerful enough to suffocate the persons in the tent —

Ex qua re, quia sicubi fumus adscendit in altum; ita sacrificulus, duplicata altiori voce, *Kännakä, kännakä!* vel aliquando *Hoo Hoo!* faciem versus orientem convertit.

Whereupon as the smoke ascends on high, the sacrificer crying with a loud voice, *Kännakä, Kännakä!* or sometimes *Hoo, Hoo!* turns his face towards the east.

While some are silent during the sacrifice, certain make a ridiculous speech, while others imitate the cock, the squirrel and other animals, and make all kinds of noises. During the shouting two roast deer are distributed.

<pre>
                    (breathing the books in)
        the acrid fumes,
                    for what they could decipher   .
        warping the sense to detect the norm, to break
        through the skull of custom
                            to a place hidden from
        affection, women and offspring — an affection
        for the burning   .
</pre>

It started in the car barns of the street railway company, in the paint shop. The men had been working all day refinishing old cars with the doors and windows kept closed because of the weather which was very cold. There was paint and especially varnish being used freely on all sides. Heaps of paint soaked rags had been thrown into the corners. One of the cars took fire in the night.

<pre>
        Breathless and in haste
        the various night (of books) awakes! awakes
        and begins (a second time) its song, pending the
        obloquy of dawn   .
                            It will not last forever
        against the long sea, the long, long
        sea, swept by winds, the "wine-dark sea"   .

        A cyclotron, a sifting   .
</pre>

And there,
in the tobacco hush : in a tepee they lie
huddled (a huddle of books)
                antagonistic,
                        and dream of
gentleness—under the malignity of the hush
they cannot penetrate and cannot waken, to be again
active but remain—books
                that is, men in hell,
their reign over the living ended

Clearly, they say. Oh clearly! Clearly?
What more clear than that of all things
nothing is so unclear, between man and
his writing, as to which is the man and
which the thing and of them both which
is the more to be valued

When discovered it was a small blaze, though it was hot but it looked as tho' the
firemen could handle it. But at dawn a wind came up and the flames (which they
thought were subsiding) got suddenly out of control—sweeping the block and head-
ing toward the business district. Before noon the whole city was doomed   —

Beautiful thing

                —the whole city doomed! And
the flames towering   .

                like a mouse, like
                a red slipper, like
                a star, a geranium
                a cat's tongue or —

[116]

thought, thought
that is a leaf, a
pebble, an old man
out of a story by

Pushkin   .

                    Ah!
rotten beams tum-
bling,

            .   an old bottle
mauled

The night was made day by the flames, flames
on which he fed—grubbing the page
                        (the burning page)
like a worm—for enlightenment

Of which we drink and are drunk and in the end
are destroyed (as we feed). But the flames
are flames with a requirement, a belly of their
own that destroys—as there are fires that
smolder
        smolder a lifetime and never burst
into flame

                            Papers
(consumed) scattered to the winds. Black.
The ink burned white, metal white. So be it.
Come overall beauty. Come soon. So be it.
A dust between the fingers. So be it.
Come tatterdemalion futility. Win through.
So be it. So be it.

An iron dog, eyes
aflame in a flame-filled corridor. A drunkenness
of flames. So be it. A bottle, mauled
by the flames, belly-bent with laughter:
yellow, green. So be it—of drunkenness
survived, in guffaws of flame. All fire afire!
So be it. Swallowing the fire. So be
it. Torqued to laughter by the fire,
the very fire. So be it. Chortling at flames
sucked in, a multiformity of laughter, a
flaming gravity surpassing the sobriety of
flames, a chastity of annihilation. Recreant,
calling it good. Calling the fire good.
So be it. The beauty of fire-blasted sand
that was glass, that was a bottle: unbottled.
Unabashed. So be it.

An old bottle, mauled by the fire
gets a new glaze, the glass warped
to a new distinction, reclaiming the
undefined. A hot stone, reached
by the tide, crackled over by fine
lines, the glaze unspoiled   .
Annihilation ameliorated: Hottest
lips lifted till no shape but a vast
molt of the news flows. Drink
of the news, fluid to the breath.
Shouts its laughter, crying out—by
an investment of grace in the sand
—or stone: oasis water. The glass
splotched with concentric rainbows
of cold fire that the fire has bequeathed
there as it cools, its flame
defied—the flame that wrapped the glass
deflowered, reflowered there by

[118]

the flame: a second flame, surpassing
heat   .

Hell's fire. Fire. Sit your horny ass
down. What's your game? Beat you
at your own game, Fire. Outlast you:
Poet Beats Fire at Its Own Game! The bottle!
the bottle! the bottle! the bottle! I
give you the bottle! What's burning
now, Fire?

The Library?

        Whirling flames, leaping
from house to house, building to building

        carried by the wind

the Library is in their path

Beautiful thing! aflame   .

        a defiance of authority
—burnt Sappho's poems, burned
by intention (or are they still hid
in the Vatican crypts?)   :
        beauty is
a defiance of authority   :

        for they were
unwrapped, fragment by fragment, from
outer mummy cases of papier mâché, inside
Egyptian sarcophagi   .

        flying papers
from old conflagrations, picked up

haphazard by the undertakers to make
moulds, layer after layer
                          for the dead

Beautiful thing

The anthology suppressed, revived even by
the dead, you who understand nothing
of this:

        Dürer's *Melancholy*, the gears
lying disrelated to the mathematics of the
machine

        Useless.

                Beautiful thing, your
vulgarity of beauty surpasses all their
perfections!

                Vulgarity surpasses all perfections
—it leaps from a varnish pot and we see
it pass — in flames!

                Beautiful thing

—intertwined with the fire. An identity
surmounting the world, its core — from which
we shrink squirting little hoses of
                          objection — and
I along with the rest, squirting
at the fire

                Poet.

                        Are you there?

How shall I find examples? Some boy
who drove a bull-dozer through
the barrage at Iwo Jima and turned it
and drove back making a path for the others —

                           Voiceless, his
action gracing a flame
                                 —but lost, lost
because there is no way to link
the syllables anew to imprison him

                        No twist of the flame
in his own image : he goes nameless
until a Niké shall live in his honor —

And for that, invention is lacking,
the words are lacking:

                       the waterfall of the
flames, a cataract reversed, shooting
upward (what difference does it make?)

The language,

                      Beautiful thing—that I
make a fool of myself, mourning the lack
of dedication

                 mourning its losses,
for you

             Scarred, fire swept
(by a nameless fire, that is unknown even
to yourself) nameless,

                drunk.

Rising, with a whirling motion, the person
passed into the flame, becomes the flame—
the flame taking over the person

                    —with a roar, an outcry
which none can afford (we die in silence, we
enjoy shamefacedly—in silence, hiding
our joy even from each other
                  keeping
a secret joy in the flame which we dare
not acknowledge)

                    a shriek of fire with
the upwind, whirling the room away—to reveal
the awesome sight of a tin roof (1880)
entire, half a block long, lifted like a
skirt, held by the fire—to rise at last,
almost with a sigh, rise and float, float
upon the flames as upon a sweet breeze,
and majestically drift off, riding the air,
                sliding
upon the air, easily and away over
the frizzled elms that seem to bend under
it, clearing the railroad tracks to fall
upon the roofs beyond, red hot
darkening the rooms
                  (but not our minds)

While we stand with our mouths open,
shaking our heads and saying, My God, did
you ever see anything like that? As though
it were wholly out of our dreams, as
indeed it is, unparalleled in our most sanguine
dreams   .
                The person submerged
in wonder, the fire become the person   .

But the pathetic library (that contained,
perhaps, not one volume of distinction)
must go down also —

BECAUSE IT IS SILENT. IT
IS SILENT BY DEFECT OF VIRTUE IN THAT IT
CONTAINS NOTHING OF YOU

That which should be
rare, is trash; because it contains
nothing of you. They spit on you,
literally, but without you, nothing. The
library is muffled and dead

But you are the dream
of dead men

Beautiful Thing!

Let them explain you and you will be
the heart of the explanation. Nameless,
you will appear

Beautiful Thing
the flame's lover —

The pitiful dead
cry back to us from the fire, cold in
the fire, crying out—wanting to be chaffed
and cherished
those who have written books

We read: not the flames
but the ruin left
by the conflagration

Not the enormous burning
but the dead (the books
remaining). Let us read   .

and digest: the surface
glistens, only the surface.
Dig in—and you have

a nothing, surrounded by
a surface, an inverted
bell resounding, a

white-hot man become
a book, the emptiness of
a cavern resounding

Hi Kid

I know you just about to shot me. But honest Hon. I have really been to busy
to write. Here there, and everywhere.

Bab I haven't wrote since October so I will go back to Oct. 31, (Oh by the way
are friend Madam B. Harris had a party the 31, but only high browns and *yellow*
so I wasn't invited)

But I pay that no mind, cause I really (pitched myself a ball) Went to the
show early in the day, and then to the dance at the club. had me a (some kinded
fine time) I was a feeling good believe me you. child.

But, child, Nov 1, I did crack you know yourself I been going full force on the
(jug) will we went out (going to Newark) was raining, car slaped on brakes, car
turned around a few times, rocked a bit and stopped facing the other way, from
which we was going. Pal, believe me for the next few days. Honey, I couldn't
even pick up a half filled bucket of hot water for fear of scalding myself.

Now I don't know which did it the jug or the car skidding but all I know is
I was nowhere on nerves. But as they say alls well that ends well   So Nov 15, I
mean Kid I was so teaed that I didn't know a from z I really mean I was teaed
Since Nov 15 I Have been at it again ever since.

But now for the (Boys)   How Raymond James People going with Sis but is
in jail for giving Joseble Miller a baby.

Robert Blocker has taken his ring from Sally Mitchell

[124]

Little Sonny Jones is supposed to be the father of a girl's baby on Liberty St.

Sally Mund Barbara H Jean C and Mary M are all supposed to be going to have kids Nelson W. a boy on 3rd St is father to 3 kids on their way.

.   .   .   .

P. S.   Kid do you think in your next letter of your you could tell me how to get over there.

Tell Raymond I said   I bubetut hatche isus cashutute
Just a new way of talking kid. It is called (Tut) maybe you heard of it. Well here hoping you can read it

D

J

B

So long.

    Later

                Beautiful thing

                                I saw you:

                                  Yes, said
the Lady of the House to my questioning.
Downstairs
           (by the laundry tubs)
                 and she pointed,
smiling, to the basement, still smiling, and
went out and left me with you (alone in the house)
lying there, ill
           (I don't at all think that you
were ill)
           by the wall on your damp bed, your long
body stretched out negligently on the dirty sheet   .

Where is the pain?
                (You put on a simper designed
not to reveal)

                —the small window with two panes,
my eye level of the ground, the furnace odor   .

                                    Persephone
gone to hell, that hell could not keep with
the advancing season of pity.

                          —for I was overcome
by amazement and could do nothing but admire
and lean to care for you in your quietness —

who looked at me, smiling, and we remained
thus looking, each at the other   .   in silence   .

You lethargic, waiting upon me, waiting for
the fire and I
        attendant upon you, shaken by your beauty

Shaken by your beauty   .
                          Shaken.

— flat on your back, in a low bed (waiting)
under the mud plashed windows among the scabrous
dirt of the holy sheets   .

You showed me your legs, scarred (as a child)
by the whip   .

Read. Bring the mind back (attendant upon
the page) to the day's heat. The page also is
the same beauty : a dry beauty of the page —
beaten by whips

          A tapestry hound
with his thread teeth drawing crimson from
the throat of the unicorn

   .   .   .   a yelping of white hounds
—under a ceiling like that of San Lorenzo, the long

painted beams, straight across, that preceded
the domes and arches
            more primitive, square edged

.   a docile queen, not bothered
to stick her tongue out at the moon, indifferent,
through loss, but   .

              queenly,
in bad luck, the luck of the stars, the black stars

       .   the night of a mine

Dear heart
        It's all for you, my dove, my
                 changeling
       But you!
       —in your white lace dress
          "the dying swan"
       and high-heeled slippers—tall
       as you already were—
          till your head
       through fruitful exaggeration
       was reaching the sky and the
       prickles of its ecstasy
          Beautiful Thing!
       And the guys from Paterson
          beat up
       the guys from Newark and told
       them to stay the hell out
       of their territory and then
       socked you one
          across the nose
          Beautiful Thing
       for good luck and emphasis
          cracking it

till I must believe that all
desired women have had each
    in the end
    a busted nose
and live afterward marked up
    Beautiful Thing
    for memory's sake
to be credible in their deeds

Then back to the party!
    and they maled
and femaled you jealously
    Beautiful Thing
as if to discover whence and
    by what miracle
there should escape, what?
still to be possessed, out of
    what part
    Beautiful Thing
should it look?
    or be extinguished—
Three days in the same dress
    up and down   .

      I can't be half gentle enough,
half tender enough
      toward you, toward you,
inarticulate, not half loving enough

BRIGHTen

        the cor

            ner

where   you   are!

        —a flame,
black plush, a dark flame.

[128]

III.

It is dangerous to leave written that which is badly written.
A chance word, upon paper, may destroy the world. Watch care-
fully and erase, while the power is still yours, I say to myself, for
all that is put down, once it escapes, may rot its way into a thou-
sand minds, the corn become a black smut, and all libraries, of
necessity, be burned to the ground as a consequence.

Only one answer: write carelessly so that nothing that is not
green will survive.

> There is a drumming of submerged
> engines, a beat of propellers.
> The ears are water. The feet
> listen. Boney fish bearing lights
> stalk the eyes—which float about,
> indifferent. A taste of iodine
> stagnates upon the law of percent-
> ages: thick boards bored through
> by worms whose calcined husks
> cut our fingers, which bleed   .

We walk into a dream, from certainty to the unascertained,
in time to see   .   from the roseate past   .   a
ribbed tail deploying

> Tra la la la la la la la la
> La tra tra tra tra tra tra

Upon which there intervenes
a sour stench of embers. So be it. Rain
falls and surfeits the river's upper reaches,
gathering slowly. So be it. Draws together,
runnel by runnel. So be it. A broken oar
is found by the searching waters. Loosened
it begins to move. So be it. Old timbers
sigh—and yield. The well that gave sweet water
is sullied. So be it. And lilies that floated
quiet in the shallows, anchored, tug as
fish at a line. So be it. And are by their
stems pulled under, drowned in the muddy flux.
The white crane flies into the wood.
So be it. Men stand at the bridge, silent,
watching. So be it. So be it.

                        And there rises
a counterpart, of reading, slowly, overwhelming
the mind; anchors him in his chair. So be
it. He turns   .   O Paradiso! The stream
grows leaden within him, his lilies drag. So
be it. Texts mount and complicate them-
selves, lead to further texts and those
to synopses, digests and emendations. So be it.
Until the words break loose or—sadly
hold, unshaken. Unshaken! So be it. For
the made-arch holds, the water piles up debris
against it but it is unshaken. They gather
upon the bridge and look down, unshaken.
So be it. So be it. So be it.

The sullen, leaden flood, the silken flood
—to the teeth
                to the very eyes
                          (light grey)

Henry's the name. Just Henry,

                                    ever'body
knows me around here: hat
pulled down hard on his skull, thick chested,
fiftyish   .

                              I'll hold the baby.

That was your little dog bit me last year.
Yeah, and you had him killed on me.
                                   (the eyes)
I didn't know he'd been killed.
                    You reported him and
they come and took him. He never hurt
anybody.
          He bit me three times.
                              They come and
took him and killed him.
                         I'm sorry but I had
     to report him   .   .

A dog, head dropped back, under water, legs
sticking up   :
                 a skin
tense with the wine of death
                                        downstream
on the swift current   :
                          Above the silence
a faint hissing, a seething hardly at first
to be noticed

          —headlong!

                         Speed!

                              —marked
as by the lines on slate, mottled by petty
whirlpools

                    [131]

(to the teeth, to the very eyes)

a formal progression

The remains—a man of gigantic stature—were transported on the shoulders of the most renowned warriors of the surrounding country .   for many hours they travelled without rest. But half way on the journey the carriers had to quit overcome by fatigue—they had walked many hours and Pogatticut was heavy. So by the side of the trail, at a place called "Whooping Boys Hollow," they scooped out a shallow hole and laid the dead chieftain down in it while they rested. By so doing, the spot became sacred, held in veneration by the Indians.

Arrived at the burial place the funeral procession was met by Pogatticut's brothers and their followers. There was great lamentation and the Kinte Kaye was performed in sadness.

Wyandach, the most illustrious brother, performed the burial sacrifice. Having his favorite dog, a much loved animal, brought forth, he killed him, and laid him, after painting his muzzle red, beside his brother. For three days and three nights the tribes mourned   .

Pursued by the whirlpool-mouths, the dog
descends toward Acheron   .   Le Néant
  .   the sewer
         a dead dog

                              turning
upon the water:
         Come yeah, Chi Chi!

                              turning
as he passes   .

It is a sort of chant, a sort of praise, a
peace that comes of destruction:
                              to the teeth,
to the very eyes
         (cut lead)
                  I bin nipped

[132]

hundreds of times. He never done anybody any
harm   .

      helpless   .

         You had him killed on me.

About Merselis Van Giesen a curious story illustrative of the superstition of the day is to this effect: His wife was ill for a long time, confined to her bed. As she lay there, a black cat would come, night after night, and stare at her through the window, with wicked, blazing eyes. An uncanny fact about this visitation was that *no one else could see the cat.* That Jane was bewitched was the belief of the whole neighborhood. Moreover, the witch who exercised this spell, and who made these weird visits to the sufferer, in the guise of a cat invisible to everybody but the bewitched, was believed to be Mrs. B. who lived in the gorge in the hill beyond.

      Happy souls! whose devils lived so near.

Talking the matter over with his neighbors, Merselis (he was called "Sale") was told that if he could shoot the spectral cat with a silver bullet he would kill the creature, and put a stop to the spells exercised over his wife. He did not have a silver bullet, but he had a pair of silver sleeve buttons.

      Who of us thinks so fast to switch the category
of our loves and hatreds?

Loading his gun with one of these buttons, he seated himself on the bed beside his wife, and declared his intention of shooting the witch cat. But how could he shoot a creature he could not see?

      Are we any better off?

"When the cat comes," said he to his wife, "do you point out just where it is, and I will shoot at that spot." So they waited, she in a tremor of hope and dread— hope that the spells afflicting her would soon be ended; dread that some new torment might come to her from this daring attempt of her husband; he, in grim determination to forever end the unholy power exercised over his wife by Mrs. B., in the guise of the invisible feline. Long and silently they waited.

      —what a picture of marital fidelity! dreaming as one.

[133]

At last, when their feelings had been wrought up, by the suspense to the highest pitch, Jane exclaimed "There is the black cat!" "Where?" "At the window, it's walking on the sill, it is in the lower left-hand corner!" Quick as a flash "Sale" raised his gun and fired the silver bullet at the black cat which he could not see. With a snarl that was a scream the mysterious creature vanished forever from the gaze of Mrs. Van Giesen, who from that hour began to recover her health.

The next day "Sale" started out on a hunt through what is now known as Cedar Cliff Park. On the way he met the husband of the suspected witch. There was the usual exchange of courteous neighborly inquiries regarding the health of their respective families. Mr. B. said his wife was troubled with a sore on her leg for some time. "I would like to see that sore leg," said "Sale." After some demur he was taken to the house, and on one plea or another was finally permitted to examine the sore. But what particularly attracted his notice was a fresh wound, just where his silver sleeve button had struck the unfortunate creature when she had last visited his wife in the form of the spectral black witch cat! Needless to say Mrs. B. never more made those weird visitations. Perhaps it was from a sense of thanksgiving for her miraculous deliverance that Mrs. Van Giesen joined the First Presbyterian Church on Confession, Sept. 26, 1823. Merselis Van Giesen was assessed in 1807 for 62 acres of unimproved land, two horses and five cattle.

    — 62 acres of unimproved land, two horses
and five cattle —

    (that cures the fantasy)

      The Book of Lead,
 he cannot lift the pages

     (Why do I bother with this
rubbish?)

      Heavy plaits
 tumbling massive, yellow into the cleft,
bellowing

[134]

    —giving way to the spread
of the flood as it lifts to recognition in a
rachitic brain

   (the water two feet now on the turnpike
and still rising)

     There is no ease.
     We close our eyes,
     get what we use
     and pay. He owes
     who cannot, double.
     Use. Ask no whys?
     None wants our ayes.

But somehow a man must lift himself
again —
    again is the magic word .
      turning the in out :
Speed against the inundation

He feels he ought to *do* more. He had
a young girl there. Her mother told her,
Go jump off the falls, who cares? —
She was only fifteen. He feels so frustrated.
I tell him, What do you expect, you
have only two hands . ?

  It was a place to see, she said, The White Shutters. He said I'd be perfectly
safe there with him. But I never went. I wanted to, I wasn't afraid but it just
never happened. He had a small orchestra that played there, *The Clipper Crew*
he called it—like in all the speakeasies of those days. But one night they came
leaping downstairs from the banquet hall tearing their clothes off, the women

throwing their skirts over their heads, and joined in the dancing, naked, with the others on the main floor. He took one look and then went out the back window just ahead of the police, in his dress shoes into the mud along the river bank.

Let me see, Puerto Plata is
the port of Santo Domingo.

There was a time when
they didn't want any whites
to own anything—to
hold anything—to say, This
is mine   .

I see things,   .   .

—the water at this stage no lullaby but a piston,
cohabitous, scouring the stones   .

                                                  the rock
floating on the water (as at Mt Katmai
the pumice-covered sea was white as milk)

One can imagine
the fish hiding or
at full speed
stationary
in the leaping stream

—it's undermining the railroad embankment

[136]

Hi, open up a dozen, make
it two dozen!   Easy girl!
You wanna blow a fuse?
All manner of particularizations
to stay the pocky moon   :

January sunshine   .

1949
Wednesday, 11
(10,000,000 times plus April)

—a red-butted reversible minute-glass
loaded with
salt-like   white crystals
flowing

for timing eggs

*Salut à Antonin Artaud pour les
lignes, très pures*   :

"*et d'évocations plas-
tiques d'éléments de*"

and
"Funeral *designs*"
(a beautiful, optimistic
word   .   .   )   and
"Plants"
in this case "plants" does NOT refer to interment.)
"Wedding bouquets"
—the association

is indefensible.

[137]

(re. C.O.E.   Panda Panda   )

Fer got sake don't so exaggerate
I never told you to *read* it.
let erlone REread it.   I didn't
say it *wuz*   !   !   *henjoyable* readin.
I sd the guy had done some honest
work devilupping his theatre technique

———————————

That don't necess/y mean making
reading matter @ all.
Enny how there must be
one hundred books (*not*
that one) that you *need* to
read fer yr/ mind's sake.

———————————

re read *all* the Gk tragedies in
Loeb. — plus Frobenius, plus Gesell.
plus Brooks Adams
ef you ain't read him all. —
Then Golding's Ovid is in
Everyman's lib.

———————————

& nif you want a readin
list ask papa—but don't
go rushin to *read* a book
just cause it is mentioned
eng passang—is fraugs.

[138]

SUBSTRATUM

Artesian well at the Passaic Rolling Mill, Paterson.

The following is the tabular account of the specimens found in this well, with the depths at which they were taken, in feet. The boring began in September, 1879, and was continued until November, 1880.

DEPTH			DESCRIPTION OF MATERIALS
65 feet.	.	.	Red sandstone, fine
110 feet.	.	.	Red sandstone, coarse
182 feet.	.	.	Red sandstone, and a little shale
400 feet.	.	.	Red sandstone, shaly
404 feet.	.	.	Shale
430 feet.	.	.	Red sandstone, fine grained
540 feet.	.	.	Sandy shale, soft
565 feet.	.	.	Soft shale
585 feet.	.	.	Soft shale
600 feet.	.	.	Hard sandstone
605 feet.	.	.	Soft shale
609 feet.	.	.	Soft shale
1,170 feet.	.	.	Selenite, 2 x 1 x 1/16 in.
1,180 feet.	.	.	Fine quicksand, reddish
1,180 feet.	.	.	Pyrites
1,370 feet.	.	.	Sandy rock, under quicksand
1,400 feet.	.	.	Dark red sandstone
1,400 feet.	.	.	Light red sandstone
1,415 feet.	.	.	Dark red sandstone
1,415 feet.	.	.	Light red sandstone
1,415 feet.	.	.	Fragments of red sandstone
1,540 feet.	.	.	Red sandstone, and a pebble of kaolin
1,700 feet.	.	.	Light red sandstone
1,830 feet.	.	.	Light red sandstone
1,830 feet.	.	.	Light red sandstone
1,830 feet.	.	.	Light red stone
2,000 feet.	.	.	Red shale
2,020 feet.	.	.	Light red sandstone
2,050 feet.	.	.	
2,100 feet.	.	.	Shaly sandstone

At this depth the attempt to bore through the red sandstone was abandoned, the water being altogether unfit for ordinary use. . . . The fact that the rock salt of England, and of some of the other salt mines of Europe, is found in rocks of the same age as this, raises the question whether it may not also be found here.

— to the teeth, to the very eyes
    .   uh,   uh

FULL STOP

—and leave the world
        to darkness
        and to
        me

When the water has receded most things have lost their
form. They lean in the direction the current went. Mud
covers them

                    —fertile(?)mud.

If it were only fertile. Rather a sort of muck, a detritus,
in this case—a pustular scum, a decay, a choking
lifelessness—that leaves the soil clogged after it,
that glues the sandy bottom and blackens stones—so that
they have to be scoured three times when, because of
an attractive brokenness, we take them up for garden uses.
An acrid, a revolting stench comes out of them, almost one
might say a granular stench—fouls the mind   .

How to begin to find a shape—to begin to begin again,
turning the inside out : to find one phrase that will
lie married beside another for delight   .   ?
—seems beyond attainment   .

 *American poetry is a very easy subject to discuss for the
simple reason that it does not exist*

Degraded. The leaf torn from
the calendar. All forgot. Give
it over to the woman, let her
begin again—with insects
and decay, decay and then insects :
the leaves—that were varnished
with sediment, fallen, the clutter
made piecemeal by decay, a
digestion takes place   .

—of this, make it of *this,* this
this, this, this, this   .

Where the dredge dumped the fill,
something, a white hop-clover
with cordy roots (of iron) gripped
the sand in its claws—and blossomed
massively, where the old farm
was and the man broke his wife's
cancerous jaw because she was
too weak, too sick, that is, to
work in the field for him as he
thought she should   .

So thinking, he composed
a song to her:
        to entertain her
in her reading:

            *   *   *

The birds in winter
and in summer the flowers
those are her two joys
—to cover her secret sorrow

Love is her sorrow
over which at heart
she cries for joy by the hour
—a secret she will not reveal

Her ohs are ahs
her ahs are ohs
and her sad joys
fly with the birds and blossom
                with the rose

—the edema subsides

Who is it spoke of April? Some
insane engineer. There is no recurrence.
The past is dead. Women are
legalists, they want to rescue
a framework of laws, a skeleton of
practices, a calcined reticulum
of the past which, bees, they will
fill with honey   .

It is not to be done. The seepage has
rotted out the curtain. The mesh
is decayed. Loosen the flesh
from the machine, build no more
bridges. Through what air will you
fly to span the continents? Let the words
fall any way at all—that they may
hit love aslant. It will be a rare
visitation. They want to rescue too much,
the flood has done its work   .

Go down, peer among the fishes. What
do you expect to save, muscle shells?

Here's a fossil conch (a paper weight
of sufficient quaintness) mud
and shells baked by a near eternity
into a melange, hard as stone, full of
tiny shells

—baked by endless desiccations into
a shelly rime—turned up
in an old pasture whose history—
even whose partial history, is
death itself

        Vercingetorix, the only
hero   .

Let's give the canary to that
old deaf woman; when he opens his
bill, to hiss at her, she'll think he
is singing   .

Does the pulp need further maceration?
take down the walls, invite
the trespass. After all, the slums
unless they are (living)
wiped out they cannot be re-
constituted   .

The words will have to be rebricked up, the
—what? What am I coming to   .

        pouring down?

When an African Ibibio man is slain in battle, married women who are his
next of kin rescue the corpse. No man may touch it. Weeping and singing songs,
the scouts bear the dead warrior to a forest glade called Owokafai—the place of
those slain by sudden death. They lay him on a bed made of fresh leaves. Then

they cut young branches from a sacred tree and wave the bough over the genital organs of the warrior to extract the spirit of fertilty into the leaves. Knowledge of the rites must be kept from men and from unmarried girls. Only married women, who have felt the fertility of men in their bodies, can know the secret of life. To them it was entrusted by their great goddess "in the days when woman, not man, was the dominant sex.   .   ; on the guarding of this secret depended the strength of the tribe. Were the rites once disclosed—few or no babies would be born, barns and herds would yield but scanty increase, while the arms of future generations of fighting men would lose their strength and hearts their courage." This ceremony is conducted to the accompaniment of low, wailing chants, which only these wives of warriors have authority to sing, or even to know.

         —in a hundred years, perhaps—
         the syllables
                    (with genius)
                           or perhaps

         two lifetimes

         Sometimes it takes longer   .

Did I do more than share your guilt, sweet woman. The cherimoya is the most delicately flavored of all tropic fruit.   .   .   Either I abandon you or give up writing   .

    I was thinking about her all day long yesterday. You know she's been dead four years? And that son of a bitch only has one more year to serve. Then he'll be out and we can't do a thing about it. — I suppose he killed her. — You *know* he killed her, just shot her to death. And do you remember that Clifford that used to follow her around, poor man? He'd do anything she asked him to—the most harmless creature in the world; he's been sick. He had rheumatic fever when he was a child and can't leave the house any more. He wrote to us to send him some dirty jokes because he can't get out to hear them himself. And we can't either of us think of one new one to send him.

        The past above, the future below
        and the present pouring down: the roar,

[144]

the roar of the present, a speech—
is, of necessity, my sole concern   .

They plunged, they fell in a swoon .
or by intention, to make an end—the
roar, unrelenting, witnessing   .
Neither the past nor the future

Neither to stare, amnesic—forgetting.
The language cascades into the
invisible, beyond and above : the falls
of which it is the visible part —

Not until I have made of it a replica
will my sins be forgiven and my
disease cured—in wax: *la capella di S. Rocco*
on the sandstone crest above the old

copper mines—where I used to see
the images of arms and knees
hung on nails (de Montpellier)   .
No meaning. And yet, unless I find a place

apart from it, I am its slave,
its sleeper, bewildered—dazzled
by distance   .   I cannot stay here
to spend my life looking into the past:

the future's no answer. I must
find my meaning and lay it, white,
beside the sliding water: myself —
comb out the language—or succumb

—whatever the complexion. Let
me out! (Well, go!) this rhetoric
is real!

[145]

BOOK FOUR

(1951)

The Run to the Sea

I.

An Idyl

Corydon & Phyllis

Two silly women!

(Look, Dad, I'm dancing!)

What's that?

I didn't say anything   .
except *you* don't look silly   .

Semantics, my dear   .

— and I know *I'm* not   .

Ouch! you have hands like a man   .   Some day,
sweetheart, when we know each other better
I'll tell you a few things   .   .
Thank you. Very satisfactory. My secretary
will be at the door with your money   .
No.   I prefer it that way

O. K.

Good-bye

Miss   .   eh

Phyllis

Tiens! I'll phone the agency   .
Until tomorrow, then, Phyllis, at the same hour.
Shall I be walking again soon, do you think?

Why not?

.   .   .   .   .   .

A Letter

Look, Big Shot, I refuse to come home until you promise to cut out the booze.
It's no use your talking about Mother needs me and all that bologney. If you
thought anything of her you wouldn't carry on the way you do. Maybe your
family did once own the whole valley. Who owns it now? What you need is
to be slapped down.

I'm having a fine time in the Big City as a Professional Woman, ahem! Believe
me there's plenty of money here — if you can get it. With your brains and
ability this should be your meat. But you'd rather hit the bottle.

That's all right with me — only I won't wrestle with you all night on the bed
any more because you got the D.Ts. I can't take it, your too strong for me. So
make up your mind — one way or the other.

.   .   .   .   .   .

Corydon & Phyllis

And how are you today, darling?

(She calls me darling now!)

What sort of life can you lead
in that horrid place   .   Rach-a-mo, did
you say?

[150]

Ramapo

                                        To be sure,
how stupid of me.

                        Right.

                                        What was that?
Really you'll have to speak louder

                        I said   .

                                        Never mind.

You mentioned a city?

                        Paterson, where I trained

                                        Paterson!
Yes, of course. Where Nicholas Murray Butler was
born   .   and his sister, the lame one. They
used to have silk mills there   .
until the unions ruined them. Too bad. Wonderful
hands! I completely forget myself   .
Some hands are silver, some gold and some,
a very few, like yours, diamonds (If only I
could keep you!) You like it here?   .   Go
look out of that window   .

That is the East River. The sun rises there.
And beyond, is Blackwell's Island. Welfare Island,
City Island   .   whatever they call it now   .
where the city's petty criminals, the poor
the superannuated and the insane are housed   .

Look at me when I talk to you

                                        — and then
the three rocks tapering off into the water   .
all that's left of the elemental, the primitive
in this environment. I call them my sheep   .

                    Sheep, huh?

Docile, are they not?

                    What's the idea?

Lonesomeness perhaps. It's a long story. Be
their shepherdess Phyllis. And I
shall be Corydon   .   inoffensively, I hope?
Phyllis and Corydon. How lovely! Do you
care for almonds?

                    Nope. I hate all kinds of
nuts. They get in your hair   .   your
teeth, I mean   .

   .   .   .   .   .   .

Lay off that stuff. I can take care of myself. And if not, so what?

This is a racket, all I got to do is give her "massage" — and what do I know
about massage? I just rub her, and how I rub her! And does she like it! And
does she pay! Oh boy! So I rub her and read to her. The place is full of books—
in all languages!

But she's a nut, of the worst kind. Today she was telling me about some rocks
in the river here she calls her three sheep. If they're sheep I'm the Queen of
England. They're white all right but it's from the gulls that crap them up all
day long.

You ought to see this place.

There was a hellicopter (?) flying all over the river today looking for the body
of a suicide, some student, some girl about my age (she says   .   a Hindu
Princess.) It was in the papers this morning but I didn't take notice. You ought
to have seen the way those gulls were winging it around. They went crazy   .

   .   .   .   .   .   .

You must have lots of boy friends, Phyllis

                     Only one

Incredible!

                     Only one I'm interested in
right now

What is he like?

                     Who?

Your lover

                     Oh him. He's married. I
haven't got a chance with him

You hussy! And what do you do together?

                     Just talk.

  .   .   .   .   .   .

Phyllis & Paterson

                     Are you happy
               Happy I've come?

               Happy? No, I'm not happy

                     Never?

            Well   .

                   [153]

                    The couch looks
            comfortable

   .   .   .   .   .   .

The Poet

Oh Paterson! Oh married man!
He is the city of cheap hotels and private
entrances   .   of taxis at the door, the car
standing in the rain hour after hour by
the roadhouse entrance   .

Good-bye, dear. I had a wonderful time.
Wait! there's something   .   but I've forgotten
what it was   .   something I wanted
to tell you. Completely gone! Completely.
Well, good-bye   .

   .   .   .   .   .   .

Phyllis & Paterson

How long can you stay?

Six-thirty   .   I've got
to meet the boy friend

Take off your clothes

No. I'm good at saying that.

              She stood
        quietly to be undressed   .

the buttons were difficult   .

[154]

This is one of my father's
best. You ought to have heard
him this morning when I
cut the tails off   .

He drew back the white
shirt   .   slid aside the
ribbons   .

                 Glory be to God   .

— then stripped her

                 and all His Saints!

                        .

        No, just broad shouldered

                        .

— on the couch, kissing and talking while his
hands explored her body, slowly   .
courteously   .   persistent   .

                        .

             Be careful   .
             I've got an awful cold

             It's the first
             this year. We went
             fishing in all
             that rain last week

Who? Your father?
— and my boy friend

Fly fishing?
No. Bass. But it isn't

the season. I know that
but nobody saw us

I got soaked to the skin
Can you fish?

Oh I have a pole and a
line and just fish along

We caught quite a few

.   .   .   .   .   .

Good morning, Phyllis. You are beautiful this morning (in
a common sort of way) I wonder if you know how lovely you
really are, Phyllis, my little Milk Maid (That's good! The
lucky man!) I dreamt of you last night.

.

I don't care what you say. Unless Mother writes me, herself, that you've
stopped drinking — and I mean *stopped drinking* — I won't come home.

.

What sort of people do you come from, Phyllis?

My father's a drunk.

[156]

That's more humility than the situation demands. Never be ashamed of your origins.

I'm not. It's just the truth.

The truth! Virtue, my dear, if one had it! is only interesting in the aggregate, as you will discover . or perhaps you have already found it so. That's our Christian teaching: not denial but forgiveness, the Prodigal Daughter. Have you ever been to bed with a man?

Have you?

Good shot! With this body? I think I'm more horse than woman. Did you ever see such skin as mine? Speckled like a Guinea hen   .

Only *their* speckles are white.

More like a toad, perhaps?

I didn't say that.

Why not? It's the truth, my little Oread. Indomitable. Let's change names. You be Corydon! And I'll play Phyllis. Young! Innocent! One can fairly hear the pelting of apples and the stomp and clatter of Pan's hoofbeats. Tantamount to nothing   .

.   .   .   .   .   .

Phyllis & Paterson

Look at us! Why do you
torment yourself?
You think I'm a virgin.

[157]

Suppose I told you
I'd had intercourse. What
would you say then?
What would you say? Suppose
I told you that   .

She leaned forward in
the half light, close to
his face. Tell
me, what would you say?

Have you had many lovers?

No one who has mauled me
the way you have. Look,
we're all sweaty   .

                    .

My father's trying to get me a horse   .

                    .

I went out, once, with a boy
I only knew him a short time

He asked me   .   .
No, I said, of course not!

He acted so surprised.
Why, he said, most girls

are crazy for it. I
thought they all were   .

You ought to have seen
my eyes. I never heard

[158]

of such a thing   .

                    .

    I don't know why I can't give myself to you. A man
like you should have everything he wants   .   I guess I care
too much, that's the trouble   .

    .   .   .   .   .   .

Corydon & Phyllis

    Phyllis, good morning. Could you stand a drink at this
early hour? I've written you a poem   .   and the worst is, I'm
about to read it to you   .   You don't have to like it. But, hell
take it, you damn well better listen to it. Look at me shake! Or
better, let me give you a short one, to begin with:

> If I am virtuous
> condemn me
> If my life is felicitous
> condemn me
> The world is
> iniquitous

Mean anything?

Not much.

Well, here's another:

> You dreamy
>   Communist
> where are you
>   going?

To world's end
       Via?
Chemistry
       Oh oh oh oh

That will
       really
be the end   .
       you

dreamy Communist
       won't it?
Together
       together

"With that she split her girdle." Gimme another shot.
I always fell on my face when I wanted to step out. But here
goes! Here it is. This is what I've been leading up to. It's called,
Corydon, a Pastoral. We'll skip the first part, about the rocks and
sheep, begin with the helicopter. You remember that?

   .   .   drives the gulls up in a cloud
Um   .   no more woods and fields. Therefore
present, forever present

             .   a whirring pterodactyl
of a contrivance, to remind one of Da Vinci,
searches the Hellgate current for some corpse,
lest the gulls feed on it
and its identity and its sex, *as* its hopes, and its
despairs and its moles and its marks and
its teeth and its nails be no longer decipherable
and so lost   .
       therefore present,
           forever present   .

The gulls, vortices of despair, circle and give
voice to their wild responses until the thing
is gone   .   then, ravening, having scattered
to survive, close again upon the focus,
the bare stones, three harbor stones, except
for that   .   useless

                                unprofaned   .

It stinks!

       If this were rhyme, Sweetheart
               such rhyme as might be made
       jaws would hang open   .

       But the measure of it is the thing   .   None
            can wish for an embellishment
and keep his mind lean,
          fit for action   .
such action as I plan

           — to turn my hand up and hold
       it open, to the rain   .
           of their deaths
       that I brood   .   and find none ready
           but mine own   .

Nuts! After that, how about a story that's a little   .
recherché, a little strong? To hide my embarrassment? O.K.?

Sure.

Skip it.

           A ring is round
           but cannot bind
           though it may bound
           a lover's mind

                                        Phyllis, I think I'm
quite well now   .   .   How would you like to go
fishing with me somewhere? You like to fish   .

        Can I bring my father?

        No, you can't bring your father. You're a big girl now. A
month with me, in the woods! I have a concession. Don't answer
at once. You've never been to Anticosti   .   ?

        What's it like, pizza?

        Phyllis, you're a bad girl. Let me go on with my poem

    .   .   .   .   .   .

Dear Pappy:

   How yuh doin'? Are you behaving? because she wants me to go fishing with
her. For a month! What do you say? You'd like that.

Is that so? Well, you know where you can get off at. And don't think you can
start coming in here. Because if you do I'll *never* go home. And you *haven't stopped
drinking!* Don't try to kid me.
                                   .
Alright, if you think I'm in danger then learn to behave yourself. Are you a
weakling or something? But I won't go through all that again. Never. Don't worry,
as I told you, I can take care of myself. And if anything happens me, so what?
Blame it on I've got a father who is a drunk.

                              Your daughter
                                   P.

    .   .   .   .   .   .

Phyllis & Paterson

                   This dress is sweaty. I'll have
                   to have it cleaned

                        [162]

It lifted past the shoulders.
Under it, her stockings

Big thighs   .

                    .

Let us read, said the King
lightly. Let us

redivagate, said the Queen
even more lightly

and without batting an eye

                    .

He took her nipples
gently in his lips. No
I don't like it

.   .   .   .   .   .

    You remember where we left off? At the entrance to the
45th Street tunnel   .   Let's see

                              .   houses placarded:
        Unfit for human habitation   etc   etc

Oh yes   .

                              Condemned   .
        But who has been condemned   .   where the tunnel
        under the river starts? *Voi ch'entrate*

revisited! Under ground, under rock, under river
under gulls   .   under the insane   .

     .   the traffic is engulfed and disappears   .
to emerge   .   never

A voice calling in the hubbub (Why else
are there newspapers, by the cart-load?) blaring
the news no wit shall evade, no rhyme
cover. Necessity gripping the words   .   scouting
evasion, that love is begrimed, befouled   .

I'd like to spill the truth, on that one.

Why don't you?

This is a POEM!

                              begrimed
          yet lifts its head, having suffered a sea-change!
          shorn of its eyes and its hair
          its teeth kicked out   .   a bitter submersion
          in darkness   .   a gelding, not to be
          listed   .   to be made ready! fit to
          serve (vermin trout, that eat the salmon eggs,
          gaze up through the dazzle   .   in glass
          necklaces   .   picturesque peasant stuff
          without value)   .   pulp

                         While in the tall
          buildings (sliding up and down) is where
          the money's made
                    up and down
                              directed missiles
          in the greased shafts of the tall buildings   .

They stand torpid in cages, in violent motion
unmoved
        but alert!
                        predatory minds, un-
affected

                       unsexed, up
and down (without wing motion) This is how
the money's made   .   using such plugs.

                            At the
sanitary lunch hour packed woman to
woman (or man to woman, what's the difference?)
the flesh of their faces gone
to fat or gristle, without recognizable
outline, fixed in rigors, adipose or sclerosis
expressionless, facing one another, a mould
for all faces (canned fish) this   .

Move toward the back, please, and face the door!

is how the money's made,
             money's made
                      pressed together
talking excitedly   .   of the next sandwich   .
reading, from one hand, of some student, come
waterlogged to the surface following
last night's thunderstorm   .   the flesh a
flesh of tears and fighting gulls   .

                      Oh I could cry!
cry upon your young shoulder for what I know.
I feel so alone   .

I think I'll go on the stage,
said she, with a deprecating laugh,
Ho, ho!

Why don't you? he replied
though the legs, I'm afraid, would
beat you   .

.   .   .   .   .   .

          .   with me, Phyllis
(I'm no Simaetha) in all your native loveliness
that these spiked rumors may not tear
                    that sweet flesh

It sounds as tho' I wanted to eat you, I'll have to change that.

Come with me to Anticosti, where the salmon
lie spawning in the sun in the shallow water

          I think that's Yeats   .

— and we shall fish for the salmon fish

          No, I think *that's* the Yeats   .

          — and its silver
shall be our crest and guerdon (what's a guerdon?)
drawn struggling   .

          Believe me, some tussle!

          from the icy water   .

[166]

I wish you'd come, dear, I've got my yacht all stocked and
ready. Let me take you on a tour   .   of Paradise!

    That I'd like to see.

    Then why not come?

    I'm not ready to die yet, not even for that.

    You don't need to.

   .   .   .   .   .   .

Dear Pappy:

    For the last time!

    All day today, believe it or not, we've been coasting along what they call up
here the North Shore on our way to the place we're going to fish at. It sounds like
an Italian dinner, Anticosti, but it's really french.

It's wild, they say, but we have a marvellous guide, an Indian I think but it's not
sure (maybe I'll marry him and stay up there for the rest of my life) Anyway
he speaks french and the Missis talks to him in that language. I don't know what
they're saying (and I don't care, I can talk my own language).

I can hardly keep my eyes open, I've been out almost every night this week. To
go on. We have wine, mostly Champagne on board. She showed it to me, 24 cases
for the party but I don't want any of it, thanks. I'll stick to my rum and coke. Don't
worry. Tell Ma everything's all right. But remember, I'm through.

   .   .   .   .   .

Phyllis & Paterson

        Do you know that tall
        dark girl with the long nose?
        She's my friend. She says
        she's going West next fall.

I'm saving every cent I
can put together. I'm going
with her. I haven't told
my mother yet   .

Why do you torment yourself? I can't
think unless you're naked. I wouldn't blame

you if you beat me up, punched me,
anything at all   .   I wouldn't do

you that much honor. What! what did you say?
I said I wouldn't do you that much

honor   .   So that's all?
I'm afraid so. Something I shall always

desire, you've seen to that. Talk to me.
This is not the time for it. Why did you let

me come? Who knows, why *did* you? I like
coming here, I need you. I know that   .

hoping I'd take it from you, lacking
your consent. I've lost out, haven't I?

You have. Pull down my slip   .
He lay upon his back upon the couch.

She came, half dressed, and straddled him.
My thighs are sore from riding   .

Oh let me breathe! After I'm married
you must take me out sometime. If that's

what you want   .

Have any of these men
you speak of   .   ?
— and has he?

No.

Good.

What's good about it?

Then you're still a virgin!

What's it to *you?*

II.

You were not more than 12, my son
               14 perhaps, the high school age
when we went, together,
            a first for both of us,
to a lecture, in the Solarium
             topping the hospital, on atomic
fission. I hoped to discover
            an "interest" on your part.
You listened   .

       Smash the world, wide!
       —if I could do it for you —
       Smash the wide world   .
       a fetid womb, a sump!
       No river! no river
       but bog, a   .   swale
       sinks into the mind or
       the mind into it, a   ?

Norman Douglas (*South Wind*) said to me, The best thing a
man can do for his son, when he is born, is to die   .

I gave you another, bigger than yourself, to contend with.

To resume:

[170]

(What I miss, said your mother, is the poetry, the pure poem
of the first parts   .   )

    The moon was in its first quarter.
                As we approached the hospital
the air above it, having taken up
                the glow through the glass roof
seemed ablaze, rivalling night's queen.

                The room was packed with doctors.
How pale and young the boy seemed
                among those pigs, myself
among them! who surpassed him
                only in experience, that drug,
sitting erect to their talk:
                valences   .

For years a nurse-girl
                an unhatched sun corroding
her mind, eating away a rind
                of impermanences, through books
remorseless   .

Curie (the movie queen) upon
                the stage at the Sorbonne   .
a half mile across! walking solitary
                as tho' in a forest, the silence
of a great forest (of ideas)
                before the assembly (the
little Polish baby-nurse) receives
                international acclaim (a
drug)

                Come on up! Come up Sister and be
    saved (splitting the atom of
    bitterness)! And Billy Sunday evangel

and ex-rightfielder sets himself
to take one off the wall   .

                              He's *on*

the table now! Both feet, singing
(a foot song) his feet canonized   .

                    .   as paid for
by the United Factory Owners' Ass'n   .

    .   to "break" the strike
and put those S.O.Bs in their places, be
Geezus, by calling them to God!

— getting his 27 Grand in the hotel room
after the last supper (at the *Hamilton*)
on the eve of quitting town, exhausted
in his efforts to split (a split
personality)   .   the plate

                    What an arm!

Come to Jesus!   .   Someone help
that old woman up the steps   .   Come to
Jesus and be   .   All together now,
give it everything you got!

                    Brighten
    .   .   the corner where you
are!

Dear Doctor:
    In spite of the grey secrecy of time and my own self-shuttering doubts in these
youthful rainy days, I would like to make my presence in Paterson known to you,
and I hope you will welcome this from me, an unknown young poet, to you, an
unknown old poet, who live in the same rusty county of the world. Not only do I
inscribe this missive somewhat in the style of those courteous sages of yore who
recognized one another across the generations as brotherly children of the muses

(whose names they well know) but also as fellow citizenly Chinamen of the same province, whose gastanks, junkyards, fens of the alley, millways, funeral parlors, river-visions—aye! the falls itself—are images white-woven in their very beards.

I went to see you once briefly two years ago (when I was 21), to interview you for a local newspaper. I wrote the story in fine and simple style, but it was hacked and changed and came out the next week as a labored joke at your expense which I assume you did not get to see. You invited me politely to return, but I did not, as I had nothing to talk about except images of cloudy light, and was not able to speak to you in your own or my own concrete terms. Which failing still hangs with me to a lesser extent, yet I feel ready to approach you once more.

As to my history: I went to Columbia on and off since 1943, working and travelling around the country and aboard ships when I was not in schools, studying English. I won a few poetry prizes there and edited the Columbia Review. I liked Van Doren most there. I worked later on the Associated Press as a copyboy, and spent most of the last year in a mental hospital; and now I am back in Paterson which is home for the first time in seven years. What I'll do there I don't know yet—my first move was to try and get a job on one of the newspapers here and in Passaic, but that hasn't been successful yet.

My literary liking is Melville in Pierre and the Confidence Man, and in my own generation, one Jack Kerouac whose first book came out this year.

I do not know if you will like my poetry or not—that is, how far your own inventive persistence excludes less independent or youthful attempts to perfect, renew, transfigure, and make contemporarily real an old style or lyric machinery, which I use to record the struggle with imagination of the clouds, with which I have been concerned. I enclose a few samples of my best writing. All that I have done has a program, consciously or not, running on from phase to phase, from the beginnings of emotional breakdown, to momentary raindrops from the clouds become corporeal, to a renewal of human objectivity which I take to be ultimately identical with no ideas but in things. But this last development I have yet to turn into poetic reality. I envision for myself some kind of new speech—different at least from what I have been writing down—in that it has to be clear statement of fact about misery (and not misery itself), and splendor if there is any out of the subjective wanderings through Paterson. This place is as I say my natural habitat by memory, and I am not following in your traces to be poetic: though I know you will be pleased to realize that at least one actual citizen of your community has inherited your experience in his struggle to love and know his own world-city, through your work, which is an accomplishment you almost cannot have hoped to achieve. It is misery I see (like a tide out of my own fantasy) but mainly the splendor which I carry within me and which all free men do. But harking back to a few sentences previous, I may need a new measure myself, but though I have a flair for your style I seldom did exactly what you are doing with cadences, line length, sometimes syntax, etc., and cannot handle your work as a solid object— which properties I assume you rightly claim. I don't understand the measure. I haven't worked with it much either, though, which must make the difference. But I would like to talk with you concretely on this.

I enclose these poems. The first shows you where I was 2 years ago. The second, a kind of dense lyric I instinctively try to imitate—after Crane, Robinson, Tate, and old Englishmen. Then, the Shroudy Stranger (3) less interesting as a poem (or less sincere) but it connects observations of *things* with an old dream of the void—I have real dreams about a classic hooded figure. But this dream has become identified with my own abyss—and with the abyss of old Smokies under the Erie R.R. tracks on straight street—so the shroudy stranger (4) speaking from the inside of the old wracked bum of a paterson or anywhere in america. This is only a half made poem (using a few lines and a situation I had in a dream). I contemplated a long work on the shroudy stranger, his wanderings. Next (5) an earlier poem, Radio City, a long lyric written in sickness. Then a mad song (to be sung by Groucho Marx to a Bop background) (6). The (7) an old style ballad-type ghost dream poem. Then, an ode to the Setting Sun of abstract (8) ideas, written before leaving the hospital, and last an Ode to Judgment, which I just wrote, but which is unfinished. (9) What will come of all this I do not know yet.

I know this letter finds you in good health, as I saw you speak at the Museum in N. Y. this week. I ran backstage to accost you, but changed my mind, after waving at you, and ran off again.

Respectfully yours,

A. G.

Paris, a fifth floor room, bread
milk and chocolate, a few
apples and coal to be carried,
des briquettes, their special smell,
at dawn: Paris   .
the soft coal smell, as she
leaned upon the window before de-
parting, for work   .

— a furnace, a cavity aching
toward fission; a hollow,
a woman waiting to be filled

— a luminosity of elements, the
current leaping!
Pitchblende from Austria, the
valence of Uranium inexplicably
increased. Curie, the man, gave up
his work to buttress her.

But she is pregnant!
Poor Joseph,

the Italians say.

Glory to God in the highest
and on earth, peace, goodwill to
men!

Believe it or not.

A dissonance
in the valence of Uranium
led to the discovery

Dissonance
(if you are interested)
leads to discovery

— to dissect away
the block and leave
a separate metal:

hydrogen
the flame, helium the
pregnant ash   .

— the elephant takes two years

Love is a kitten, a pleasant
thing, a purr and a
pounce. Chases a piece of
string, a scratch and a mew
a ball batted with a paw   .
a sheathed claw   .

Love, the sledge that smashes the atom? No, No! antagonistic
cooperation is the key, says Levy   .

Sir Thopas (The Canterbury Pilgrims) says (to Chaucer)
                    Namoor—
                    Thy drasty rymyng is not
                    worth a toord
—and Chaucer seemed to think so too for he stopped and went
on in prose   .

REPORT OF CASES

CASE I.—M. N., a white woman aged 35, a nurse in the pediatric ward, had
no history of previous intestinal disturbance. A sister who lived with her suffered
with cramps and diarrhea, later found by us to be due to amebiasis. On Nov. 8,
1944 a stool submitted by the nurse for the usual monthly examination was found
to be positive for Salmonella montevideo. The nurse was at once removed from
duty with full pay, a measure found to be of advantage in having hospital personnel
report diarrheal disturbances without fear of economic reprisal.

            — with ponderous belly, full
            of thought! stirring the cauldrons
            .   in the old shed used
            by the medical students for dissections.
            Winter. Snow through the cracks

                        Pauvre étudiant   .
            en l'an trentième de mon âge
            Item   .   with coarsened hands
            by the hour, the day, the week
            to get, after months of labor   .

            a stain at the bottom of the retort
            without weight, a failure, a
            nothing. And then, returning in the
            night, to find it   .

                    LUMINOUS!

On Friday, the twelfth of October, we anchored before the land and made
ready to go ashore   .   There I sent the people for water, some with arms,
and others with casks: and as it was some little distance, I waited two hours for
them.

During that time I walked among the trees which was the most beautiful thing
which I had ever known.

.   knowledge, the contaminant

Uranium, the complex atom, breaking
down, a city in itself, that complex
atom, always breaking down   .
to lead.

            But giving off that, to an
exposed plate, will reveal   .

And so, with coarsened hands
                              she stirs

And love, bitterly contesting, waits
that the mind shall declare itself not
alone in dreams   .

A man like you should have everything he wants   .

                    not half asleep
            waiting for the sun to part the labia
            of shabby clouds   .   but a man (or
            a woman) achieved

                        flagrant!
            adept at thought, playing the words
            following a table which is the synthesis
            of thought, a symbol that is to him,

sun up! a Mendelief, the elements laid
out by molecular weight, identity
predicted before found! and   .

Oh most powerful connective, a bead
to lie between continents through
which a string passes   .

Ah Madam!
this is order, perfect and controlled
on which empires, alas, are built

But there may issue, a contaminant,
some other metal radioactive
a dissonance, unless the table lie,
may cure the cancer   .   must
lie in that ash   .   Helium plus, plus
what? Never mind, but plus   .   a
woman, a small Polish baby-nurse
unable   .

Woman is the weaker vessel, but
the mind is neutral, a bead linking
continents, brow and toe

                    and will at best take out
its spate in mathematics
                              replacing murder

Sappho vs Elektra!

The young conductor gets his orchestra
and leaves his patroness
                    with child.

.   *les idées Wilsoniennes nous*
gâtent   .   the vague irrelevances
and the destructive silences
                        inertia

As Carrie Nation
            to Artemis
                        so is our life today   .

They took her out West on a photographing
expedition
            to study chiaroscuro
                        to Denver, I think.
Somewhere around there   .
                        the marriage
was annulled. When she returned
                        with the baby
                                    openly
taking it to her girls' parties, they
                        were shocked

—and the Abbess Hildegard, at her own
funeral, Rupertsberg, 1179
had enjoined them to sing the choral, all
women, she had written for the occasion
and it was done, the peasants kneeling
in the background   .   as you may see

[180]

MONEY : JOKE (i.e., crime
          under the circumstances : value
          chipped away at accelerated pace.)

— do you joke when a man is dying
                    of a brain tumor?

Take up the individual misfortune
by buffering it into the locality — not
penalize him with surgeon's fees
and accessories at an advance over the
market price for
                    "hospital income"

Who gets that? The poor?
                    What poor?
— at $8.50 a day, ward rate?
          short of the possibility of recovery

And not enrich the widow either
                    long past fertility

Money: Uranium (bound to be lead)
throws out the fire   .
— the radium's the credit — the wind in
the trees, the hurricane in the
palm trees, the tornado that lifts
oceans   .
Trade winds that broached a continent
drive the ship forward   .

Money sequestered enriches avarice, makes
poverty: the direct cause of
disaster   .
                    while the leak drips

Let out the fire, let the wind go!
Release the Gamma rays that cure the cancer
.   the cancer, usury. Let credit
out   .   out from between the bars
before the bank windows

            .   credit, stalled
in money, conceals the generative
that thwarts art or buys it (without
understanding), out of poverty of wit, to
win, vicariously, the blue ribbon

                        to win
the Congressional Medal
for bravery beyond the call of duty but
not to end as a bridge-tender
on government dole   .

                    Defeat may steel us
in knowledge : money : joke
to be wiped out sooner or later at stroke
of pen   .

.   just because they ain't no water fit to drink in that spot (or
you ain't found none) don't mean there ain't no fresh water to be
had NOWHERE   .   .
        .

            —and to Tolson and to his ode
            and to Liberia and to Allen Tate
            (Give him credit)
            and to the South generally
                    Selah!

            — and to 100 years of it — splits
            off the radium, the Gamma rays

will eat their bastard bones out who
are opposed
                    Selah!

Pobres bastardos, misquierdos
                    Pobrecitos
            Ay! que pobres

— yuh wanna be killed with your
face in the dirt and a son-of-a-bitch
of a *Guardia Civil* giving you the
                coup de (dis)grace
right in the puss   .   ?

            Selah! Selah!

Credit!   I hope you have a long credit
            and a dirty one
                    Selah!

What is credit?   the Parthenon

What is money?   the gold entrusted to Phideas for the
                statue of Pallas Athena, that he "put aside"
                for private purposes

        — the gold, in short, that Phideas stole
        You can't steal credit : the Parthenon.

— let's skip any reference, at this time, to the Elgin marbles.

            Reuther — shot through a window, at whose pay?

— then there's Ben Shahn   .

            Here follows a list of the mayors of
            120 American cities in the years following

the Civil War.　　.　　or the War Between
the States, if you prefer　　.　　like
cubes of fat in the *blutwurst* of the
times　　　　.

Credit.　　Credit.　　Credit.　　Give them all credit. They were
the fathers of many a later novelist, no worse than the rest.

> Money : Joke
> could be wiped out
> at stroke
> of pen
> and was when
> gold and pound were
> devalued

> Money : small time
> 　　　　　reciprocal action relic
> precedent to stream-lined
> 　　　　turbine : credit

> Uranium : basic thought — leadward
> 　　　　Fractured : radium : credit

> Curie : woman (of no importance) genius : radium

THE GIST

credit : the gist

IN
　venshun.
O.KAY
　　In　venshun

and seeinz az how yu hv/started. Will you consider
a remedy of a lot :
                    i.e. LOCAL control of local purchasing
                                                    power .

                                                    ?   ?

Difference between squalor of spreading slums
and splendour of renaissance cities.

                    Credit makes solid
                    is related directly to the effort,
                    work: value created and received,
                    "the radiant gist" against all that
                    scants our lives.

III.

Haven't you forgot your virgin purpose,
the language?

What language? "The past is for those who
lived in the past," is all she told me.

Shh!   the old man's asleep

—all but for the tides, there is no river,
silent now, twists and turns
in his dreams   .

                            The ocean yawns!
It is almost the hour

—and did you ever know of a sixty year
woman with child   .   ?

                        Listen!
someone's coming up the path,   .   perhaps
it is not too late? Too late   .

JONATAN, bap. Oct. 29, 1752; m. Gritie (Haring?). He was born and brought
up at Hoppertown (Hohokus), but in 1779 was running the grist and saw-mill at
Wagaraw, now owned by the Alyeas. On the night of April 21, 1779, his wife
was aroused by a noise as of someone trying to get into the lower part of the mill,
where, for better security, he kept his horses. "Yawntan," said she in Dutch,

"someone is stealing your horses." Lighting a lantern, he threw open the upper half-door and challenged the marauders. Instantly a shot was fired through the lower half-door, wounding him in the abdomen. He staggered back into the house and fell upon a bed, covering himself up in the blankets. A party of Tories, masked and disguised, rushed in, and, compelling his young wife to hold a candle, they savagely attacked the prostrate form. Once he seized one of the bayonettes and holding it for a moment, cried at his assailant: "Andries, this is an old grudge." With redoubled fury the inhuman savages bayonetted him, until with a groan he expired. His two infant children who were wont to sleep in a trundle bed beneath his, were horrified spectators of their father's massacre. After the murderers were gone, his wife and a neighbor took the blood out of the bed in double handfuls. The murdered man had received nineteen or twenty cruel bayonette thrusts. It was believed that some neighbor had led the Tories to the attack, less from political or pecuniary considerations than from motives of private revenge. Hopper was a captain in the Bergen County militia. One of his children was Albert, bap. Oct. 6, 1776. It is said that Jonathan's children removed to Cincinnati, and there attained some prominence.

Come on, get going. The tide's in

*Leise, leise! Lentement! Che va piano,
va lontano!* Virtue,
my kitten, is a complex reward in all
languages, achieved slowly.

.   which reminds me of
an old friend, now gone   .

—while he was still in the hotel business, a tall and rather beautiful young woman came to his desk one day to ask if there were any interesting books to be had on the premises. He, being interested in literature, as she knew, replied that his own apartment was full of them and that, though he couldn't leave at the moment — Here's my key, go up and help yourself.

She thanked him and went off. He forgot all about her.

After lunch he too went to his rooms not remembering until he was at the door that he had no key. But the door was unlatched and as he entered, a girl was lying naked on the bed. It startled him a little. So much so that all he could do was to remove his own clothes and lie beside her. Quite comfortable, he soon fell into a heavy sleep. She also must have slept.

They wakened later, simultaneously, much refreshed.

[187]

                              —another, once gave me
an old ash-tray, a bit of
                    porcelain inscribed
with the legend, *La Vertue*
                    est toute dans l'effort
baked into the material,
                              maroon on white, a glazed
Venerian scallop   .   for
                    ashes, fit repository
for legend, a quieting thought:
                    Virtue is wholly
in the effort to be virtuous   .
                              This takes connivance,
takes convoluted forms, takes
                    time!   A sea-shell   .
Let's not dwell on childhood's
                    lecherous cousins. Why
should we? Or even on
                    as comparatively simple
a thing as the composite
                    dandelion that
changes its face overnight   .   Virtue,
                    a mask: the mask,
virtuous   .

Kill the explicit sentence, don't you think? and expand our meaning—by verbal
sequences. Sentences, but not grammatical sentences: dead-falls set by schoolmen.
Do you think there is any virtue in that? better than sleep? to revive us?

          She used to call me her
                              country bumpkin
          Now she is gone I think
                              of her as in Heaven
          She made me believe in
                              it   .   a little
          Where else could she go?

                    [188]

There was
Something grandiose
                about her   .
Man and woman are not
                much emphasized as
such at that age: both
                want the same
thing   .   to be amused.
                Imagine *me*
at her funeral. I sat
                way back. Stupid,
perhaps but no more so
                than any funeral.
You might think she had
                a private ticket.
I think she did; some
                people, not many,
make you feel that way.
                It's in them.

Virtue, she would say   .
                (her version of it)
is a stout old bird,
                unpredictable. And
so I remember her,
                adding,
as she did, clumsily,
                not being used to
such talk, that —
                Nothing does, does
as it used to do
                do do! I loved her.

        All the professions, all the arts,
        idiots, criminals to the greatest
        lack and deformity, the stable parts

making up a man's mind — fly
after him attacking ears and eyes:
small birds following marauding
crows, in ecstasies   .   of fear
and daring

The brain is weak. It fails mastery,
never a fact.

            To bring himself in,
hold together wives in one wife and
at the same time scatter it,
the one in all of them   .
                    Weakness,
weakness dogs him, fulfillment only
a dream or in a dream. No one mind
can do it all, runs smooth
in the effort: *toute dans l'effort*

            The greyhaired President
(of Haiti), his women and children,
                at the water's edge,
sweating, leads off finally, after
delays, huzzahs, songs for pageant reasons
over the blue water   .
in a private plane
            with his blonde secretary.

Scattered, the fierceness
of knowledge comes flocking down again—

            souvenir of childhood,
the skull of the white stone   .

There was Margaret of the big breasts
and daring eyes who carried
her head, where her small brain rattled,
as the mind might wish,
at the best, to be carried. There was
Lucille, gold hair and blue eyes, very
straight, who
to the amazement of many, married a
saloon keeper and lost her modesty.
There was loving Alma, who wrote a steady
hand, whose mouth never wished for
relief. And the cold Nancy, with small
firm breasts   .

           You remember?

                        .   a high
forehead, she who never smiled more
than was sufficient but whose broad
mouth was icy with pleasure startling
the back and knees! whose words were
few and never wasted. There were
others — half hearted, the over-eager,
the dull, pity for all of them, staring
out of dirty windows, hopeless, indifferent,
come too late and a few, too drunk
with it — or anything — to be awake to
receive it. All these
and more — shining, struggling flies
caught in the meshes of Her hair, of whom
there can be no complaint, fast in
the invisible net — from the back country,
half awakened — all desiring. Not one
to escape, not one   .   a fragrance
of mown hay, facing the rapacious,
the "great"   .

The whereabouts of Peter the Dwarf's grave was unknown until the end of the last century, when, in 1885, P. Doremus, undertaker, was moving bodies from the cellar of the old church to make room for a new furnace, he disinterred a small coffin and beside it a large box. In the coffin was the headless skeleton of what he took to be a child until he opened the large box and found therein an enormous skull. In referring to the burial records it was learned that Peter the Dwarf had been so buried.

Yellow, for genius, the Jap said. Yellow
is your color. The sun. Everybody looked.
And you, purple, he added, wind over water.

My serpent, my river! genius of the fields,
Kra, my adored one, unspoiled by the mind,
observer of pigeons, rememberer of
cataracts, voluptuary of gulls! Knower
of tides, counter of hours, wanings and
waxings, enumerator of snowflakes, starer
through thin ice, whose corpuscles are
minnows, whose drink, sand   .

Here's to the baby,
may it thrive!
Here's to the labia
that rive

to give it place
in a stubborn world.
And here's to the peak
from which the seed was hurled!

In a deep-set valley between hills, almost hid
by dense foliage lay the little village.
Dominated by the Falls the surrounding country
was a beautiful wilderness where mountain pink
and wood violet throve: a place inhabited only
by straggling trappers and wandering Indians.

A print in colors by Paul Sandby, a well known
water color artist of the eighteenth century,
a rare print in the Public Library
shows the old Falls restudied from a drawing
made by Lieut. Gov. Pownall (excellent work) as he
saw it in the year 1700.

The wigwam and the tomahawk, the Totowa tribe   .
On either side lay the river-farms resting in
the quiet of those colonial days: a hearty old
Dutch stock, with a toughness to stick and
hold fast, although not fast in making improvements.

Clothing homespun. The people raised their own
stock. Rude furniture, sanded floors, rush
bottomed chair, a pewter shelf of Brittania
ware. The wives spun and wove — many things
that might appear disgraceful or distasteful today
The Benson and Doremus estates for years were
the only ones on the north side of the river.

Dear Doc: Since I last wrote I have settled down more, am working on a Labor
newspaper (N. J. Labor Herald, AFL) in Newark. The owner is an Assemblyman
and so I have a chance to see many of the peripheral intimacies of political life
which is in this neighborhood and has always had for me the appeal of the rest of
the landscape, and a little more, since it is the landscape alive and busy.

Do you know that the west side of the City Hall, the street, is nicknamed
the Bourse, because of the continual political and banking haggle and hassel that
goes on there?

Also I have been walking the streets and discovering the bars—especially around
the great Mill and River streets. Do you know this part of Paterson? I have seen
so many things—negroes, gypsies, an incoherent bartender in a taproom overhang-
ing the river, filled with gas, ready to explode, the window facing the river painted
over so that the people can't see in. I wonder if you have seen River Street most
of all, because that is really the heart of what is to be seen.

I keep wanting to write you a long letter about deep things I can show you,
and will some day—the look of streets and people, events that have happened here
and there.

                                                                    A.G.

  .   .   .   .   .   .

[193]

There were colored slaves. In 1791 only ten
houses, all farm houses save one, The Godwin
Tavern, the most historic house in Paterson,
on River Street: a swinging sign on a high
post with a full length picture of Washington
painted on it, giving a squeaking sound when
touched by the wind.

Branching trees and ample gardens gave
the village streets a delightful charm and
the narrow old-fashioned brick walls added
a dignity to the shading trees. It was a fair
resort for summer sojourners on their way
to the Falls, the main object of interest.

The sun goes beyond Garret Mountain
as evening descends, the green of its pine
trees, fading under a crimson sky until
all color is lost. In the town candle light
appears. No lighted streets. It is as dark
as Egypt.

There is the story of the cholera epidemic
the well known man who refused to bring his
team into town for fear of infecting them
but stopped beyond the river and carted his
produce in himself by wheelbarrow — to the
old market, in the Dutch style of those days.

Paterson, N. J., Sept. 17—Fred Goodell Jr., twenty-two, was arrested early this
morning and charged with the murder of his six-months-old daughter Nancy, for
whom police were looking since Tuesday, when Goodell reported her missing.

Continued questioning from last night until 1 a.m. by police headed by Chief
James Walker drew the story of the slaying, police said, from the $40-a-week
factory worker a few hours after he refused to join his wife, Marie, eighteen, in
taking a lie detector test.

At 2 a.m. Goodell led police a few blocks from his house to a spot on Garrett

Mountain and showed them a heavy rock under which he had buried Nancy, dressed only in a diaper and placed in a paper shopping bag.

Goodell told the police he had killed the child by twice snapping the wooden tray of a high chair into the baby's face Monday morning when her crying annoyed him as he was feeding her. Dr. George Surgent, the county physician, said she died of a fractured skull.

There was an old wooden bridge to Manchester, as
Totowa was called in those days, which
Lafayette crossed in 1824, while little
girls strewed flowers in his path. Just
across the river in what is now called the Old
Gun Mill Yard was a nail factory where
they made nails by hand.

I remember going down to the old cotton
mill one morning when the thermometer was
down to 13 degrees below on the old bell
post. In those days there were few steam
whistles. Most of the mills had a bell post
and bell, to ring out the news, "Come to work!"

Stepping out of bed into a snow drift
that had sifted in through the roof; then,
after a porridge breakfast, walk
five miles to work. When I got there I
did pound the anvil for sartin', to keep
up circulation.

In the early days of Paterson, the breathing
spot of the village was the triangle square
bounded by Park Street (now lower Main St.)
and Bank Street. Not including the Falls it
was the prettiest spot in town. Well shaded
by trees with a common in the center where
the country circus pitched its tents.

[195]

On the Park Street side it ran down to
the river. On the Bank Street side it ran
to a roadway leading to the barnyard of
the Goodwin House, the barnyard taking up
part of the north side of the park.

The circus was an antiquated affair, only
a small tent, one ring show. They didn't
allow circuses to perform in the afternoon
because that would close up the mills. Time
in those days was precious. Only in the
evenings. But they were sure to parade their
horses about the town about the time the
mills stopped work. The upshot of the
matter was, the town turned out to the circus
in the evening. It was lighted

in those days by candles especially
made for the show. They were giants fastened
to boards hung on wires about the tent,
a peculiar contrivance. The giant candles
were placed on the bottom boards, and two
rows of smaller candles one above the other
tapering to a point, forming a very pretty
scene and giving plenty of light.

The candles lasted during the performance
presenting a weird but dazzling spectacle
in contrast with the showy performers —

Many of the old names and some of the
places are not remembered now: McCurdy's
Pond, Goffle Road, Boudinot Street. The
Town Clock Building. The old-fashioned
Dutch Church that burned down Dec. 14, 1871
as the clock was striking twelve midnight.

Collet, Carrick, Roswell Colt,
Dickerson, Ogden, Pennington   .   .
The part of town called Dublin
settled by the first Irish immigrants. If
you intended residing in the old town you'd
drink of the water of Dublin Spring. The
finest water he ever tasted, said Lafayette.

Just off Gun Mill yard, on the gully
was a long rustic winding stairs leading
to a cliff on the opposite side of the river.
At the top was Fyfield's tavern — watching
the birds flutter and bathe in the little
pools in the rocks formed by the falling
mist — of the Falls   .   .

Paterson, N. J., January 9, 1850:—The murder last night of two persons living
at the Goffle, within two or three miles of this place has thrown our community
into a state of intense excitement. The victims are John S. Van Winkle and his
wife, an aged couple, and long residents of this county. The atrocious deed was
accomplished as there appears no doubt by one John Johnson, a laboring farmer,
and who at the time was employed by some of his neighbors in the same capacity.
So far as we have been able to gather the particulars, it would seem that Johnson
effected an entrance into the house through an upper window, by means of a ladder,
and descending to the bedroom of his victims below, accomplished his murderous
purpose by first attacking the wife who slept in front, then the husband, and again
the wife.

The second attack appears to have immediately deprived the wife of life; the
husband is still living but his death is momentarily expected. The chief instrument
used appears to have been a knife, though the husband bears one or more marks of
a hatchet. The hatchet was found next morning either in bed or on the floor, and
the knife on the window sill, where it was left by the murderer in descending to
the ground.

A boy only slept in the same dwelling. . . . . The fresh snow, however, enabled
his pursuers to find and arrest their man. . . . . His object was doubtless money
(which, however, he seemed not to have obtained).

Johnson inquired why they had tied him, "what have I done?" . . . . He was
taken to the scene of murder and shown the objects of his barbarous cruelty, but
the sight produced no other sensible effect than to extort from him an expression
of pity, he denying any knowledge of participation in the inhuman butchery.

Trip a trap o'troontjes
De vaarkens in de boontjes—
De koeien in de klaver—
De paarden in de haver—
De eenden in de waterplas,
        Plis! Plas!
Zoo groot mijn kleine Derrick was!

You come today to see killed
                    killed, killed
as if it were a conclusion
                    —a conclusion!
a convincing strewing of corpses
—to move the mind

            as tho' the mind
can be moved, the mind, I said
by an array of hacked corpses:

                    War!
a poverty of resource   .   .

            Twenty feet of
guts on the black sands of Iwo

            "What have I done?"

—to convince whom? the sea worm?
They are used to death and
jubilate at it   .   .

Murder.

        —you cannot believe
that it can begin again, again, here
again   .   here

Waken from a dream, this dream of
the whole poem   .   sea-bound,
                    rises, a sea of blood

—the sea that sucks in all rivers,
                            dazzled, led
by the salmon and the shad   .

Turn back I warn you
                (October 10, 1950)
from the shark, that snaps
at his own trailing guts, makes a sunset
of the green water   .

But lullaby, they say, the tame sea is
no more than sleep is   .   afloat
with weeds, bearing seeds   .

                    Ah!

float wrack, float words, snaring the
seeds   .

I warn you, the sea is *not* our home.
                    the sea is not our home

The sea *is* our home whither all rivers
(wither) run   .

                    the nostalgic sea
sopped with our cries
                Thalassa! Thalassa!
calling us home   .

[199]

I say to you, Put wax rather in your
ears against the hungry sea
                    it is not our home!

.   draws us in to drown, of losses
and regrets   .

Oh that the rocks of the Areopagus had
kept their sounds, the voices of the law!
Or that the great theatre of Dionysius
could be aroused by some modern magic
                              to release
what is bound in it, stones!
that music might be wakened from them to
melt our ears   .

The sea is not our home   .

—though seeds float in with the scum
and wrack   .   among brown fronds
and limp starfish   .

Yet you will come to it, come to it! The
song is in your ears, to Oceanus
where the day drowns   .

                    No! it is not our home.

You will come to it, the blood dark sea
of praise. You must come to it. Seed
of Venus, you will return   .   to
a girl standing upon a tilted shell, rose
pink   .

                    Listen!

Thalassa!   Thalassa!
            Drink of it, be drunk!
                    Thalassa
immaculata: our home, our nostalgic
mother in whom the dead, enwombed again
cry out to us to return   .
                        the blood dark sea!
nicked by the light alone, diamonded
by the light   .   from which the sun
alone lifts undamped his wings
                              of fire!

.   .   not our home! It is NOT
our home.

                        What's that?
—a duck, a hell-diver? A swimming dog?
What, a sea-dog? There it is again.
A porpoise, of course, following
the mackerel   .   No. Must be the up-
end of something sunk. But this is moving!
Maybe not. Flotsam of some sort.

A large, compact bitch gets up, black,
from where she has been lying
under the bank, yawns and stretches with
a half suppressed half whine, half cry   .
She looks to sea, cocking her ears and,
restless, walks to the water's edge where
she sits down, half in the water   .

When he came out, lifting his knees
through the waves she went to him frisking
her rump awkwardly   .

[201]

Wiping his face with his hand he turned
to look back to the waves, then
knocking at his ears, walked up
to stretch out flat on his back in
the hot sand   .   there were some
girls, far down the beach, playing ball.

—must have slept. Got up again, rubbed
the dry sand off and walking a
few steps got into a pair of faded
overalls, slid his shirt on overhand (the
sleeves were still rolled up) shoes,
hat where she had been watching them under
the bank and turned again
to the water's steady roar, as of a distant
waterfall   .   Climbing the
bank, after a few tries, he picked
some beach plums from a low bush and
sampled one of them, spitting the seed out,
then headed inland, followed by the dog

John Johnson, from Liverpool, England, was convicted after 20 minutes con-
ference by the Jury. On April 30th, 1850, he was hung in full view of thousands
who had gathered on Garrett Mountain and adjacent house tops to witness the
spectacle.

This is the blast
the eternal close
the spiral
the final somersault
        the end.

BOOK FIVE

(1958)

To the Memory

of

HENRI TOULOUSE LAUTREC,

Painter

I.

In old age
       the mind
              casts off
         rebelliously
      an eagle
from its crag

         — the angle of a forehead
             or far less
     makes him remember when he thought
        he had forgot

                 — remember

      confidently
  only a moment, only for a fleeting moment —
      with a smile of recognition   .   .

    It is early   .   .   .
    the song of the fox sparrow
  reawakening the world
    of Paterson
          — its rocks and streams
    frail tho it is
from their long winter sleep

    In March —

[205]

                    the rocks
                    the bare rocks
          speak!

— it is a cloudy morning.
              He looks out the window
                    sees the birds still there —

Not prophecy! NOT prophecy!
              but the thing itself!

                    — the first phase,
Lorca's *The Love of Don Perlimplín,*
          the young girl
                    no more than a child
leads her aged bridegroom
              innocently enough
                    to his downfall —

                              —at the end of the play, (she was a hot
little bitch but nothing unusual—today we marry women who are past their
prime, Juliet was 13 and Beatrice 9 when Dante first saw her).

Love's whole gamut, the wedding night's promiscuity in the girl's mind, her
determination not to be left out of the party, as a moral gesture, if ever there
was one

The moral
              proclaimed by the whorehouse
                              could not be better proclaimed
          by the virgin, a price on her head,
                    her maidenhead!
                              sharp practice
to hold on to that
              cheapening it:
                              Throw it away! (as she did)

The Unicorn

                    the white one-horned beast
                                        thrashes about
        root toot a toot!
                        faceless among the stars
                                        calling
        for its own murder

        Paterson, from the air
                        above the low range of its hills
                                        across the river
        on a rock-ridge
                        has returned to the old scenes
                                        to witness

        What has happened
                        since Soupault gave him the novel
                                        the Dadaist novel
        to translate —
                        The Last Nights of Paris.
                                "What has happened to Paris
        since that time?
                        and to myself"?

                        A WORLD OF ART
        THAT THROUGH THE YEARS HAS

                                SURVIVED!

        — the museum became real
                        The Cloisters —
                                        on its rock
        casting its shadow —
                        "la réalité! la réalité!
                                la réa, la réa, la réalité!"

                                [207]

Dear Bill:

I wish you and F. could have come. It was a grand day and we missed you two, one and all missed you. Forgetmenot, Wild columbine, white and purple violets, white narcissus, wild anemones and yards and yards of delicate wild windflowers along the brook showed up at their best. We didn't have hard cider or applejack this time but wine and vodka and lots of victuals. The farm buildings are not "long gone" but exactly as you saw them. The erstwhile chicken house has been a studio for years, one D.E. envied when he saw it and it has been occupied by one person or another writing every summer when I am here which has been pretty continuously for some time. The barn too has a big roomy floor which anyone who finds a table and a chair in space enlivening is welcome to. E's even fondled the idea of "doing something" about the barn and I wish they would. Their kids went in bathing in the brook, painted pictures and explored. If you ever feel like coming and get transportation please come. E's will be up again before leaving Princeton in June. They will be in H. next year. J.G. is occupying the "Guest House" now.

How lovely to read your memories of the place; a place is made of memories as well as the world around it. Most of the flowers were put in many years ago and thrive each spring, the wild ones in some new spot that is exciting to see. Hepatica and bloodroot are now all over the place, and trees that were infants are now tall creatures filled this season with orioles, some rare warblers like the Myrtle and magnolia warbler and a wren has the best nest in the garage (not to be confused with any uptodate shelter) where I had a coat lined with sheepskin hanging and the wren simply used it to back her nest against where she is sitting warm and pretty on five eggs.

    Best wishes and love from everyone who was here

                                Josie

           The whore and the virgin, an identity:
— through its disguises

        thrash about — but will not succeed in breaking free   .
                    an identity

        Audubon (Au-du-bon), (the lost Dauphin)
                    left the boat
                                downstream
        below the falls of the Ohio at Louisville
                    to follow

                          [208]

a trail through the woods
                  across three states
                                northward of Kentucky   .   .

He saw buffalo
                and more
                              a horned beast among the trees
in the moonlight
                following small birds
the chicadee
                in a field crowded with small flowers
.   .   its neck
                circled by a crown!
                              from a regal tapestry of stars!
lying wounded wounded on his belly
                legs folded under him
the bearded head held
                regally aloft   .
                        What but indirection
will get to the end of the sphere?
                Here
is not there,
                and will never be.
                      The Unicorn
has no match
                or mate   .   the artist
                has no peer   .
Death
                has no peer:
wandering in the woods,
                a field crowded with small flowers
in which the wounded beast lies down to rest

                We shall not get to the bottom:
                death is a hole

in which we are all buried
Gentile and Jew

The flower dies down
and rots away   .
But there is a hole
in the bottom of the bag.

It is the imagination
which cannot be fathomed.
It is through this hole
we escape   .   .

So through art alone, male and female, a field of
flowers, a tapestry, spring flowers unequaled
in loveliness,

through this hole
at the bottom of the cavern
of death, the imagination
escapes intact

.   he bears a collar round his neck
hid in the bristling hair.

Dear Dr. Williams:

Thanks for your introduction. The book is over in England being printed, and
will be out in July sometime. Your foreword is personal and compassionate and
you got the point of what has happened. You should see what strength & gaiety
there is beyond that though. The book will contain . . . I have never been
interested in writing except for the splendor of actual experience etc. bullshit,
I mean I've never been really crazy, confused at times.

.   .   .   .

I am leaving for the North pole this time on a ship in a few weeks. . . .
I'll see icebergs and write great white polar rhapsodies. Love to you, back in Oc-
tober and will pass thru Paterson to see family on my first trip to Europe. I have
NOT absconded from Paterson. I have a whitmanesque mania & nostalgia for cities
and detail & panorama and isolation in jungle and pole, like the image you pick

up. When I've seen enough I'll be back to splash in the Passaic again only with a body so naked and happy City Hall will have to call out the Riot Squad. When I come back I'll make big political speeches in the mayoralty campaigns like I did when I was 16 only this time I'll have W. C. Fields on my left and Jehovah on my right. Why not? Paterson is only a big sad poppa who needs compassion. . In any case Beauty is where I hang my hat. And reality. And America.

There is no struggle to speak to the city, out of the stones etc. Truth is not hard to find . . . I'm not being clear, so I'll shut up . . . I mean to say paterson is not a task like milton going down to hell, it's a flower to the mind etc   etc

A magazine will be put out . . . etc.
.   .   .   .
Adios.   A.G.

IF YOU DON'T HAVE ANY TIME FOR ANYTHING ELSE
PLEASE READ THE ENCLOSED
SUNFLOWER SUTRA

— the virgin and the whore, which
most endures? the world
of the imagination most endures:

Pollock's blobs of paint squeezed out
with design!
pure from the tube. Nothing else
is real   .   .

WALK in the world
                    (you can't see anything
from a car window, still less
from a plane, or from the moon!? Come
off of it.)
              — a present, a "present"
world, across three states (Ben Shahn saw it
among its rails and wires,
and noted it down) walked across three states
for it   .   .
              a secret world,

[211]

a sphere, a snake with its tail in
its mouth
     rolls backward into the past

. . .   The whores grasping for your genitals, faces almost pleading—"two
dolla, two dolla" till you almost go in with the sheer brute desire straining at your
loins, the whisky and the fizzes and the cognac in you till a friend grabs you . . .
"No . . . to a real house, this is shit." A real house, a real house? *Casa
real? Casa de putas?* And then the walk through the dark streets, joy of living,
in being drunk and walking with other drunks, walking the streets of dust in a
dusty year in a dusty century where everything is dust but you are young and you
are drunk and there are women ready to love for some paper in your pocket.
Through the streets with dozens of bands of other soldiers (they are soldiers even
with civilian clothes, soldiers as you are but different and this band is different
because you are you — and drunk and Baudelaire and Rimbaud and a soul with a
book in it and drunk) A woman steps into the open door of a cafe and puts her
hand between her legs and smiles at you . . . at you a whore smiles! And
you yell back and all yell back and she yells and laughs and laughter fills . . .
the . . . guitar soaked night air.

    And then the house, . . . and see a smooth faced girl against a door,
all white . . . snow, the virgin, O bride . . . crook her finger and
the vestal not-color of it, the clean hair of her and the beauty of her body in the
orchid stench, in the vulgar assailing stench the fragility and you walk and sway
across the floor, and reel against the dancers and push away the voice that embraces
your ear and find her, still standing against the door and she is smooth-faced and
wants four dollars but you make it three but four she says you argue and her hand
on your belly and she moves it and four and you can hear the music spinning out
its tropical redness the beer you gulp and touch the breast, the firmness FOUR no
three and smile a girl is carried out of the room by a soldier (bride eternal) smile
FOUR no three the hand! the breast, you touch grasp hold lust feel the curve of a
buttock silent-smooth sliding under your palm, the dress, the hand!

    high heels clack clack laughs noise and her eyes are black and four? please and
you pay four? no . three . and then yes four cuatro . . . cuatro
dolares but twice, I go twice, 'andsome, come on, 'andsome. A child you follow
her, the light whirling in your eyes the noise the other girls in the babel friend's
voice unintelligible, edged with laughter his face at which you smile though there
is nothing to smile at but smile absurdly because making love to a whore is funny
but it is not funny as her blood beneath flesh, her fingers fragile touches yours in
rhythm not funny but heat and passion bright and white, brighter-white than
lights of whorehouses, than the gin fizz white, white and deep as birth, deeper
than death.

                                                G.S.

        A lady with the tail of her dress
        on her arm   .   her hair is

slicked back showing the round
head, like her cousin's, the King,
the royal consort's, young as she   .
in a velvet bonnet, puce,
slanted above the eyes, his legs
are in striped hose, green and brown.

The lady's brow is serene
to the sound of a huntsman's horn

— the birds and flowers, the castle showing through the leaves of the trees, a
pheasant drinks at the fountain, his shadow drinks there also

     .   cyclamen, columbine, if the art
with which these flowers have been
put down is to be trusted — and
again oak leaves and twigs
that brush the deer's antlers   .   .
          the brutish eyes of the deer
          not to be confused
          with the eyes of the Queen
          are glazed with death   .
     .   a rabbit's rump escaping
through the thicket   .

One warm day in April, G.B. had the inspiration to go in swimming naked with
the boys, among whom, of course, was her brother, a satyr if there ever was one,
to beat anybody up who presumed to molest her. It was at Sandy Bottom, near
Willow Point where in later years we used to have picnics. That was before she
turned whore and got syphilis. L.M. about that time, a young sailor, went to Rio
unafraid of "children's diseases" as the French (and others) called them — but it
was no joke as Gauguin found out when his brains began to rot away

     .   the times today
          are safer for the fornicators
             the moral's
as you choose but the brain
          need not putrefy

[213]

                         or petrify
for fear of venereal disease
               unless you wish it

"Loose your love to flow"
               while you are yet young
                              male and female
(if it is worth it to you)
               'n cha cha cha
                              you'd think the brain
'd be grafted
               on a better root

II.

"   .   I am no authority on Sappho and do not read her poetry particularly well. She wrote for a clear gentle tinkling voice. She avoided all roughness. 'The silence that is in the starry sky,' gives something of her tone,   .   "

A.P.

Peer of the gods is that man, who
face to face, sits listening
to your sweet speech and lovely
        laughter.

It is this that rouses a tumult
in my breast. At mere sight of you
my voice falters, my tongue
        is broken.

Straightway, a delicate fire runs in
my limbs; my eyes
are blinded and my ears
        thunder.

Sweat pours out: a trembling hunts
me down. I grow paler
than dry grass and lack little
        of dying.

13 Nv   Oke Hay   my BilBill   The Bull Bull, ameer.

Is there anything in Ac Bul 2/   vide enc that seems cloudy to you, or
INComprehensible/

or that having comprehended you disagree with?

The hardest thing to discover is WHY someone else, apparently not an ape or a Roosevelt cannot understand something as simple as 2 plus 2 makes four.

McNair Wilson has just writ me, that Soddy got interested and started to study "economics" and found out what they offered him wasn't economics but banditry

Wars are made to make debt, and the late one started by the ambulating dunghill FDR has been amply successful.

                                        and the stink that elevated
him still emits a smell.

Also the ten vols/ treasury reports sent me to Rapallo show that in the years from departure of Wiggin till the mail stopped you suckers had paid ten billion for gold that cd/ have been bought for SIX billion.

                                Is this clear or do you still want DEEtails?

That sovereignty inheres in the POWER to issue money, whether you have the right to do it or not.

                        don't let me crowd you.

If there is anything here that is OBskewer   ,   say so.

don't worry re Beum,

He didnt say you told him to send me the book, merely that he had metChu. let the young   educ   the young.

  Only naive remark I found in Voltaire wuz when he found two good books on econ/   and wrote   :   "Now people will understand it." end quote.

But if the buzzards on yr(and Del M's) list   had been CLEAR I wdn't have spent so much time clarifying their indistinctnesses.

You   agree   that   the   offering   da   shittahd   aaabull   instead   of   history   is
            undesirable   ??????

                There is a woman in our town
                walks rapidly, flat bellied

                in worn slacks upon the street
                where I saw her.

                    Neither short
nor tall, nor old nor young
her
    face would attract no

adolescent. Grey eyes looked
straight before her.
                    Her

                        hair
was gathered simply behind the
ears under a shapeless hat.

Her
    hips were narrow, her
                        legs
thin and straight. She stopped

me in my tracks — until I saw
her
    disappear in the crowd.

                    .
An inconspicuous decoration
made of sombre cloth, meant
I think to be a flower, was
pinned flat to her
                    right

breast — any woman might have
done the same to
say she was a woman and warn
us of her mood. Otherwise

she was dressed in male attire,
as much as to say to hell

with you. Her

                    expression was
serious, her
                feet were small.

And she was gone!

.   if ever I see you again
as I have sought you
daily without success

I'll speak to you, alas
too late! ask,
What are you doing on the

streets of Paterson? a
thousand questions:
Are you married? Have you any

children? And, most important,
your NAME! which
of course she may not

give me — though
I cannot conceive it
in such a lonely and

intelligent woman

.   have you read anything that I have written?
It is all for you

                or the birds   .
or Mezz Mezzrow

                who wrote   .

Knocking around with Rapp and the Rhythm Kings put the finishing touches on me and straightened me out. To be with those guys made me know that any white man, if he thought straight and studied hard, could sing and dance and play with the Negro. You didn't have to take the finest and most original and honest music in America and mess it up because you were a white man; you could dig the colored man's real message and get in there with him, like Rapp. I felt good all over after a session with the Rhythm Kings, and I began to miss that tenor sax.

Man, I was gone with it — inspiration's mammy was with me. And to top it all, I walked down Madison Street one day and what I heard made me think my ears were lying. Bessie Smith was shouting the *Downhearted Blues* from a record in a music shop. I flew in and bought up every record they had by the mother of the blues — *Cemetery Blues, Bleedin' Hearted*, and *Midnight Blues* — then I ran home and listened to them for hours on the victrola. I was put in a trance by Bessie's mournful stories and the patterns of true harmony in the piano background, full of little runs that crawled up and down my spine like mice. Every note that woman wailed vibrated on the tight strings of my nervous system; every word she sang answered a question I was asking. You couldn't drag me away from that victrola, even to eat.

                     .   .   or the Satyrs, a
pre-tragic play,
        a satyric play!
               All plays
were satyric when they were most devout.
        Ribald as a Satyr!

Satyrs dance!
        all the deformities take wing
            Centaurs
leading to the rout of the vocables
        in the writings
of Gertrude
        Stein — but
               you cannot be
an artist
        by mere ineptitude
The dream
        is in pursuit!
The neat figures of
        Paul Klee

     fill the canvas
but that
    is not the work
      of a child   .
the cure began, perhaps
    with the abstraction
      of Arabic art
Dürer
    with his *Melancholy*
      was aware of it—
the shattered masonry. Leonardo
    saw it,
      the obsession,
and ridiculed it
    in *La Gioconda*.
      Bosch's
congeries of tortured souls and devils
    who prey on them
      fish
swallowing
    their own entrails
Freud
    Picasso
      Juan Gris.
A letter from a friend
    saying:
      For the last
three nights
    I have slept like a baby
      without
liquor or dope of any sort!
    we know
      that a stasis
from a chrysalis
    has stretched its wings .
      like a bull

or a Minotaur
            or Beethoven
                        in the scherzo
    from the Fifth Symphony
            stomped
                        his heavy feet
I saw love
            mounted naked on a horse
                        on a swan
    the tail of a fish
            the bloodthirsty conger eel
                        and laughed
    recalling the Jew
            in the pit
                        among his fellows
    when the indifferent chap
            with the machine gun
                        was spraying the heap   .
    he had not yet been hit
            but smiled
    comforting his companions   .
            comforting
                        his companions
    Dreams possess me
            and the dance
                        of my thoughts
    involving animals
            the blameless beasts

(Q. Mr. Williams, can you tell me, simply, what poetry is?

A.   Well   .   .   .   I would say that poetry is language charged with emo-
     tion. It's words, rhythmically organized   .   .   .   A poem is a com-
     plete little universe. It exists separately. Any poem that has worth expresses
     the whole life of the poet. It gives a view of what the poet is.

Q.   All right, look at this part of a poem by E. E. Cummings, another great
     American poet:

[221]

```
(im)c-a-t(mo)
b,i;l:e

FallleA
ps!fl
OattumblI

sh?dr
IftwhirlF
(Ul) (lY)
&&&
```

Is this poetry?

A.   I would reject it as a poem. It may be, to him, a poem. But I would reject it. I can't understand it. He's a serious man. So I struggle very hard with it — and I get no meaning at all.

Q.   You get no meaning? But here's part of a poem you yourself have written: . . . "2 partridges/ 2 mallard ducks/ a Dungeness crab/ 24 hours out/ of the Pacific/ and 2 live-frozen/ trout/ from Denmark . . ." Now, that sounds just like a fashionable grocery list!

A.   It is a fashionable grocery list.

Q.   Well — is it poetry?

A.   We poets have to talk in a language which is not English. It is the American idiom. Rhythmically it's organized as a sample of the American idiom. It has as much originality as jazz. If you say "2 partridges, 2 mallard ducks, a Dungeness crab" — if you treat that rhythmically, ignoring the practical sense it forms a jagged pattern. It is, to my mind, poetry.

Q.   But if you don't "ignore the practical sense" . . . you agree that it is a fashionable grocery list.

A.   Yes. Anything is good material for poetry. Anything. I've said it time and time again.

Q.   Aren't we supposed to understand it?

A.   There is a difference of poetry and the sense. Sometimes modern poets ignore sense completely. That's what makes some of the difficulty . . . The audience is confused by the shape of the words.

Q.   But shouldn't a word mean something when you see it?

A.   In prose, an English word means what it says. In poetry, you're listening to two things . . . you're listening to the sense, the common sense of what it says. But it says more. That is the difficulty.

.   .   .   .   )

III.

Peter Brueghel, the elder, painted
a Nativity, painted a Baby
new born!
among the words.

                    Armed men,
savagely armed men
                      armed with pikes,
halberds and swords
whispering men with averted faces
got to the heart
                  of the matter
as they talked to the pot bellied
greybeard (center)
the butt of their comments,
looking askance, showing their
amazement at the scene,
features like the more stupid
German soldiers of the late
war

— but the Baby (as from an
illustrated catalogue
in colors) lies naked on his Mother's
knees

— it is a scene, authentic
enough, to be witnessed frequently

[223]

among the poor (I salute
the man Brueghel who painted
what he saw —
            many times no doubt
among his own kids but not of course
in this setting

The crowned and mitred heads
of the 3 men, one of them black,
who had come, obviously from afar
(highwaymen?)
by the rich robes
they had on — offered
to propitiate their gods

Their hands were loaded with gifts
— they had eyes for visions
in those days — and saw,
saw with their proper eyes,
these things
to the envy of the vulgar soldiery

He painted
the bustle of the scene,
the unkempt straggling
hair of the old man in the
middle, his sagging lips

— — incredulous
that there was so much fuss
about such a simple thing as a baby
born to an old man
out of a girl and a pretty girl
at that

But the gifts! (works of art,

where could they have picked
them up or more properly
have stolen them?)
— how else to honor
an old man, or a woman?

— the soldiers' ragged clothes,
mouths open,
their knees and feet
broken from 30 years of
war, hard campaigns, their mouths
watering for the feast which
had been provided

Peter Brueghel the artist saw it
from the two sides: the
imagination must be served —
and he served
            dispassionately

It is no mortal sin to be poor — anything but this featureless
tribe that has the money now — staring into the atom, com-
pletely blind — without grace or pity, as if they were so many
shellfish. The artist, Brueghel, saw them   .   :   the
suits of his peasants were of better stuff, hand woven, than we
can boast.

— we have come in our time to the age of shoddy, the men are
shoddy, driven by their bosses, inside and outside the job to be
done, at a profit. To whom? But not true of the Portuguese
mason, his own boss "in the new country" who is building a
wall for me, moved by oldworld knowledge of what is "virtu-
ous"   .   "that stuff they sell you in the stores now-a-days,
no good, break in your hands   .   that manufactured stuff,
from the factory, break in your hands, no care what they turn
out"

The Gospel according to St. Matthew, Chapter 1, verse 18, — Now the birth of Jesus Christ was on this wise: When as his mother Miriam was espoused to Joseph before they came together she was found with child of the Holy Ghost.

19 Then Joseph her husband, being a just man, and not willing to make her a public example, was minded to put her away privately.

20 But while he thought on these things, behold, the angel of the Lord, appeared to him in a dream, saying, Joseph, thou son of David, fear not to take unto thee Miriam thy wife: for that which is conceived in her is of the Holy Ghost.

Luke   .   .   And Mary kept all these sayings, pondering them in her heart.

> .   no woman is virtuous
> who does not give herself to her lover
> — forthwith

Dear Bill:

.   .   .   .

I am told by a dear friend in Paris, G.D. who is married to Henri Matisse's daughter, and who is the one vibrant head I have met in Europe, that France today is ruled by the gendarme and the concierge. In socialist Denmark I knew a highly intelligent author, a woman, who had come to America and there had a child by a wretched scribbler. Poor and forsaken she had returned to Copenhagen, where she earned her niggard indigence doing reviews for the Politiken, and giving occasional lectures on Middle English and early Danish. She lived in the slummy part of that beautiful city, trying to support a wonderful boy, sturdy, loving, and very masculine. It was my joy to bring him oranges, chocolate, and those precious morsels which his mother could not afford. She told me that the socialist police had called on her one night, asking why she had not paid her taxes to the government. Poverty was her reply. Do you recall the epitaph on Thomas Churchyard's tombstone? 'Poverty and Obscurity doth this tomb enclose.' A week later they returned, threatening to remove her furniture and have it impounded by the government. When she again pleaded that if she gave what Kroners she had her little boy would starve, the police said: 'We went to the Vin Handel last evening, and learned from the proprietor that you had bought a bottle of wine; if you can afford to drink wine you certainly can pay your taxes.' She then said 'I am so poor, and so driven to despair by it that I had to have a bottle of wine to relieve me of my melancholia.'

I am quite sure too that people only have the kind of government that their bellies crave. Furthermore, I cannot cure one soul in the earth. Plato took three journeys to Dionysius, the Tyrant of Syracuse, and once was almost killed and on another occasion was nearly sold into slavery because he imagined that he influenced a devil to model his tyranny upon The Republic. Seneca was the teacher of Nero, and Aristotle tutored Alexander of Macedon. What did they teach?

We are content here because it is cheap; my wife can eat chateaubriand for seven pesetas, about 15 or 16 cents. Going to the shops in the morning is a ritual; there is the greeting from the woman who runs the Panaderia, and the salutation (courtesy always eases the spirit and relieves the nervous system), from the man or his wife at the lecheria (where you get milk), and an expansive smile from the humble woman who sells you three pesetas worth of helio, ice. . . .

Edward

Paterson has grown older

        the dog of his thoughts
has shrunk
to no more than "a passionate letter"
to a woman, a woman he had neglected
to put to bed in the past   .
            And went on
living and writing
         answering
letters
     and tending his flower
garden, cutting his grass and trying
to get the young
        to foreshorten
their errors in the use of words which
he had found so difficult, the errors
he had made in the use of the
poetic line:

"   .   the unicorn against a millefleurs background,   .   "

There's nothing sentimental about the technique of writing. It can't be learned, you'll say, by a fool. But any young man with a mind bursting to get out, to get down on a page even a clean sentence — gets courage from an older man who stands ready to help him — to talk to.

A flight of birds, all together,
seeking their nests in the season

[227]

a flock before dawn, small birds
"That slepen al the night with open yë,"
moved by desire, passionately, they
have come a long way, commonly.
Now they separate and go by pairs
each to his appointed mating. The
colors of their plumage are undecipherable
in the sun's glare against the sky
but the old man's mind is stirred
by the white, the yellow, the black
as if he could see them there.

Their presence in the air again
calms him. Though he is approaching
death he is possessed by many poems.
Flowers have always been his friends,
even in paintings and tapestries
which have lain through the past
in museums jealously guarded, treated
against moths. They draw him imperiously
to witness them, make him think
of bus schedules and how to avoid
the irreverent — to refresh himself
at the sight direct from the 12th
century what the old women or the young
or men or boys wielding their needles
to put in her green thread correctly
beside the purple, myrtle beside
holly and the brown threads besides:
together as the cartoon has plotted it
for them. All together, working together —
all the birds together. The birds
and leaves are designed to be woven
in his mind eating and   .   .
all together for his purposes

— the aging body
    with the deformed great-toe nail
makes itself known
    coming
       to search me out — with a
       rare smile
among the thronging flowers of that field
     where the Unicorn
       is penned by a low
wooden fence
    in April!
       the same month
when at the foot of the post
     he saw the man dig up
the red snake and kill it with a spade.
      Godwin told me
       its tail
would not stop wriggling till
     after the sun
       goes down —
he knew everything
     or nothing
       and died insane
when he was still a young man

The (self) direction has been changed
     the serpent
       its tail in its mouth
"the river has returned to its beginnings"
     and backward
      (and forward)
it tortures itself within me
     until time has been washed finally under:
     and "I knew all (or enough)
it became me . "

                    — the times are not heroic
since then
                    but they are cleaner
                                and freer of disease
the mind rotted within them   .
            we'll say
                        the serpent
has its tail in its mouth
                AGAIN!
                            the all-wise serpent

Now I come to the small flowers
                    that cluster about the feet
                            of my beloved
— the hunt of
            the Unicorn and
                        the god of love
of virgin birth

                    The mind is the demon
                    drives us   .   well,
                    would you prefer it to
                    turn vegetable and

                    wear no beard?

— shall we speak of love
            seen only in a mirror
                        —no replica?
reflecting only her impalpable spirit?
            which is she whom I see
                        and not touch her flesh?

        The Unicorn roams the forest of all true
lovers' minds. They hunt it down. Bow wow! sing hey the
green holly!

— every married man carries in his head
                    the beloved and sacred image
                              of a virgin
      whom he has whored   .
                    but the living fiction
                              a tapestry
      silk and wool shot with silver threads
                    a milk white one horned beast
                              I, Paterson, the King-self   .
      saw the lady
                    through the rough woods
                              outside the palace walls
      among the stench of sweating horses
                    and gored hounds
                              yelping with pain
      the heavy breathing pack
                    to see the dead beast
                              brought in at last
      across the saddle bow
                    among the oak trees.
                              Paterson,
      keep your pecker up
                    whatever the detail!
                              Anywhere is everywhere:
      You can learn from poems
                    that an empty head tapped on
                              sounds hollow
      in any language! The figures
                    are of heroic size.
                              The woods
      are cold though it is summer
                    the lady's gown is heavy
                              and reaches to the grass.

All about, small flowers fill the scene.

A second beast is brought in
wounded.
And a third, survivor of the chase,
lies down to rest a while,
his regal neck
fast in a jeweled collar.
A hound lies on his back
eviscerated
by the beast's single horn.
Take it or leave it,
if the hat fits —
put it on. Small flowers
seem crowding to be in on the act:
the white sweet rocket,
on its branching stem, four petals
one near the other to
fill in the detail
from frame to frame without perspective
touching each other on the canvas
make up the picture:
the cranky violet
like a knight in chess,
the cinque-foil,
yellow faced —
this is a French
or Flemish tapestry—
the sweetsmelling primrose
growing close to the ground, that poets
have made famous in England,
I cannot tell it all:
slippered flowers
crimson and white,
balanced to hang
on slender bracts, cups evenly arranged upon a stem,
foxglove, the eglantine
or wild rose,

pink as a lady's ear lobe when it shows
        beneath the hair,
                campanella, blue and purple tufts
small as forget-me-not among the leaves.
        Yellow centers, crimson petals
           and the reverse,
dandelion, love-in-a-mist,
        cornflowers,
           thistle and others
the names and perfumes I do not know.
        The woods are filled with holly
           (I have told you, this
is a fiction, pay attention),
        the yellow flag of the French fields is here
           and a congeries of other flowers
as well: daffodils
        and gentian, the daisy, columbine
           petals
myrtle, dark and light
        and calendulas

The locust tree in the morning breeze
        outside her window
           where one branch moves
quietly
        undulating
           upward and about and
back and forth
        does not remind me more
           than of an old woman's smile
— a fragment of the tapestry
        preserved on an end wall
           presents a young woman
           with rounded brow
lost in the woods (or hiding)

announced   .   .
               (that is, the presentation)
by the blowing of a hunter's horn where he stands
        all but completely hid
               in the leaves. She
interests me by her singularity,
        her courtly dress
               among the leaves, listening!

The expression of her face,
        where she stands removed from the others
— the virgin and the whore,
        an identity,
               both for sale
to the highest bidder!
        and who bids higher
               than a lover? Come
out of it if you call yourself a woman.

I give you instead, a young man
        sharing the female world
               in Hell's despight, graciously
— once on a time   .
        on a time:

        Caw!   Caw!   Caw!
           the crows cry!

        In February! in February they begin it.
        She did not want to live to be

        an old woman to wear a china door-knob
        in her vagina to hold her womb up — but

        she came to that, resourceful, what?
        He was the first to turn her up

and never left her till he left her
with child, as any soldier would

until the camp broke up.

She maybe was "tagged" as Osamu
Dazai and his saintly sister

would have it

She was old when she saw her grandson:
                You young people
                                think you know everything.
She spoke in her Cockney accent
                and paused
                                looking at me hard:
The past is for those that lived in the past. Cessa!

— learning with age to sleep my life away:
saying   .

                The measure intervenes, to measure is all we know,

                        a choice among the measures   .   .

                                        the measured dance
                "unless the scent of a rose
                                startle us anew"

                Equally laughable
                                is to assume to know nothing, a
                                                chess game
                massively, "materially," compounded!

                        Yo ho! ta ho!

We know nothing and can know nothing
                          but
the dance, to dance to a measure
contrapuntally,
              Satyrically, the tragic foot.

Appendix A

———————————•••————————————

BOOK VI (c. 1961)

Jan.4/61   Paterson 6   The intimate name you were known as
          to your intimates in that reaks was The Genius, before
your enimies got hold of you

          you knew the Falls and read Greek fluently
          It did not stop the bullet that killed you - close after dawn
          at Weehawken that September dawn

- you waned to or daninize the country so that we should all
stick together and make a little money

          a rich man

John Jay, James Madison   .   let's read about it!

          Words are the burden of poems, poems are made of wods

1/8/61   the dandelion – tions-tooth – ineffegee
of fience old Hudson Rver work, might as
well have been of Paterson

a crude cheap cheap jary made to contain
pickeled peaches or eder berries

casually with all the art of domestic
husbandry or the kitchen shelf
a royal bluecurving
on itself to make a simple flour design

to decorate my bedroom wall

come out of itself to be an abstract desigs withou design
to be anything but itself for than a ¢hinese poem who
drowned embracing the reflection of the mbon in the river

– or the image of a frostyy elm outlined in ¢y gayest of
of all pantomimes

Dance, dance! loosen your limbs rom that art which holds you
faster than the drugs which hold you fater – dandelion on
my bedroom wall.

[238]

7/1/61

As Weehawken is to Hamilton

is to Provence we'll say, he hated it

of which he knew nothing and cared less

and used it inhis scheems - so

founding the counding which was to
try

increase to be the wonder of the world
in its day

which was to exceed his London on which he patterened it

(A key figure in the development)

                     If any one is important more important
                    - point of a dagger-
than the edge of a knife or a poem is: or an irrelevance

in the life of a people: see Da Da or the murders of a

Staline

          or a Li Po

                    or an obscre Montezuma

or a forgotten Socrates or Aristotle before the destruction

of the library of Alexandria (as note derisively by Berad Shaw)

by fire in which the poes of Sappho were lost

          and brings us (Alex was born out of wedlock)

     illegitimately perversion righed though that alone

does not a make a poet or a statesman

 - Wahington was a six foot four man with a wekk voice and a slow
mind which made it inconvenient for him to move fast - and so he
stayed. He had a will bred in the slow woods so that when he
moved the world moved out of has way.

[239]

Paterson 6

Book 6

Lucy had a womb
            like every other woman
                        her father sold her
so she told me
            to Charlie
                        for 3 hundred dollars
she couldn't read or write
            fresh out of
                        the old country
she hadn't had her changes yet
            I delivered her
                        of 13 children
before she came around
            she was vulgar
but fiercely loyal to me
            she had a friend
                        Mrs. Blackinger
an ##### Irish woman
            who could tell a story
                        when she'd a bit taken

Appendix B

A Note on the Text

Paterson has a textual history that is a suitable parallel to the colorful past of the city that is its focus. But this is also a textual history that immensely complicates the preparation of a new edition. These complications include the serial composition and publication of the poem over twenty years, its author's declining health over that time, its text being reset serially for a popular edition that its author gave progressively less attention to, and a number of posthumous changes to the text of the poem's later books.

Until the present edition, the reset text of the popular edition, as repaginated in 1969, has been the only collected text of the poem in print, but this 1969 text is very problematic. From the beginning of the 1950s, even before his first serious stroke, Williams evidently became impatient with checking the entirely reset, collected printings of *Paterson* that New Directions issued as the limited first edition printings of each book became sold out. Mrs. Williams wrote to David McDowell of New Directions on April 5, 1950, that the printers handling the "reprint of Paterson III are pretty much at sea about the whole thing. The spacing – the paging – etc–etc," and that Williams, "no proof reader . . . threw it aside saying—'To hell with it—let it wait until Jim [Laughlin] gets back.' " Mrs. Williams requests that when McDowell next meets with Williams "if the subject comes up—set him straight—if my suspicions are correct—that he should not be concerned with re-prints" (Harry Ransom Center, University of Texas). Unfortunately, the reset text was no mere reprint, and the spacing and other visual elements of Book III suffered a good deal of corruption in the popular edition.

By the time of Book V in 1958, Williams' capacity to check his work and that of his typists was quite limited, especially by vision problems. He also experienced increasing difficulty with the act of typing itself. His condition had deteriorated even further when he was forced to abandon work on the projected Book VI in early 1961.

In 1963, the first edition text of Book V was subjected to more than sixty post-humous revisions when reset for the first complete collected *Paterson*. Subsequently the spacing of many passages throughout the 1963 text suffered corruption when in 1969 it was cut and pasted for a reprinting that reduced the pagination by forty pages.

These complications are compounded by the selective degree of attention Williams gave to different parts of individual books. When checking the retyped drafts of *Paterson*, and the stages of its printing, Williams always gave the prose sections of his poem less attention than he did the poetry. The manuscripts show this tendency increasing with the later books. Thus not only does the serial nature of the poem's composition and publication produce different degrees of authorial attention to the different books in their different printings over time, but during composition the author looked at some parts of his poem more carefully than at others. In fact, most of the textual problems I have faced in preparing this new edition occur in the areas of the poem's prose, and in the spacing corruptions introduced by the reset printings.

In view of Williams' limited attention to the reset printings of his poem, for this edition I have taken the first editions of each book as copy text. The design and pagination of this new text are also based on the first editions. At the same time, I have incorporated such revisions of the first edition texts as Williams appears to have authorized, and have made individual decisions on the very small number of changes that occur between the late typescripts and the first printed version. I have also tried to be sensitive to the way that Williams' compositional process has left its mark on the text of all six books, and have weighed this aspect of the poem in making decisions that also involve considering the more limited degree of authorial involvement in the prose, in the reset texts, and in the first edition of Book V.

My editorial decisions were further complicated by not all the necessary evidence being available, although fortunately the gaps are mostly from material associated with the earlier books. In looking at the wealth of material that is available, I have consulted the manuscripts of the various parts of the poem held by Kent State University, the University of Virginia, the Houghton Library of Harvard University, SUNY Buffalo, and the Beinecke Library at Yale. I have also consulted a number of private archives, including the New Directions files in New York and Norfolk, and the papers of figures in some way connected to the poem, where I was able to track down the family or literary executor. Through these materials much of the history of the poem's composition can be traced.

Kent State holds a version of the Book I typescript that went to the printer, and that is dated by Williams March 1, 1945. The library holds the galleys that were set up from this version, and upon which Williams made many excisions, cutting about a tenth of his text. The library also holds a set of page proofs set up from these edited galleys. These materials came through a private donor, and originally through the New York dealer House of Books. (Vivienne Koch notes in the preface to her 1950 study *William Carlos Williams* that she possesses "the emended galley proofs of Book I given to her by James Laughlin.") In addition, Kent State holds a late typescript of Book III, dated May 18, 1949, by Williams, and inscribed by him to David Ignatow.

The University of Virginia received the material sold in 1964 by Kathleen Hoagland, Williams' friend, novelist, and local historian, who typed some of the late drafts of Books I–IV. The library holds the carbons of these drafts, with valuable annotations added by Ms. Hoagland, probably at the time of the sale. The Hoagland material also includes some of the poem's source materials—letters and historical summaries—with which she was involved.

The New Directions materials at The Houghton Library include the printer's typescript of Book IV, for Book V the printer's typescript and a typescript for magazine excerpts, page proofs of the first edition of Book V, and the galleys of Book V's reset text for the 1963 collected *Paterson*.

Most of the poem's manuscripts are with the major repositories of the poet's material, at Buffalo and Yale. In general, Buffalo holds most of the material associated with the first three books (including another set of page proofs for Book I), and Yale the material for the last two, although Yale holds some early drafts of the first three books, and Buffalo early drafts of Book IV. In the Neil Baldwin and Steven Meyers catalogue of the Buffalo collection, the *Paterson* material covers E1 to E30. At Yale the *Paterson* manuscripts are numbered Za 186 to Za 190, although a few early drafts of Book V material are filed with some currently uncatalogued papers donated by John Thirlwall in the late 1960s.

The major gaps in the material for preparing an edition are the lack of a late draft, galleys or page proofs for Book II, the lack of galleys or page proofs for Book III, or galleys for Book IV. Some of this material could be in private hands, although my study of sale catalogues and queries to booksellers produced no leads. Fortunately, I was able to consult one copy of the page proofs of Book IV at Dartmouth College Library, where Richard Eberhart had donated the set he received for a *New York Times* book review.

Also unavailable to me were some of the source materials for the poem's prose, and while this complicated a few editorial decisions, the main effect of these gaps was to limit the record I hoped to provide of the differences between the source materials and the poem's version of them. The letters from Alva N. Turner and Edward Dahlberg excerpted in Book I are not with the collections of their correspondence to Williams at Buffalo and Yale, and the originals of the letters from Marcia Nardi used in Book II are not filed with her other letters to Williams in the two collections. I was also unable to find the sources of a few of the prose passages. But generally I was able to record the source, thanks to the excellent pioneer work of such scholars as Benjamin Sankey, Mike Weaver, John Thirlwall and Ralph

Nash. In addition, Williams sometimes provided clues himself in his notes on the manuscripts, and I was further helped by being able to consult the copies of the poem owned and annotated by Thirlwall and Norman Holmes Pearson, both close friends of the poet, and by the annotations of Kathleen Hoagland on her carbons at Virginia. With the help of the manuscripts and these sources, I was also able to clarify and correct some attributions that have appeared in earlier scholarship.

Two additional sources for the poem's prose that might have been very helpful for the edition are also missing. John Thirlwall told both Norman Holmes Pearson (in a letter of October 27, 1953, private collection) and Benjamin Sankey (see p. 228 of his *Companion to Paterson*) that Williams owned a bound file of *The Prospector*. Within the pages of this newspaper, which reprinted articles on local history, Williams and Kathleen Hoagland found some of the historical sources used in the poem. Sankey, citing Thirlwall, records Williams' holdings as "for 1935–1936," whereas Thirlwall told Pearson "Bill has bound together the issues from Friday, July 3, 1936 to Thursday, November 12, 1936." The more exact description covers exactly the run of *The Prospector* during which its contents were devoted almost entirely to local history, rather than contemporary local news. But whatever the particular issues, I have been unable to track down Williams' copy. Equally fruitless has been my attempt to find Kathleen Hoagland's copy of the paper (which could be the same item that Thirlwall refers to). When she offered her Williams material for sale in 1964, she also offered a run of *The Prospector*. Unfortunately, Clifton Waller Barrett, who purchased the Hoagland material for the University of Virginia, chose not to purchase what might have seemed at the time a publication only tangential to *Paterson*, and my attempts to trace the fate of the item through dealers' records have been to no avail. While I have been able to study other copies of the newspaper, Williams' and Ms. Hoagland's own copies may well have had a particular value for tracing and recording the sources of the poem.

The missing Marcia Nardi letters in Book II brought their own textual and annotation problems. At the Harry Ransom Center, University of Texas, among the papers purchased from Ms. Nardi in 1966 is a version of the long letter that, in a revised form, is the source of the prose ending Book II. The question here is, who did the revising? Although some scholars have argued that Williams revised Nardi's prose, citing what appears to have been a copy of this Texas version, supplied by Nardi herself, Williams' practice generally in *Paterson* is to cut and edit letters, but very rarely to make verbal changes, and even then of only a word or two. My full reasons for treating the Texas material as an earlier draft by Nardi and not as a copy of a source document subsequently revised by Williams, are spelled out in the textual notes. In the absence of the original letter, and of the other Nardi letter excerpted in Book II, I treat the earliest Buffalo transcription of them as a source from which to record subsequent changes (chiefly excisions). This is also the route I take with other missing source documents—turning to what appears to be the earliest version available, although of course that version may well already have been shaped by Williams.

A further complication in my attempt to record the relationship of the prose sources to the final text concerns the missing papers of the late Bloomfield historian and artist Herbert Fisher. Mr. Fisher's involvement with the poem was uncovered by Mike Weaver in preparing his 1971 study *William Carlos Williams: The American Background*. Fisher wrote to Weaver that c. 1938–1940 Williams "stopped by our house . . . with a friend, said he had heard of me and wanted to make my acquaintance." At that time Williams

> borrowed some notes, not a manuscript, of mine which he used in his *Paterson*. He was making an outline for his poem. When his book came out I was surprised (not angry) to find he had copied word for word. However, the material was not original with me! I had obtained the material from William Nelson, William Scott, Mr. Longwell, and other historians.
>
> Kitty Hoagland typed the manuscript for Mr. Williams. She had borrowed my notes and recognized them as mine and mentioned the fact to Mr. Williams.
>
> Later, a rumor got around that Mr. Williams had stolen the material for his book from me. He did not. The material he used he could have obtained from the original sources and I never considered it as stolen material. I freely loaned it to him. I hope this will put the record straight on that score.

Mr. Fisher's manuscripts had disappeared by the time he was writing to Weaver, evidently the result of his 1963 move to Hot Springs, S.D. My enquiries to Mr. Fisher's friends in Hot Springs, and my visits to the Bloomfield Public Library and the Bloomfield Historical Society failed to turn them up.

But the role of Mr. Fisher's notes in even the earliest existent drafts of the poem is unclear. Mr. Fisher's account, and the commentary he provided to Weaver over a number of letters, led Weaver to speculate in some of his own annotations to the poem that the verbal differences between the poem and some of its sources were the result of Mr. Fisher's mistranscription or Williams misreading his handwriting (see Weaver 118–119). But Williams, to my knowledge, never mentions Mr. Fisher in his accounts of the poem's development, and although Kathleen Hoagland annotates Mr. Fisher three times in her notes on the Virginia typescripts, the references are all to the opening pages of Book I.

Mr. Fisher's letters to Weaver are replete with a deep knowledge of local history and lore, and in the early 1960s Mr. Fisher published a long series of newspaper articles on the subject. But my study of the *Paterson* typescripts has led me to conclude that the connection here is looser than he recalled writing to Weaver twenty-five years later. While many of the historical narratives that appear in the poem are repeated almost verbatim in various histories of Paterson and New Jersey, including the sources cited by Mr. Fisher in his letters, a close study of Williams' earliest available transcription usually reveals which particular source he used, and this is not always the version Mr. Fisher cites to Weaver. Sometimes Mr. Fisher recalls prose passages as his particular synthesis from a variety of sources, but Williams' typescripts and revisions clearly reveal a different source and development. Williams' changes from his sources can be traced through the various retypings, as noted above. It appears that Mr. Fisher, along with Kathleen Hoagland and probably others, provided Williams with direction and what amounted to a bibliography of historical sources, that he then, for the most part, went on to study himself. This part of his thinking on the poem thus took its place alongside the collage-like letters of David Lyle, a correspondent from Paterson, Ms. Hoagland's historical writing, and his own trials and experiments, to bring about his growing conception of the poem's final form.

Within the limitations imposed by what I was able to find, I record the differences between the prose sources and the *Paterson* version in the notes, and record any evidence of authorial revision behind the changes. Most of the small verbal differences that are introduced into the various retypings are probably transcription slips by Williams or the typists who helped him. On the whole in the first four books I have let them stand, since their presence reflects Williams's compositional methods. The typescripts also provide ample evidence that if a retyped sentence contained an obvious error, Williams revised for sense rather than going back to the source or even to the previous typescript (see, for example, the prose from the first Marcia Nardi letter in Book I, or the first Allen Ginsberg letter in Book IV). I have, however, corrected a handful of proper names and dates, where Williams' own transcription accurately followed his source and the error crept in in subsequent retypings (for example, I have corrected the name of the Rev. Hooper Cumming, the date in the first line of Book I's eel harvest, and the date of Sam Patch's fatal dive—the last example discovered by Weaver and corrected for the 1968 printing).

I concluded, however, that the prose of Book V had to be treated as a special case. This was also the conclusion of the New Directions staff, guided by a number of well-intentioned readers, when Book V was reset for the collected *Paterson* in 1963. Williams' own typed first transcription drafts are usually close to his source, although as was his practice, some sentences or paragraphs are omitted. But more than any other book, the prose of Book V goes through verbal changes in subsequent retypings that display all the characteristics of mistranscription. (Mrs. Williams commented to James Laughlin in a 1963 letter suggesting changes to Book V's extract from Mezz Mezzrow, "the typist . . . I remember did that part under pressure" [New Directions archives].) As noted above, Williams' capacity to check the work of his typists was severely diminished by 1957, and correspondence at the Ransom Center reveals that among those who helped him review the typescripts was Louis

Zukofsky. The main attention of both poets clearly went into checking the accuracy of the poetry.

I felt that I had to reject the solution arrived at for Book V's prose in the 1963 and subsequent printings, which amounted to a rather piecemeal and inconsistent restoration of the language of the original sources in Book V (and in some of Book IV). These changes were made possible by the source letters from Allen Ginsberg, Josephine Herbst, and Ezra Pound having turned up among the Williams papers at Yale. In addition, Gilbert Sorrentino forwarded a few revisions for the prose sketch of his included in Book V, to make sense of some garbled sentences. But all these changes went unrecorded, sometimes added new printing errors, and were evidently made without consulting the typescripts. The hope, reasonably, was to try to rescue Williams' intentions in those parts of the poem prepared when his physical handicaps impaired him, but the result was that identified prose sources and letters from well-known writers were thus altered, largely in Books III, IV, and V, whereas the prose in the other books remained untouched—although it, too, differs from its sources. And little notice was taken of possible spacing errors in Book V or in the reset versions of the earlier books.

A few additional posthumous changes to Book V occurred through suggestions by John Thirlwall, who was solicited for his comments. Some further revisions, such as the Sam Patch date noted above, occurred in 1968 as a result of a note from Mike Weaver to James Laughlin following his study of the manuscripts. These changes were mostly in the nature of correcting dates and proper names, changes which I have retained, for the reasons noted above.

Guided by my attempt to try to remain sensitive to the way the poem's compositional history, its author's own history, and his concerns and attitudes, are built into the fabric of the text, I have sought a compromise for the prose of Book V that I hope comes closer to these aims than the 1963 solution, and I have included that compromise within my larger general treatment of the poem's typescripts and printed versions. If Book V's prose were to be returned to the language of its sources, then the same treatment would need to be applied to the other four books, and this would clearly be far too much editorial intrusion. James Laughlin voiced a similar concern as coming from Mrs. Williams, when writing to Mike Weaver in January 1967: "Correcting Bill's texts is a rather tricky business. I always consult with Mrs. Williams when a correction is suggested, and generally speaking, unless it is an obvious 'typo,' she prefers that things should remain as Bill wrote them. She feels, as I understand it, that his idiosyncrasies were very much part of his style, and I can see her point" (carbon in New Directions archives). Of course, with a poem like *Paterson*, the question of what parts of the poem "Bill wrote" is itself an issue, both editorial and critical.

For Book V's prose I concluded to use as copy text the version as first transcribed and typed by Williams, while accepting later changes that carry evidence of his having authorized them. The result is to bring the prose of Book V in the present edition much closer to the sources than in the first edition, but not as close as in the collected edition printed in 1963 and subsequently. For verbal and spacing issues in the poetry of Book V I have been guided much more by the late typescripts and the first edition.

I have given more authority to the reset editions of Books I and II than to the reset editions of Books III and IV, and as indicated above, still less to the posthumous reset printing of Book V. In a small number of examples in the later books I restore the reading of the printer's typescript where no evidence exists that Williams directed a change in the printed version (for example "the tame sea" for "the time sea" of all editions, Book IV, iii, and Phyllis's missed "to" in one of her Book IV letters). I have not interfered, as the posthumous printings did, with such features of the poem as Williams' reproducing an error that appears in his source (the "Jonatan" of Book IV, iii). I have allowed all Williams' typescript revisions to stand, even where they are based erroneously on the assumption of a typing error in the retyped script, for example his changing Allen Ginsberg's "seldom dig exactly what you are doing" to "seldom did exactly what you are doing," no doubt because he was unfamiliar with the usage. A further example is Williams' cutting in the prose of Book V a repetition of Gilbert Sorrentino's included for stylistic purposes.

In cases where the retyping of the prose produces a substitute word, either directly or through Williams' response to a typing error, I leave the word, but I correct typographical errors that are not words. Mike Weaver drew New Directions' attention to the "castor hat" of Cornelius Doremus in Book I that became a "Kastor hot," but the text was not changed. This transformation happened a letter at a time in the typescripts, and could serve as a good example of the changes the prose undergoes. I have given Cornelius back his hat. But I have let "throsh" stand in Alva N. Turner's letter in Book I, even though the earlier drafts, and probably the missing letter itself, read "thrash."

The general principles governing the selection of textual and background annotations can be found at the head of Appendix C. Limitations of space and the complexity of recording non-verbal variants have made it impossible to record all differences between printings or all non-verbal corrections to the text. I have generally not recorded the following kinds of variants, unless they appear to have important critical significance:

1) changes in punctuation. I let Williams' punctuation stand as printed, being guided by the late typescripts, even when—as in some instances from Book I, following the revised galleys—the usage appears to be an unintended result of revision. A common punctuation problem is the dropping in later printings of some of the poem's periods within or at the end of a line where they occur in Williams'

idiosyncratic usage following or surrounded by a space. A similar fate had met this usage in the reprintings of the shorter poems from the 1940s and 1950s (and continues to plague this editor with the reprintings of Volume II of the *Collected Poems*!).

2) changes of spacing between stanzas, and changes in the positioning of a line or a stanza. The spacing of Book III, as Mrs. Williams noticed, was corrupted the most by the resetting for the collected texts, although the repagination of 1969 added many more examples throughout the poem.

3) changes in hyphenation and spelling variants. I have usually retained the usage of the first edition.

4) corrections to foreign languages made in Williams' lifetime.

Because of the irregular stanza form that is a central characteristic of Williams' poetics in *Paterson* it can be difficult to tell whether the end of a page marks the close of a stanza. In this edition the following pages end with a space:

3	10	11	13	18	19	20	21	23	25	26	27
29	30	31	33	36	37	43	44	45	46	47	50
51	52	54	55	56	57	60	62	63	64	65	67
68	70	71	72	77	78	79	80	81	82	83	86
95	96	99	100	101	103	104	106	109	110	113	115
116	117	120	121	122	123	125	129	131	133	136	140
141	142	149	150	151	153	154	155	156	158	159	160
161	162	165	166	167	168	170	174	175	176	178	179
181	184	190	191	192	195	198	199	201	207	218	228
230	234	235									

Appendix C

Annotations and
Textual Notes

These notes record the verbal variants between the printed versions of *Paterson*, including the extracts from the poem published in journals, and they also present—usually in more general terms—the verbal differences between Williams' prose sources and the *Paterson* version of the material. I have identified the probable sources where these are known. The annotations are not intended to be "complete," or to record all of WCW's comments on the poem or parts of it. Extensive comments by WCW on *Paterson* can be found in John Thirlwall's "William Carlos Williams' 'Paterson': The Search for the Redeeming Language—A Personal Epic in Five Parts," *New Directions* 17 (1961): 252–310, and in numerous published interviews with WCW conducted in the 1950s. The pioneer studies by Sankey and Weaver listed below also contain additional comments by WCW, and amplify some of the annotations recorded here. I have reprinted in the "Preface" to this edition WCW's statement in a 1951 press release on the poem, and also his comments to New Directions on his intentions for the fifth book. I do note the comments by WCW that appeared with the first editions of each book, and provide such additional comments or notes on context as might be particularly helpful to a reader, or that have not hitherto appeared in print.

In keeping with the principles governing the annotations to the two volumes of WCW's *Collected Poems*, I have usually excluded matters of general cultural knowledge that can be found in standard dictionaries, or the *Encyclopedia Britannica*. I have not repeated full bibliographical information that can be found in Emily Wallace's *A Bibliography of William Carlos Williams*, and I have kept the bibliographic citations as concise as possible. Annotations are keyed to page numbers throughout.

The following abbreviations are used in the annotations:

A   *The Autobiography of William Carlos Williams* (1951)

BH   John Barber and Henry Howe, *Historical Collections of the State of New Jersey* (1844)

BUFFALO   Neil Baldwin and Steven L. Meyers, *The Manuscripts and Letters of William Carlos Williams in the Poetry Collection of the Lockwood Memorial Library, State University of New York at Buffalo: A Descriptive Catalogue* (1978)

CP1   *The Collected Poems of William Carlos Williams, Volume I: 1909–1939* (1986)

CP2   *The Collected Poems of William Carlos Williams, Volume II: 1939–1962* (1988)

IST   The first, limited printing of *Paterson,* in individual books

HARVARD   The Williams archive at the Houghton Library, Harvard University

HRC   The Williams archive at the Harry Ransom Humanities Research Center, University of Texas at Austin

KH   Kathleen Hoagland, friend, historian, and typist of the *Paterson* drafts now at University of Virginia

KS   The Williams archive at Kent State University

MARIANI   Paul Mariani, *William Carlos Williams: A New World Naked* (1981)

NC   The New Classics reset text of *Paterson* that followed the first editions

ND ARCHIVES   Files of New Directions Publishing Corporation, New York and Norfolk, CT.

NELSON   William Nelson, *History of the City of Paterson and the County of Passaic New Jersey* (1901)

1963   The first, 1963, printing of all five books of *Paterson* in a single volume

NS   William Nelson and Charles A. Shriner, *History of Paterson and its Environs: The Silk City,* 3 vols. (1920)

SANKEY   Benjamin Sankey, *A Companion to William Carlos Williams's Paterson* (1971)

SL   *The Selected Letters of William Carlos Williams,* ed. John C. Thirlwall (1957)

UVA   The Williams archive at the University of Virginia

WCW/JL   *William Carlos Williams and James Laughlin, Selected Letters,* ed. Hugh Witemeyer (1989)

WEAVER   Mike Weaver, *William Carlos Williams: The American Background* (1971)

YALE   The Williams archive at the Beinecke Rare Book and Manuscript Library, Yale University

BOOK I (1946)

The first edition carried an "Author's Note" following the title page: "This is the first part of a long poem in four parts—that a man in himself is a city, beginning, seeking, achieving and concluding his life in ways which the various aspects of a city may embody—if imaginatively conceived—any city, all the details of which may be made to voice his most intimate convictions. Part One introduces the elemental character of the place. The Second Part will comprise the modern replicas. Three will seek a language to make them vocal, and Four, the river below the falls, will be reminiscent of episodes—all that any one man may achieve in a lifetime."

The note was reprinted, with minor changes for context, in the NC printing of Books I and II in 1949, and in all subsequent printings.

WCW incorporated forty-four lines of his 1927 poem "Paterson" into Book I. In the present edition the material appears on pp. 6–7, 9–10, and 27. For the 1927 poem, which appeared in *The Dial*, see CP1 263–66.

3   Paterson: Book I/ Paterson   (5th printing of 1963 text, in 1969, and subsequent printings)

3   "Rigor of beauty . . . remonstrance?"   WCW's own prose. On the 1945 KS galleys WCW cut two additional sentences that were also contained within the quotation marks: "It is not in the things nearest us unless transposed there by our employment? Make it free, then, by the art you have, to enter these starved and broken pieces."

4   the slot of/ hollow suns risen   WCW told his friend Fred Miller in 1945 that the lines included a reference to the view from the back window at 9 Ridge Road, WCW's home. See Weaver 201. The letter Weaver quotes from is at UVA.

4   and the craft   The lower-case "a" is an example of the legacy of the slashed KS galleys (see "A Note on the Text"). WCW cut the first two and a half lines of this stanza—which had begun with a capital.

6   Paterson lies . . . unroused   "Information from Herb Fisher's [manuscript] book on Paterson," note by KH on the UVA typescripts. Herbert Fisher (1907–

1977), a local historian and painter, was a prominent figure in nearby Bloomfield, New Jersey, whose interests included the history and legends of the Passaic. See his obituary in *The Independent Press* [Bloomfield, N.J.], January 20, 1977, p. 1, and Weaver 118–119. Although Fisher's manuscript histories are now lost, he published 149 articles on local history and lore in *The Independent Press* from June 1960 to April 1963, including articles on Paterson and on the Passaic. See also "A Note on the Text."

7   A man like . . . a city   These lines served as an epigraph to "For the poem *Patterson*" [*sic*], a sequence of fifteen numbered poems WCW published in *The Broken Span* in 1941, when his concept of the poem was still close to the *Detail & Parody for the poem Paterson* typescript he prepared in 1939. See CP2 14 and the accompanying note.

7   In regard . . . the like   Adapted from a four-page handwritten letter from Marcia Nardi to WCW, April 9, [1942], (Yale uncat.). Marcia Nardi (1901–1990), then living in New York, had telephoned and subsequently visited WCW some days before, possibly at the suggestion of Harvey Breit, for advice concerning her son. During her visit she left some of her poems with WCW for his possible comments.

WCW admired Nardi's work, replying on the following day to the April 9 letter "these poems have in them definitely some of the best writing by a woman (or by anyone else) I have seen in years. . . . What I'd like to see you do is to copy them all out clean and let me have a copy of *all* of them" (HRC). WCW encouraged the publication of some of Nardi's poems in *New Directions Number Seven* (1942), and wrote an introduction to the selection that appeared there. Their exchanges over the next ten months included more than thirty letters, but in February 1943 WCW terminated his side of the correspondence, which subsequently resumed from 1949 to 1956. For further details of the correspondence and of MN's own writing career see Theodora R. Graham, " 'Her Heigh Compleynte': The Cress Letters of William Carlos Williams' *Paterson*," in *Ezra Pound and William Carlos Williams: The University of Pennsylvania Conference Papers* (Philadelphia, 1983), ed. Daniel Hoffman, pp. 164–193, and Elizabeth O'Neil, "Marcia Nardi: Woman of Letters," in *Rossetti to Sexton: Six Women Poets at Texas* (Austin, 1992), pp. 73–111, a special issue of *The Library Chronicle of the University of Texas at Austin*, Vol. 22, 1 & 2.

WCW considered a number of ways of using Nardi's letters in *Paterson* (see, for example, Buffalo E19, where they were intended at one stage as an "Interlude"). Eventually he included in Book II parts of two additional letters, dating from 1943, see pp. 45, 48, 64, 76, 82, and 87–91.

As he did with much of the prose in Book I, WCW cut this material considerably on the 1945 KS galleys, which had reproduced much more of the original letter. The paragraphs from which the material in the galleys and final version are taken read as follows in the original letter (with material omitted before the galley stage in square brackets):

But I was, believe me, in a most desperate situation that Sunday. I didn't know a soul except H.B. (at least no respectable person) outside the world where only standardized conceptions of parenthood prevail; and there I was faced with an investigation of my decidedly irregular private life which would have amounted, for me, to the most ghastly kind of inquisition [—especially since my son, by the way, is illegitimate.]

[Fortunately I was able to stave all that off. I won't burden you with the details (quite a long story). But that boy of mine is now out of that God forsaken psychopathic ward and up in the mountains with a nice simple wholesome family;] and my [own] doors are bolted forever (I hope forever) against all public welfare workers, professional do-gooders, and the like. [But thank you more than I can express for having let me come. I otherwise might have been completely robbed of my wits, and thus have been unable to straighten out the situation.]

In regard to the poems I left with you: will you be so kind as to return them to me at my new [12th Street] address? And without bothering to comment upon them if you should find that embarrassing—for it was the human situation and not the literary one that motivated my phone call and visit. Besides I know myself to be more the woman than the poet; and to concern myself less with the problems of poetry than with [those of] living; and to have always been prevented [by the latter] from doing any really concentrated and thoughtful work 'in what, under happier circumstances, would have been the field of my choice.' [And] also I think [that with rare exceptions (such as Emily Dickinson and Marianne Moore) even] a talented woman writer depends, much more than a man, upon her social environment and her personal relationships, to gain definition for her personality and to develop her own minor creative potentialities. Andre Gide makes this true of most of his women; and the great disillusionment of the male characters in his books is when they find that those qualities of mind and soul which they love in some particular woman have been little more than a couch on which she could lay her thoughts next to theirs. That Gide's male characters are homosexual enables them of course to understand this [easily—galley reads "desire"] about women, since they thus escape being hoodwinked by desire.

The *Paterson* text's "publishers of poetry" for MN's "problems of poetry" runs through all the typescripts and probably stems from a misreading of MN's difficult handwriting by WCW or his typist in the transcription, and is marked with a query on Buffalo E7. WCW subsequently deleted "those of" and added an ellipsis to make sense of the sentence (one example of many of his correcting the poem's prose for sense after a retyping, but not against the source).

"But they set up an investigation"   is WCW's own summary.

9   In February 1857 . . . open the shell   No source found. To judge by an
article in the *Bulletin of the Passaic County Historical Society* of November 1956,
pp. 38–39, 44, this prose conflates two stories. Jacob and John Quackenbush found
and sold to Tiffany what became known as the "Queen Pearl." The article cites
The Paterson Guardian of May 1, 1857. The article goes on to tell the story of "a
South Paterson citizen . . . One account names him as a poor shoemaker . . . one
David Hower. Another source names him as Daniel Howell, carpenter." Hower/
Howell brought home mussels for dinner, found them tough and fried them, and
while subsequently eating them bit into the 400-grain pearl—which had been
ruined by "too much cooking. . . . it was, by far, the largest pearl ever found in
fresh water mussels." K. H. cites Herbert Fisher (UVA).

10   A gentleman of . . . on either side"   From BH (1844), 407, with minor
differences, noted below. (The passage is replaced by an illustration of Paterson in
the 1865 printing.) BH (1844) is specifically cited in an early version of the poem
on Buffalo E10, where two characters named "Doc and Willie" read this passage
from the book.

Differences from BH wording:

> gentleman of the/ gentleman with the
> the community/ this vicinity
> in human/ in a human
> around the upper/ round the upper
> his voice/ and his voice is
> body is/ body is only
> sit up/ stand or sit up
> on pillows/ on large pillows

With two exceptions the BH wording appears in the early Buffalo typescripts
E4 and E10, but all the differences appear in later retypings and in the UVA and
Yale Za186 versions. None of the changes reflect revisions marked by WCW and
are probably accidents of retyping. BH's "on large pillows" becomes "on pillows"
in UVA and Za186, and appears thus on the KS typescript and galleys—but the
page proofs and all printings have "in." I have restored "on."

A footnote in Nelson, 100, notes that the BH source material, an eighteenth-
century military journal, actually records the size of the face as twenty inches.

10   From the ten houses . . . 170 Swiss   Weaver 202 records "from Herbert
A. Fisher's notes on Paterson census records." The language of the passage is close

[256]

to that of W. Clayton's *History of Bergen and Passaic Counties* (Philadelphia, 1882), 406—in a section written by William Nelson. The numbers in Clayton record 1429 German, and 3347 English. The material is typed as if poetry on the KS typescript.

11   The twaalft . . . "The Monster Taken"   With a few minor verbal differences, including a revision by WCW ("one seven feet" for "a sturgeon seven feet") the passage appears in Nelson, 387–388.

12–13   If there was not beauty . . . region was called   Probably WCW's own prose. *The Prospector* of 3 July 1936 printed a special Ringwood issue, and the Buffalo E1 typescripts contain a promotional folder on Ringwood. Some of this passage is in verse in earlier typescripts, and the material is generally much reworked.

13   Cromwell . . . Irish brogue   As Sankey and Weaver note, from Seamus MacCall's *Thomas Moore* (London, 1935), 94. WCW begins in mid-sentence, cutting the "who" that follows "Cromwell" and substituting "others" for MacCall's "negro slaves" on a typescript filed with Yale Za186.
   The other differences from MacCall are present in early drafts:

   some thousands/ thousands
   sold/ sold there
   asserted to/ asserted that to

13   a *Geographic* picture   Between pp. 180 and 181 Weaver reproduces and cites the probable source, *The National Geographic Magazine* 49: 6 (June 1926), 716. However, the photograph is of six wives, and they are squatting, but not on a log.

14   Mrs. Sarah Cumming . . . to Newark   From BH 412–413 with slight changes and the omission of fifteen lines. BH, what is probably WCW's transcription typescript filed with Yale Za186, and the early Buffalo E4 typescript correctly spell Hooper, which I have restored. Later typescripts and all previous printings read Hopper.
   Following "district of Maine" BH has "she was a lady of an amiable disposition, a well-cultivated mind, distinguished intelligence, and most exemplorary piety; and she was much endeared to a large circle of respectable friends and connections." No source material is omitted between "on the following day" and "On Monday morning" (on a Buffalo E14 typescript WCW added a second period, and this punctuation was reproduced as an ellipsis on the galleys in what is a consistent pattern for this book).

[257]

Following "and his wife was gone!" the *Paterson* text omits these lines from the opening of the next paragraph:

Mrs. Cumming had complained of a dizziness early in the morning; and, as her eyes had been some time fixed upon the uncommon objects before her, when she moved with the view to retrace her steps, it is probable she was seized with the same malady, tottered, and in a moment fell, a distance of 74 feet, into the frightful gulf!

Following "caught him once more" the text omits from BH "and held him till reason had resumed her throne. He then left him, to call the neighboring people to the place."

The omitted final paragraph reads:

On Wednesday, her funeral was attended by a numerous concourse of people. Her remains were carried into the church, where a pathetic and impressive discourse, happily adapted to the mournful occasion, was delivered by the Rev. James Richards. Solemn indeed was the scene. A profound silence pervaded the vast assembly. Every one seemed to hang upon the lips of the speaker. In every quarter, the sigh of sympathy and regret echoed to the tender and affecting address.

Other differences:
two months   Original and typescripts read 2 months.
Rev. Cumming rode/ Mr. Cumming rode
event to/ event which was to
flight/ flights
stairs (the Hundred Steps)/ stairs
view of/ view of most of
length of time/ time

The apparently early Yale Za186 typescript contains all the verbal differences and omissions in the final text except the sentences following "and his wife was gone!" which WCW cut on the 1945 galley. The Rev./ Mr. difference occurs because the Yale and subsequent typescripts read "1812, rode," and WCW added "Rev. Cumming" on Buffalo E14.

15   Some things can be done as well as others   On the UVA typescripts KH notes the source for this, and for "There's no mistake in Sam Patch" (p. 16), as the *Dictionary of American Biography*. Patch's entry in Volume 14 (1934) records: "He was generally taciturn but when in his cups would parrot his two apothegems, 'There's no mistake in Sam Patch' and 'Some things can be done as well as others'." These details are not in the Longwell source, see below.

15   Noah . . . Faitoute   In 1938 WCW started corresponding with David Lyle, a resident of Paterson interested in communication systems. In going over some of Lyle's letters for possible inclusion in *Paterson*, WCW changed Lyle's opening salutation, "Dr. Williams," and his closing signature, variously to "Noah" and "Faitoute" (Yale uncat.). See Mariani 468–71 and Weaver 122–27.

15–16   So far everything . . . he jumped   Adapted with omissions and some rearrangement from Charles P. Longwell's *A Little Story of Old Paterson as Told by an Old Man* (Paterson, 1901), 37–41 (see Weaver 203–204). As Weaver notes, in Longwell's account the "robust" Tim Crane is compared to "the large, rugged stature of Sam Pope"—not Sam Patch.

The omitted material amounts to about twenty-eight lines of the original, and no further excisions from Longwell are made on the KS galley. Following the fourth paragraph—"The shows exhibited on the Falls grounds from 1825, and continued from time to time until 1835. They also exhibited in the old trangle [*sic*] square called Passaic Garden, except in winter, when they used the old wigwam, after that famous structure of the war times was built." The "to get to. . . . Crane" ellipsis omits "But any one wanting to go to Tim's had to go over to Manchester and make a roundabout tour through the Red woods. So old Tim conceived the idea of putting a bridge across the chasm at his own expense. It was the first bridge put across the chasm, but it was a good investment, as every one who crossed the bridge paid a penny toll until Tim Crane was repaid for his trouble. This penny toll continued for some years before the residents of the town could get on the Falls ground free. The Crane tavern was a very old style house, and after he left it it stood vacant for many years until torn down." Following the comparison of Crane to Patch/ Pope, a new paragraph begins: " 'After leaving the tavern and grounds, which he sold to Peter Archdeacon, he built himself, about the year 1837, a log-cabin in the woods nearby. Now I have drifted away from my subject a little,' he said, 'but it is best that you should know this, so I told you. Now I will go back to my story of the first bridge.' " What follows in Longwell, from "So far everything . . ." to "placed in position" WCW moves to the beginning of the account, and Longwell's text then continues with "When the word. . . ."

Other differences:

for old Paterson/ in old Paterson
so to give/ so it gave
resident in/ resident of
various times/ different times
in the basement under the bank   Not in Longwell
in the town/ in town
the "hundred steps" . . . the river   Not in Longwell
over six/ and over six

other citizens/ older citizens
his manner/ this manner
were the words/ are the words

16   After this start . . . down stream   Largely WCW's own prose, adapted
from details and language in the *Dictionary of American Biography*.

16   1829 / 1826 (IST, NC)   Corrected in the fourth printing of the 1963
text, 1968, as a result of Weaver's correspondence with James Laughlin, January
1967 (ND Archives). The dating error stems from the earliest typescripts.

25–26   While at 10,000 feet . . . end of the street.)   WCW's first trip by air,
traveling to Puerto Rico in 1941. See A 313–14, which also gives the story of
"Uncle Carlos."

26   I was over . . . T.   The postscript of a letter to WCW from Alva N. Turner
(1878–1963). WCW originally intended to use the letter itself as well as the
postscript, but cut the material on the 1945 galleys.
  The anthology *Poetry Out of Wisconsin* (New York, 1937), edited by August
Derleth and Raymond Larsson, included a one-paragraph biographical note on
Turner which he copied out and sent to WCW with a letter in 1937: "Alva Turner
was born in Spring Garden township, Illinois, in 1878. He spent from 1921 to
1923 in Wisconsin. He has been a minister, a school teacher, a laborer. His celeb-
rity, as a poet, is due chiefly to Harriet Monroe and William Carlos Williams. He
has contributed to *Poetry*, *The Editor*, *Judge*, etc. etc. was represented in *Others*.
He now lives in Illinois" (Buffalo F644).
  WCW had published Turner in *Others* in July 1919, and the two maintained
a correspondence for almost forty years. The original letter is missing, and is not
filed with Turner's letters in the Buffalo or Beinecke collections. The version in
Yale Za188 appears to be the earliest, although the addressee already reads "Dear
Pat:" and it concludes, before the P.S., "Le votre T"—obviously WCW's language.
WCW marked the first paragraph of the letter for omission on the Za188 draft.
  The Za188 version of the material retained until cut on the galleys is printed
below.

Now about the purchase of my home. This home is at the edge of the village.
There is a house across the road from me. There is one East—a quarter of a mile
that is just inside of the village limits. There is no other house, on this side of the
road—southside—from here to the rail-road, a quarter of a mile west. But there
are houses on the north side of the road clear over the rail-road. The schoolhouse
is one of them, and my mother's home is near the schoolhouse, north, on the
east side of Elm Street.

[260]

For years, my mother, whom I have been caring for for years, has been saying I could not live there, when she is dead, because my absentmindedness might leave an oil stove on and burn the house down. My sister, whom I cared for for two years—until she obtained a job at the school, cooking and canning has been telling me she would not live with me.

Moreover, my brother and sister in St. Louis, and my dead brother's daughter, intend to deed their part to my eccentric sister, because she has no heir. This sister has been at me for years to get out—that's why I went to East St. Louis last year. She didn't want me to run my typewriter, or do anything but wash dishes three times a day, mow the lawn, tend the garden, sweep the porches and the house and mop, and clean yards, keep up the repairs and pay all the grocery bills, but ten dollars per month, which I did, until I became tired of it. So my mother told me to buy me a home while I had the money. I did. This three roomed house has been built five years. I have painted it, tarred the kitchen roof, which is not shingled like the other two rooms, and made a lot of improvements. I am not through yet.

This house was built by an Ina father for his son, on ten acres of land. I bought two lots. This son was run over by the train, near Bonnie, just above Ina, last spring and was cut in two. I bought part of the furniture and curtains and blinds—a heavy library table and a heavy chair to match it. I also bought a kitchen table, cabinet and two rugs. But I have a new rug on the front room. I did not buy that from the widow. I tied the knot between this couple, several years ago.

The editor of the Ina Observer has given me several write-ups in his paper about me and my new home.

I am enclosing the poem I promised you. It is the first I have written since I have occupied the hermitage.

Le votre

T

WCW makes some minor editorial changes on the Buffalo E13 typescript. The sentence on the schoolhouse becomes "The schoolhouse, north, on the east side of Elm Street," probably because the typist skipped a line in retyping. The identifying references to Ina were cut on the early typescripts, and the postscript's remaining references to St. Louis and East St. Louis and "Skip" changed to "Hartford" and "Billy" at the page proof stage. "Billy" was actually the name of Turner's cat, about whom he sent WCW a poem that WCW in turn passed on to *View*, where it appeared in the Feb.–March 1942 issue, p. 5, with a note by WCW.

Billy/Skip was Turner's sister Eva Forest Getsbacher (1894–1948). Turner wrote to WCW of her death, enclosing an obituary he had written himself, on June 19, 1948 (Yale uncat.). Turner writes, "Skip is the sister I once wrote you about—the one that forced me to move out. . . . but in the last few years she had subdued the vixen that was in her and manifested the devotee. I will miss her very much."

throsh   Turner probably wrote "thrash," the reading on the earlier Buffalo typescripts.

On the postscript that remains in the final text, the Buffalo E13 retyping skips a line following "helped wash"; the line reads "and even did it by myself, carried in coal, water, carried out slop," on Za188.

obsessed with fire   As the April 1957 issue of *Poetry* reported, in printing Turner's poem "Unmolested Beauty," the Ina house "burned down to the ground last summer and he lost everything he owned, including his radio and his typewriter." And see Weaver 204, who gives a 1954 date.

28   I positively feel . . . E. D.   From a letter [1943?] to WCW from Edward Dahlberg, the first of two letters from Dahlberg in *Paterson* (see 226–227). Not filed with Dahlberg's letters to WCW at HRC or Yale, and not included in his volume of selected letters, *Epitaphs of Our Times*. As with the Nardi and Turner letters used in Book 1, WCW originally intended to use much more of the letter, but cut the material down on the 1945 KS galleys.

A version of the letter filed with the Yale Za186 typescripts appears to be the original transcription typescript, although a page of the letter is missing, probably because WCW had never intended to use it. The first fourteen lines of this version are crossed through. The Za186 typescript continues with the paragraphs that are substantially unchanged until they appear on the 1945 galleys, where they are cut:

I have always abhorred busy people, being too busy to talk, to be able to sit down a few minutes the way the Brahma or the Sacred Cow sits, to put together a letter, which is a way of arranging the pieces of one's spirit, it is just a hoax, and you ought to know that, and if you don't you ought to spend some time finding it out, even, if you have to damn me for pointing it out to you.

Frankly, I don't know what you are saying when you put the past into a frozen theorem, separate and apart from the present. I know of no such past or present; I only know of Nero, of Abraham sitting underneath the terebinth, or Modigliani painting glandular physiognomies, or Socrates prattling in the Symposium, or Sherwood Anderson walking through one of those blighted and noisesome downtown sections, and answering me, as I said to him, 'Consider with what malice this city must have been conceived.' 'Oh, it just happened,' as of one kind of human continuum. Time to me is an infant's conception, which Heraclitus so detested. Time is something you mention when you have sick nerves and cannot stand still or sit in quiet either to paint, or smile or talk or listen to somebody else. It's an occidental fraud, in the main, and there are no people in the world so concerned as the American, who positively has no time, with the clock. It always appeared to me that it was no accident that the glum little Swiss were clock-makers, and that the inhabitants of Königsberg set their watches soon as they saw the apriori Immanuel Kant. The hatred, by the

[262]

way, of the past, all human lore and poetry, is best illustrated by the modern state which always commemorates and canonizes its own murder-uses by starting a year one for the people. But enough.

The paragraphs finally included in the poem differ from the Za186 version only in minor punctuation changes and the spelling of some proper names—the latter changed through various reprintings. The first edition and NC printings read T.J. for E.D., the change coming with the 1963 printing.

Dahlberg wrote to John Thirlwall on Jan 21, 1955: "I knew nothing of the *Paterson* letter until Charles Olson, a friend of Williams and myself, told me Williams had printed something of mine in his poem. I was not troubled so much because he did this without my knowledge; what disturbed me were the initials T.J. I am not T.J., or am I? Yes, I am a Jew, and Williams' grandmother was. . . . The worst antisemites are half-Jews, for they know not which of their origins are more truthful or savory" (uncatalogued correspondence to Thirlwall, Yale). While Dahlberg admired WCW's *In the American Grain*, he was no fan of *Paterson*, writing to Robert McAlmon in 1953: "I think his *Paterson* . . . is a fraud. The man is very spongy, and imagines by repeating the word rock about a hundred and thirty-five times that he can become hard or give the effect of having ophidian intellect," *Epitaphs of Our Times*, 137.

32   He was more . . . anxious parent   Noted as WCW's prose by Thirlwall in his own copy of *Paterson*. The early Buffalo manuscripts contain many revisions.

32–33   In time of . . . who sleep   KH notes on the UVA typescript, underlining the lines on the French maid and the pet Pomeranians: "references to the Gould heiress, ref through Musya [and Charles] Sheeler." Weaver 205 notes that WCW mentions the Tarrytown estate of Princesse de Talleyrand, née Gould, in A 334, where the context is WCW's close friends the Sheelers.

33   Cornelius Doremus. . . .50 cents.   Nelson 386 and NS 138–139 print this list identically, but the source is almost certainly Nelson. A second list that is cut on the KS typescript, and that is also in both sources, reproduces a raised footnote number when first transcribed on Za186 that is only in Nelson.

The list suffered some unintended changes of small details in the original transcription and the Buffalo retypings. I have restored the correct spelling of Acquackanonk (Acquackonock in all printings), and corrected the "Kastor hot" of all printings to "castor hat"—both reflecting transcription errors in early typescripts. The source largely omits "cents" after the monetary figure, as does Za186. The change occurs on the Buffalo typescripts.

Other significant differences from Nelson:

and died/ and who died   Word omitted in Za186 transcription

Following "comfort" WCW cuts "Here is the list of his wardrobe, etc." on
    Za186.

4 pillow cases, $2.12   Nelson reads "4 pairs pillow cases, $2.12½": transcription
    error Buffalo E13

a handkerchief, $1.75   Nelson reads "2 handkerchiefs .75": transcription errors
    in Yale 186 and Buff E14

1 pair andirons, $2.00/   Buffalo E14 reads $.00, which is what appeared in
    IST. For NC and subsequent printings this was changed to $1.00. I have
    restored the Nelson and Za186 amount.

The Calendar of Wills in *Documents Relating to the Colonial, Revolutionary,
and Post-Revolutionary History of the State of New Jersey*, First Series, Vol. 39,
10 (Trenton, 1946) 134 records that in an 1801 will Doremus left his lands to his
seven surviving children and the heirs of his eighth.

34–35   By nightfall . . . work went on   Taken from a longer article, "Drain-
ing the Lake at Lakeview," that appeared in *The Prospector*, 28 August 1936, 4.
In all printings of the poem the opening date is given as "nightfall of the 28th."
I have restored "the 29th," the date in the source and in the apparent transcription
typescript, Za186. The change occurs in the retypings.

WCW reproduces about two-thirds of the article, and not all the omissions are
marked by an ellipsis. He omits the opening twenty-two lines concerning the con-
tract to drain the lake. A sentence summarizing the details is cut on the galleys.

Other omissions: between

drawn off—a black crowd: "Mr. Van Riper had prepared a wire screen and
    nets and endeavored to rescue the fish in the earlier part of the day and Mr.
    Regnor and others had nets ready; but they were only moderately successful.
    The fish did not run into their nets to any extent, although they got all they
    wanted before they left. But a crowd of men and hoodlums gathered."

bottom—some hundred: "It was an exciting scene after 4 o'clock, for the
    bottom for"

dam—the whole: "had been drained so that men could wade in the mud, and
    the fight for the eels began."

still there—There seemed: "gleaning the remainder. One man passed the eight
    o'clock train from Paterson on his way up with a snapping turtle in one hand,
    three great eels in another and his boys with all they could carry."

the eels—Those who: "It was a funny circumstance at the lake on the night of
    the 29th, that"

roadway—Little boys: "All Madison Park seemed to be out."

and eels—four wagon: "and the heaps everywhere comprised one of the queerest sights to be imagined. Mr. Mace who was present, and had with the others watched the affair, said."

carried away—At least: "The man who secured the larger ones gave the smaller ones to little boys to carry away"

in the mud—Night: "Sometimes two men racing after one big eel and finally tumbling down upon him together causing great amusement to those on shore."

WCW also omits the final five lines.

Other differences between *Paterson* and *The Prospector*:

> the water mostly had/ the water had mostly
> into the nets/ into their nets
> a black crowd/ a black cloud
> strike at them/ strike them
> Those who prepared the nets/ those who had prepared nets
> he filled it/ he filled it with eels
> the men/ and the men

All verbal differences and omissions are present in the Za186 typescript, although only the last is a revision marked by WCW.

35   Shortly before . . . all that day   Adapted from a much longer article in *The Prospector*, November 12 1936, 1, 4.

WCW originally intended to include a longer adaptation from the article, but cut the following, which preceded the present two paragraphs, on the KS galleys:

> The bells ringing out the hour of worship on Sunday morning, August 15, 1875, had scarcely done tolling before the news of a drowning of three men had spread throughout the city; and at once and thenceforth throughout the day crowds wended their way to the grounds to learn the shocking particulars.
>
> About twenty minutes past ten, application was made to Mr. Oswald Bleackly, who kept a small grocery and spruce-beer store at No. 345 Totowa Avenue, by James Grogan—a man about forty years of age, well-known in social circles as a skilled cricketer and employed at the Phoenix Mill as a "loom fixer"—for the use of his boat to take two friends on a short row up the river. Mr. Bleackly, had but a few moments previous denied the same request from a neighbor because of the danger of such amusement when the stream was swollen about the Falls, and on this application from his fellow workmen offered similar objections, claiming it was unsafe in the present condition of the river to venture out especially at such a perilous location as that occupied by his boat.
>
> The only reply to the advice was a hearty laugh, as Grogan, confident of his own power and strength stretched out his brawny arm, exclaiming, "O, a fine fellow like me afraid to go on the water? I am young and not to be compared with

you." The attempt to prevail upon the three to give up their proposed enjoyment was useless, and disliking to refuse his intimate friends when they pressed him to allow them the privilege, he finally consented. So the three with oars, rudder and key started down Wayne Avenue to the river. The boat borrowed was a well-built, flat bottom craft, painted a light pink color, red striped, and amply capable of holding the party.

The boat lay chained to the west bank of the river about thirty feet above the Society's dam below the carriage bridge. (Spruce St.)

They were all in exuberant spirits at the prospect of a splendid morning's enjoyment, and loosing the chain that bound the boat to the shore pushed out into the stream before they had made any preparations whatever for guiding the boat in the strong current that was dashing down with its oily wave but a few feet distant. Quickly all hands went to work at manning the boat, perceiving the immediate danger in which they had placed themselves, and with the crowd of spectators on the bridge and along the opposite shore shouting warnings to beware of the current, they exerted themselves to the utmost to bring the oars into working order to "back water." Not a man but Grogan, in the boat, was used to boating, nor had any knowledge of the use that might be made of rudder or oar in turning a craft, or the ensuing accident might possibly have been averted. They were soon impelled toward the rushing current through their own efforts to prevent getting farther from shore, and the bow of the boat turned down stream toward the dam. Here the three men jumped from the boat, sending it with a new momentum dashing on faster than ever. It overturned and a second afterward it had shot over the dam, at that place about six feet in height, and righting again below the rocks it passed toward the basin on the west shore and half filled with water remained safe out of the current. The men in the meantime struggled hard to reach the banks but they too one after the other followed the boat and were carried over the dam. The current there was rushing at tremendous speed and fully three feet in depth. (This dam of which the narrator is speaking, lies above the Falls proper not more than a hundred feet or so from its brink).

The alarm and consternation among the many visitors on the grounds was now intense and all ran towards the falls to catch a glimpse of the helpless castaways as they passed over, but their curiosity was disappointed as the bodies, on authentic statements, were not seen after the three heads disappeared in the wild seething mass in the basin under the dam.

The remaining *Paterson* text follows *The Prospector* to "the body being lodged," but then omits and summarizes some material. WCW makes the changes on Buffalo E13. *The Prospector* reads:

the body being lodged in a very curious manner between two logs, one a very large one that had been placed across the chasm by the workmen, and lodged across it in a very extraordinary manner. It was in the "crotch" of these logs that the body was wedged. From the position of the body it was thought impossible to remove the body without risk of life, but the river was rapidly falling which later made possible the recovery of the body.

A coat of one of the men was also found lodged in Broomhead's water wheel at the West Street bridge.

The news of finding the body hanging on the edge of the Falls, attracted a very large number of visitors. The sight of the human body hanging over the precipice was indeed one which was as novel as it was awful in appearance.

37   Your interest . . . product.   In a notebook in which he began the notes for his *Autobiography* WCW records: "Pound's story of my being interested in the loam whereas he wanted the finished product" (Buffalo D7). WCW instructed on the KS galleys that the nine lines from "What do I care" to "ruin" "must all appear on same page." But both the NC and fifth and subsequent printings of the 1963 text (1969) split the material.

38   a tranquility/ a still tranquility IST

38   "The 7th . . . ensued."   From BH 50. WCW keeps the quotation marks that are in BH, but omits the source BH provides—"*Smith's History of New Jersey.*" On the KS galley WCW cuts two further passages describing earthquakes; one another passage from BH, and the other a longer piece that KH annotates as "Mt. Pelee—eruption of Mount Pelee" (UVA). For the eruption of Mount Pelée, "which wiped out the last of my mother's family," see A 71.

40   "In order . . . morality"   WCW cites the 1880 New York, Harper edition. This passage was added to Book I very late and does not appear on the galleys or typescripts. On the KS page proof WCW noted: "center this note on a page of its own at end of book." See WCW/JL 112–114, 116. The passage follows its source save for the spelling of "meter," the addition of quotation marks, and "communicated" for "communicate." The verbal and spelling differences are as in the version sent by WCW to James Laughlin on June 14, 1945.

BOOK II (1948)

The first edition carried an "Author's Note": "The present is the second of four books on a single theme, PATERSON; the first appeared in 1946, the others will follow shortly."

43 the Park   Garret Mountain Park, Paterson

44 the ugly legs . . . beeves and   WCW quotes from (and slightly alters) his early poem "The Wanderer," first published in 1914. These lines appear in the section originally titled "Paterson—The Strike." See CP1 31, 112.

45 The body is . . . aided   As Weaver 206 notes, from Beckett Howorth, "Dynamic Posture," *Journal of the American Medical Association* 131, 17 (24 August 1946), 1402–03. Weaver reprints Fig. 6B. Page 1402 is pasted onto a sheet now filed with Buffalo E22.

45 Despite my . . . condition   Extract from a letter from Marcia Nardi, see note to p. 7. WCW and MN had continued to correspond since MN's first letter, of April 9, 1942, extracts of which appear in Book I, and subjects had included MN's writing and her search for employment. The two met for dinner in New York City in June. MN's share of the correspondence became increasingly dominant, and on February 17, 1943 WCW sent a short note (HRC):

> Though I have tried to find work for you I have not succeeded, under present circumstances my best advice would be for you to apply to one of the Federal Employment Bureaus and let them instruct you.
>   There's nothing more that I can do or say. This brings our correspondence to a close as far as I am concerned.

But MN continued to write to WCW. A handwritten draft, or copy, of a letter to WCW among MN's papers at HRC, dated February 22, 1943, begins: "This is no continuation of the correspondence you wish ended. It is merely my own 'last word' in that correspondence." A postcard on March 5 tells WCW that she has found employment, "a job that I like (and one connected with books)" and that she has used his name as a reference (Yale uncat.).

The three paragraphs on p. 45 of *Paterson* are from a long letter transcribed in the Buffalo E5 and E19 typescripts. Further extracts from the letter appear on pp. 48, 64 and 76. The original letter (April 1943?) is not filed with any of WCW's correspondence or typescripts, to my knowledge. The Buffalo E5 typescript has some characteristics of a transcription. A blank space is left, for example, the word added in manuscript, possibly where MN's difficult handwriting could not be deciphered. In a section that WCW does not use, MN refers to the job and to using WCW's name in applying for it, and so this letter certainly dates from after the March postcard. Extracts from another, later, letter appear on pp. 82 and 87–91.

On the UVA typescript KH notes "letter used almost verbatim, made him change it somewhat," and see Reed Whittemore, *William Carlos Williams: Poet from Jersey* (Boston, 1975) 291.

46 *I asked . . . occupation* As Sankey 76 points out, noted as the "Temple incident" on early typescripts, e.g. Yale Za187.

46 No fairer day . . . Dean and From *The Prospector*, November 12, 1936, 5, excerpted from a much longer article on Dean McNulty. The Buffalo E20 draft contains considerably more of the *Prospector* text, covering the Dean and Dalzell's escape, and Dalzell's trial and acquittal, material WCW marks there to omit. On E20 the cut-off point was to be at "bewildered." The E21 draft matches the final version, incorporating this and other excisions.

Most of the differences from *The Prospector* occur with the E21 version:

than May/ than on May
garden/ gardens

cheek. . . . Some WCW cuts "which inflamed the already hostile mob. Coroner William S. Hurd tried to calm the mob by making a speech, and while he was talking,"

[to] WCW adds the square brackets on Buff E21 after E20's "out of the barn and he succeeded in reaching the house of" is revised to the final version. *The Prospector* reads "out of the house" for "out of the barn."

Following "half furlong away" WCW cuts: "Chief of Police Graul arriving with the aid of policemen could not quiet the raging mob."

"a great beast" WCW's addition.

join/ join in
The crowd then/ The mob then

While in *Prospector* has "While at," change caused by typing error. "While it" on E20 that becomes "While in" on E21. This is one example of many in the typescripts of a change made on a subsequent typescript without consulting the original.

Sergeant/ police sergeant
of Saint/ of the St.
Joseph's/ Joseph
seating/ seated

Dean and In the *Prospector* and E20 the sentence concludes, "his display of Christian charity, for he was the highest prelate of the Catholic Church in Paterson and the man he was befriending had been prominent among the Orangemen."

47 Chapultepec! grasshopper hill! See Sankey 77, who reproduces a photograph of a carved grasshopper from Chapultepec.

The line is omitted in the selection from Book II published in *Partisan Review* (Feb. 1948).

48   by the mind's/ of the mind's   *Partisan Review*, which also adds a following line "Walking:—".

48   If that situation . . . for us   A continuation of the same letter [April 1943?] from Marcia Nardi quoted on p. 45. See note to that page.

Z   Reads "H" on E5, probably Harvey Breit.

49   Shortly after midnight . . . fun   From *The Prospector*, October 29, 1936, 4. The minor verbal differences from the source—table at/ table of, too small/ rather too small, the cellar/ a cellar, a lightning/ lightning—occur with the Buffalo retypings.

53–54   Dear B . . . kill   Although KH annotates as "Bill's cousin in Greenpoint" [Brooklyn] on the UVA typescripts, Thirlwall's copy of *Paterson* identifies "B" as Betty Stedman "a Post-Grad Hospital nurse." Betty Stedman is the source of a later prose passage, see note to p. 144.

Thirlwall's identification is confirmed by Mr. Stanley Stedman, who writes in a letter to Christopher MacGowan, December 15, 1990:

There was a letter about our dog Musti but it has long since disappeared. We were away from home and our neighbor Florence Plarey was taking care of our dog. Sometime after we returned we noticed that the dog was swelling and my wife suspected that [the] dog might be pregnant. She questioned Florence about it and received an evasive answer. Florence was a sweet girl without too much backbone so she went home and wrote the letter. This was in 1935 or 36.

I don't recall whether we knew Dr. Williams then or not. At any rate the letter was a gem and we saved it and eventually Elizabeth showed it to Dr. Williams. He said he would use it in Paterson and we waited eagerly for the book to come out. When it did we compared it to the original. There were minor differences and we felt that the original was superior to the published version.

A longer version of the letter appears in the UVA and Buffalo E25 typescripts. WCW marks most of the excisions on one of the E25 drafts. In the longer version the second sentence begins, "Also I did not want to shove the blame onto George [Florence's husband] but . . ." Between "beat it" and "George" WCW cuts "and I was afraid he would bite me when he was in that mood. George was working so he wasn't of any help. Gosh I'm nervous I can't talk—I mean, write." The words "had happened" are underlined in the earlier version, which then reads to its end:

I'm so excited I even left a piece here that I must write in now. I've been watching her and would have soon told you if you hadn't already asked. Please forgive my carelessness and don't be angry although I know you'll be cursing like a son-of-a-gun and probably won't ever speak to me again for not having told you. But it just goes to show that I have no backbone and if I have it must be one of a jelly-fish. Don't think I haven't been worrying about Musty. No doubt that's why I've been losing weight. She's occupied my mind every day since that awful event. You won't think so highly of me now and feel like protecting me. Instead I'll bet you could kill me.

Well let's get off on another subject unless I get a crying spell from sheer nervousness.

These early typescripts read "plenty hell" for the printed version's "plenty of hell."

(Readers might be relieved to hear that Mr. Stedman reports to the editor that Musti went on to complete a successful pregnancy, and give birth to five puppies.)

57   the lost/ Eisenstein film   Weaver 207 cites a version of *Que Viva Mexico!* shown in New York in late 1941 and titled *Time in the Sun.*

62   I see they . . . undermine us?   Thirlwall's copy of *Paterson* annotates as [August] Walters (see p. 180), as does Norman Holmes Pearson's copy—although Pearson received much of his information via Thirlwall. Weaver 207 offers the plausible suggestion that the passage is from a letter by WCW's friend Fred Miller, who edited the left-wing magazine *Blast* (see Weaver 71). But the comments are not in the approximately one hundred letters from Miller to WCW filed at Yale and Buffalo.

The passage may be WCW's own prose, perhaps a record of a friend's comment. On Buffalo E17, possibly the first appearance of this passage, the lines are handwritten, rather than typed in the manner of the transcribed letters, and the passage undergoes revision more radical than WCW's usual treatment of letters. The E17 version reads:

I see the Senate is trying to throw out Lillienthal and deliver the bomb to a few choice industrialists. I don't think they will succeed but even those party leaders here who hope to be elected to power are among them. That's what I mean when I refuse to the oppose the communists. *Are* they any worse than the shits who are trying to undermine us?
It is terrifying to think how easily we can be destroyed.

The Buffalo E23 version is also quite different from the printed version. For David E. Lilienthal's comment to Weaver see Weaver 207.

64   an old man   Thirlwall wrote to Sankey that the sermon was based on one "Williams heard at Lambert Tower 'sometime before the war'" Sankey 92.

64   There are people . . . upon me   A further extract from the April 1943 [?] Marcia Nardi letter, see note to p. 45. On Buffalo E5 the paragraph reads as in the printed version except that "few months" reads "past few months" and "maladjustments" reads "maladjustments, if necessary." WCW omits the final sentence of the paragraph: "And my economic situation has been involved, of course." On the Buffalo E25 draft the text is as the printed version.

66   The detectives . . . detective said   With the Buffalo E16 typescripts is an October 19, 1943, letter from WCW's Paterson correspondent David Lyle (for Lyle see note to p. 15), which begins: "I remember your saying once you had thought of going around with detectives etc, on their duties, but abandoned it as being all the same thing. Here's a going around, cut and indexed to be absorbed in ten minutes, of a going around in Paterson."

67   Hamilton saw . . . worse than any . . . Especially . . . Jefferson   Possibly WCW's own prose summary. In early Buffalo typescripts the language is included with prose material that is clearly WCW's.

68   America the golden . . . in hand   See Weaver 207–208 for an extensive annotation on this parody, which is to the tune of "America the Beautiful," and for background detail on John Peter Altgeld, governor of Illinois in the early 1890s.

69   As with some of the prose, the periods in the poetry mark WCW's omissions from his own earlier drafts.

69–70   As a corollary . . . manufactury   Although Sankey 95 cites the Federal Writers' Project's Stories of New Jersey (New York, 1938), this passage is closer to the version in the four pages of the Federal Writers' Project publication Stories of New Jersey, December 1936, School Bulletin #11—"prepared for use in public schools."

The first paragraph in the passage may be WCW's version of the source's "Though the Revolution had left America politically independent of Great Britain, leading minds soon realized that the fruits of liberty would be bitter if the new country could not secure her industrial independence as well."

The next two paragraphs follow the language of the 1936 text closely, with the exception of some minor changes in punctuation and definite and indefinite articles that occur through the retyping and rearrangement of these passages, and of the differences noted below.

Between the two paragraphs in *Stories of New Jersey* appears a sentence on Washington's coat at his inaugural that WCW revises and inserts as verse in a subsequent prose passage from this material, see p. 74. Other major differences:

Hamilton/ Alexander Hamilton   WCW's revision, on Buffalo E25
a great Federal City   Added by WCW. The title of the *Stories of New Jersey* article is "Paterson, 'The Federal City.'"
a national manufactury   Added by WCW, picked up from a later passage in the source that WCW inserts into *Paterson*, see p. 74.

72   that cold blooded . . . get it   The details fit the crime and hanging of John Johnson, see notes to pp. 197 and 202.

73   The Federal . . . high taxes   Extracts from a mimeographed sheet—addressed to "Dear Citizen"—put out by Alfredo and Clara Studer and dated January 1947, see Sankey 98–99 for more details. WCW includes further excerpts below, and excerpts from the pamphlet "Tom Edison on the Money Subject" which accompanied the sheet. The Studer sheet is filed with Buffalo E17 and marked by WCW at the top, "Following the preacher's clownish talk."

Clara Studer wrote to WCW on April 18, 1946, telling him that she had written to Pound and received "back several little notes" which included a request "to write and tell you what he 'actually did say' . . . [in] his [Italian] broadcasts." Studer asks if WCW is interested in receiving some Social Credit materials (Yale uncat.). For Social Credit and WCW's attitude and involvement see Weaver 103–114.

WCW's second paragraph reproduces the third paragraph of the sheet with two minor differences, which are present in the Buffalo typescripts. The source reads "over and over and over," and "in war or peace." The first paragraph reads in full: "The Federal Reserve System is a private enterprise. Ever since 1863 (1863 to 1913 it went under the name of National Banks) a private monopoly has had the power—given to it by a spineless Congress of that time—to issue and regulate all our money."

The paragraph WCW omits charges that "this was an act of treason" that "surrendered, to a handful of merchants, the most sacred right given to the people of the United States in Article 1 of the Constitution"; a "treason . . . committed as a result of pressure by . . . [the] Bank of England."

73   Witnessing the Falls . . . they called it   Probably WCW's own prose, see note to p. 67.

74   The newspapers . . . his place   Apart from one verbal difference ("all the cotton"), verbatim from *Stories of New Jersey*, see note to pp. 69–70.

74   The prominent . . . goods   From BH 408, the only remaining sentence from the earlier drafts of what was originally a longer extract from their entry for Paterson. BH reads "cotton cloths," as do the drafts up to Buffalo E25.

74   In other . . . work   The fourth paragraph of the Studer mimeographed sheet, which reads "the Government of ours" for "our Government" (as Studer on Buffalo E23, but as printed on E18).

74   In all . . . up   Sentences taken and rearranged from the pamphlet that accompanied the Studer sheet, "Tom Edison on the Money Subject." The original pamphlet, about two thousand words, is filed with Buffalo E23. The pamphlet reads "If people ever" and capitalizes "per cent to the stated cost." The differences are on the Buffalo typescripts. For fuller details of the pamphlet see Joel Conarroe, *William Carlos Williams' "Paterson": Language and Landscape* (Philadelphia, 1970) 156.

76   Whatever . . . fashion   From the same Marcia Nardi letter quoted elsewhere in Book II, see note to p. 45. WCW omits two paragraphs between this and the previous extract, on p. 64, paragraphs in which MN discusses her difficulties in obtaining employment.

> that note of yours   WCW's note of February 17, 1943, ending his side of the correspondence.
> part . . . Nor   WCW omits "For you to consent to see me as you might consent to see one of your patients outside of office hours, in that entirely impersonal way—no, thanks; not that for me." WCW marks the excision on the Buffalo E19 typescript.

The Buffalo E5 version has four other differences from the printed text. The differences occur through the E19 and E25 retypings:

> mechanical/ the mechanical
> at your office/ there at your office
> some of/ some one of
> written you/ written to you

78–79   The descent . . . indestructible   WCW printed as a separate poem in his 1954 volume *The Desert Music*. See CP2 245–246, and the accompanying note on page 486 in which WCW links these lines to his concept of "the variable foot."

are towards/ are toward   *Partisan Review* (1948), *Pictures from Brueghel*
to waken/ to awaken   *Desert Music, Pictures from Brueghel*

80   Missing was . . . age   From Mary McCarthy, *The Company She Keeps*
(New York, 1942), 239. McCarthy's prose continues: "Jim reread these masters
and tried to reproduce the tone by ear, but he could not do it. He became frightened
and went back to the public library; perhaps, as someone had suggested, the ma-
terial was under-researched." The remaining eleven words of the *Paterson* prose
passage appear as verse in early drafts.

82   My feelings . . . damned thing   From the beginning of a letter by Marcia
Nardi, [May?] 1943. See note to p. 45. The original letter is not filed with any
of WCW's correspondence or typescripts, to my knowledge, although the Buffalo
E5 typescript contains a longer version, which may be a transcription, and the Buf-
falo E19 typescript also contains this particular passage. The long prose section that
closes Book II is from this letter, see note to p. 87, which also discusses a version of
this letter at HRC.
   In the three typed drafts of this paragraph on E5 and E19 "responsibility" reads
"all responsibility."

85   Seventy-five . . . last week   Possibly a reference to one of the international
conferences held by Princeton University in 1946 to mark its bicentennial.

86   full octave/ slow octave   *Partisan Review* (1948)

87–91   My attitude . . . pages   A continuation of the letter from Marcia Nardi
begun on p. 82, see note above. A blank page preceded this prose in IST.

   Although, as noted above, the original of this letter is not among WCW's papers,
the HRC holds a version in MN's hand that she sometimes claimed many years
later was a copy of what she sent WCW. The HRC document differs in a number
of ways from the Buffalo E5 version and the printed version, and some of these
differences have been discussed by Theodora R. Graham in " 'Her Heigh Com-
pleynte': The Cress Letters of William Carlos Williams' *Paterson*," in *Ezra Pound
and William Carlos Williams: The University of Pennsylvania Conference Pa-
pers* (Philadelphia, 1983), ed. Daniel Hoffman, pp. 164–193. Professor Graham,
working with what appears to have been a copy of the HRC document provided by
MN, suggests that WCW rewrote parts of the letter to produce the printed version.
   However, my own conclusion is that the HRC document is probably a draft of
the letter MN eventually sent to WCW, and that the Buffalo E5 typescript of the

letter is, in the absence of the letter itself, the closest to the source document currently available, and the textual notes to this section of the poem are based upon this conclusion. Thus I note the verbal differences between the printed version and the E5 typescript below, but not the differences between the HRC document and the *Paterson* text. (Interested readers may consult Professor Graham's article, in which all the examples quoted match the HRC document.)

Since WCW's treatment of this letter has been the subject of some critical debate, I record below the reasons for my own conclusion:

1) WCW's practice elsewhere in *Paterson* with letters is to cut and condense, but not to add substantial material of his own. Changes he makes to letters can be traced in the various typescripts of the poem, but for this letter no changes beyond the cuts noted below can be documented in the Buffalo typescripts.

2) The HRC document itself contains a number of revisions of vocabulary and style that are consistent with the letter being composed and revised as it is being written. It does not have the character of a copy of a letter already written, and indicates an on-going involvement with the process of composition that also makes unlikely the subsequently sent letter being copied verbatim from the HRC draft. On the other hand, Buffalo E5 has some characteristics of a transcription. The differences between the HRC document and E5 could be explained as amplification and clarification by MN of her points as she rewrites from a draft.

3) MN made contradictory statements concerning the relationship of the HRC material to the printed version in *Paterson*. In material held privately, she asserts in one letter that the HRC document is an "exact copy" of the printed version, but in another that WCW made only trivial changes to what she sent him. Both comments are in letters written forty years after the event. In addition, the 1966 letter from the HRC agreeing to purchase material from MN, including this document, describes the items purchased as letters from WCW, and drafts of letters to WCW.

4) A number of the passages present in the E5 version but not the HRC document concern details either that WCW could not be expected to know, or that he is unlikely to have added to the letter. In one example he is unlikely to have invented—the references to Miss Fleming, ST and SS—WCW has to disguise identities, including that of Harvey Breit, for the printed version (see note to pp. 87–88 below). In his correspondence with MN, WCW is very careful in his references to her aborted relationship with Breit, a mutual acquaintance, and WCW never mentions MN in his letters to Breit. In another passage that is part of a longer section WCW cut from E5, but which is not in the HRC document, MN discusses her relationship with her son and includes details that

WCW would be unlikely to invent. A collation of the HRC document with E5 reveals a number of similar examples.

5) The HRC document does not contain the postscripts of the printed version, although its final page contains space for the first postscript to be started. The missing postscripts support the possibility that MN rewrote and revised the letter from the HRC draft, and—in her continuing concern to strike the right tone and convey what she wanted to communicate—she added the postscripts before sending off the letter. The postscripts also contain information, concerning the circumstances of the stolen money order, for example, that WCW would be unlikely to know or invent.

6) MN's papers, privately held, indicate that on occasion she would write a preliminary draft before the sent version of a letter. This is the case with the letter of March 30, 1949, to WCW noted below.

87   the Introduction to your Paterson   In the early 1940s WCW was calling the whole poem as then conceived an "Introduction."

woman's need to/ woman's needing to

"sail free in her own element"   MN paraphrases WCW in his review of Anaïs Nin's *The Winter of Artifice*. The review appeared in *New Directions Seven* (1942), 434.

relationships with other women/ friendships with other women
awareness/ awarenesses
doctor/ Dr. P.

88   almost in/ in almost
W/ Woodstock [New York]
so simple / as simple

Miss Fleming   HRC and E5 read Hawkins. WCW had written to Iris Barry, Film Library Director at the Museum of Modern Art, New York, in December 1942 concerning a possible position for MN and the letter had been passed on to Frances Hawkins, who—as she wrote to WCW on March 9, 1943—handled personnel matters at the Museum, and she offered to talk to MN (Yale uncat.). In the fall of 1942 Marianne Moore also made some job inquiries on MN's behalf at WCW's request (Moore to WCW, October 1942 and October 11, 1942 (Yale uncat.).

S.T. and S.S. . . . Clara . . . Jeanne   E5 reads H.B. for S.T. but the other initials are unchanged. Harvey Breit's wife was named Clara, and S.S. may be Sydney Salt, who, as Elizabeth O'Neil has pointed out to me, dedicates two books of his poetry to "Jeanne." Salt lived close to MN in Greenwich Village at this time. In other letters to WCW, MN refers to a "Sydney."

89 I asked for/ I asked you for
    and maybe/ and then maybe
    And then   All previous printings have a printer's error "And the"
    Miss X/ Miss Hawkins

so badly   On E5 the paragraph continues for twenty additional lines, discussing the poor employment prospects at the Office of War Information, and "at the Museum itself," and MN's relationship with her son.

    That I'm in the/ I'm in the
    with the social/ with social
    welfare   All previous printings and E5 have "wellfare," but MN spells
        correctly on HRC
    kind at all/ sort at all

90 acceptably/ acceptedly
    I was able/ I was then able
    like measles/ like the measles

that introduction to my poems   In *New Directions Seven* (1942), 413–414.

91 the only thing/ the only happy thing

La votre C.   WCW alludes to Criseyde's signature in writing to Troilus in Chaucer's *Troilus and Criseyde*, see SL 233.

21 Pine Street   The letter is written from 21 Grove Street, New York.

    Brown's/ [James] Laughlin's
    is dead now/ is now dead
    he took any/ he who took any
    or antisocial/ or any antisocial
    I'm reminded/ I am reminded
    A.N./ Anaïs Nin   See note to p. 87 above.
    those pages/ these pages

On March 30, 1949, the correspondence between WCW and MN resumed when MN wrote of discovering her letters in *Paterson II* while browsing in a Woodstock bookstore (ND Archives). This resumption continued until 1956 when WCW was forced to curtail most of his correspondence following his strokes.

WCW's final letter, congratulating MN on having a book of her poems published by the Swallow Press, concludes: "You are one of the hardiest women and one of the most gifted and generous women I know. I am happy at your success" (October 5, 1956, HRC).

BOOK III (1949)

The dust jacket of the first edition carried "A Note on Paterson Book III" by WCW, dated September 28, 1949:

Paterson is a man (since I am a man) who dives from cliffs and the edges of waterfalls, to his death—finally. But for all that he is a woman (since I am not a woman) who *is* the cliff and the waterfall. She spreads protecting fingers about him as he plummets to his conclusions to keep the winds from blowing him out of his path. But he escapes, in the end, as I have said.

As he dies the rocks fission gradually into wild flowers the better to voice their sorrow, a language that would have liberated them both from their distresses had they but known it in time to prevent catastrophe.

The brunt of the four books of *Paterson* (of which this is the third, 'The Library') is a search for the redeeming language by which a man's premature death, like the death of Mrs. Cumming in Book I, and the woman's (the man's) failure to hold him (her) might have been prevented.

Book IV will show the perverse confusions that come of a failure to untangle the language and make it our own as both man and woman are carried helplessly toward the sea (of blood) which, by their failure of speech, awaits them. The poet alone in this world holds the key to their final rescue.

94 Cities . . . Santayana From George Santayana, *The Last Puritan: A Memoir in the Form of a Novel* (New York, 1936) 140. (The next two sentences in Santayana read: "No: for him cities were congested spots, ugly, troublesome and sad. Boston, when he first passed through it, seemed to him nothing but Great Falls multiplied.")

sets up her trophies Santayana's text reads "sets up all her trophies"

95 Avery Samuel Putnam Avery (1822–1904), who made a fortune advising American buyers of European art, see Weaver 209.

97–98 Blow! . . . from the reading In *12th Street* (December 1949) WCW published material from various parts of Book III as a single piece under the title

"Paterson Book III: Preface." In addition to this passage the material included "The 'Castle' too . . . So be it" p. 99, "Papers . . . Unabashed. So be it" pp. 117–118, "Upon which . . . So be it. So be it. So be it" p. 130.

97   So be it   WCW told Pound "the 'so be it' I copied verbatim from a translation of a Plains Indian prayer. . . . It meant what it says: if it so is then so let it be. In other words, to hell with it" (December 1949, Lilly Library, Indiana University).

97   Cyclone, fire/ and flood   On February 8, 1902, a devastating fire consumed much of central Paterson, destroying the Danforth Free Public Library (and most of its contents) among other buildings. Nelson and Shriner record "there was a strong gale blowing . . . [which] acted like a huge bellows" (505). The following month the Passaic river "which flows through a large part of the city" flooded. "With the enormous volume of water that poured down the river bed and the territory adjacent, came huge floes of ice, carrying destruction wherever they went" (507). Later in the year a freak tornado struck the city. The library was rebuilt on a new site, and reopened in 1905.

98   no wind/ no winds   *12th Street* (1949)

doors . . . hands   In *12th Street* reads "doors/ that the wind holds; wrenches from our hands/—and arms."

98   Old newspaper files . . . Works   As Weaver 209 notes, the various details are from 1936 issues of *The Prospector*: "two little girls, firmly locked in each other's arms," July 10, p. 6; a photograph of the Paterson Cricket Club in 1896, August 21, p. 6; the story of the "two local millionaires" appears in the issue of October 9; the "Indian rock shelter" is described in the October 2 issue; the August 28 issue carried an article on the Rogers Locomotive Works.

no language   In *12th Street* "So be it" refrain follows here, and is omitted following "home"
reels . . . So be it   In *12th Street* reads

> reels—caught still in its wrappings,
> wind-held. So be it. Starts back amazed
> from the reading.

98–99   Gently! . . . hat!   These lines are part of a poem WCW published in 1937 titled "Patterson: Episode 17" [*sic*], seventy-eight lines of which are incorporated into Book III. Further material from the poem is on pp. 104–105 and 127–128. In "Patterson: Episode 17," the concept of "Beautiful Thing" is first linked to a figure beating a carpet on a church lawn, but the two opening stanzas that describe the figure, and a concluding stanza, are omitted from the material incorporated into *Paterson*. An early draft of the 1937 poem now at Harvard is titled "To a Tall Young Colored Woman." For the 1937 poem see CP1 439–43.

99   The "Castle" . . . Lambert   Catholina Lambert (1834–1923) was born in Yorkshire, England, and became one of Paterson's richest mill owners. He built his Castle residence "Belle Vista" in 1892. It was sold to the city in 1925 and now houses the Passaic County Park Commission and the Passaic County Historical Society. In the winter of 1936 the art gallery wing, by then in disrepair, was demolished, despite the opposition of two fierce editorials in *The Prospector*. For the story of Lambert and the Castle see the richly illustrated *Silk and Sandstone: The Story of Catholina Lambert and His Castle*, by Flavia Alaya (Passaic County Historical Society, 1984).

99   The "Castle" . . . be it"   *12th Street* carries an additional line before this passage, "Come death! Come clean death!" and adds following the passage "Come wind! Come flood! Come cleansing/ fire. So be it. Come end of the world:"

99   Rose and I . . . now   WCW told his friend Robert Carlton Brown (1886–1959) on September 10, 1948, "Paterson III is stalled for the moment. I'm going to use your letter about Gurlie Flynn and the others in it" (Southern Illinois Univ. Library). Rose was Brown's second wife. The letter has not been found, but a Yale Za188 version of this passage is headed "Excerpt from letter" and begins with an additional sentence: "Your Paterson, Book II should sell because it hits the semi-documentary groove." On February 25 [1950?] Brown wrote to WCW of his enthusiastic reading of Book III, adding "I called Rose to my side to look at the damned thing now" (Yale uncat.). The famous "Paterson Pageant" was staged in New York's Madison Square Garden in 1913 for the benefit of the Paterson strikers.

Za 188 reads "on the Pagent," and "the Union Hall."

102–103   The Indians . . . among us"   The story appears in "Extracts From a Work Called 'Breeden Raedt'" in *New York Documentary History IV*, 67–68, although it is unclear if this is WCW's source. WCW's first paragraph summarizes the language of this account, and then follows it almost verbatim—although omitting some specific details of the torture. A much shorter account appears in both Nelson and NS, although only Nelson 38 gives the New York source.

103–104   From 1869 . . . assembled . . . A spectator . . . adventures.   WCW's own prose, in verse in early drafts. KH and Thirlwall both note *The Prospector* as the source of the information in this passage. The August 7, 1936, issue carried a long article on the tightrope performances over the Falls of DeLave, Leslie, and Dobbs, including a photograph of one of Leslie's performances. The article contains the central details of WCW's passage.

110   the Englishman   WCW's father, William George Williams, who died in 1918 and who figures more extensively here in earlier drafts of the poem. New Barbadoes is an area in Bergen County, New Jersey.

114   to it . . . mother?)   These lines are spaced differently on the Yale Za188 and KS typescripts and in the first edition. The change occurs with the first printing of NC:

> to it not by intellection but
>
> by sub-intellection (to want to be
> blind as a pretext for
>
> saying, We're so proud of you!
> A wonderful gift! How *do*
>
> you find the time for it in
> your busy life? It must be a great
>
> thing to have such a pastime.
> But you were always a strange
>
> boy. How's your mother?)

114–115   With due ceremony . . . distributed   Adapted and rearranged from material in Nelson 35–38. The NS 51–54 version is almost the same, but Za188 follows Nelson where they differ.

115–116   It started . . . night . . . When discovered . . . doomed   Source not found, but possibly WCW's summary of information in NS 505 and elsewhere. The passages are extensively revised in Za188.

115   song/ songs   *The Tiger's Eye* (1949)

118   An iron dog   Weaver 210 cites an article on "The Brass Dog" (actually made of sheet-iron) that is probably WCW's source, *Passaic County Historical Society Bulletin* (November 1944), 19–20. The dog hung outside a tin-shop. "At 12.30 a.m. December 9, 1846 the shop was completely burned out, together with several buildings along side, but the dog kept watch over the place never to move

from the spot." WCW's copy of this issue of the *Bulletin* is with his papers at Yale (Za W677).

118   iron dog/ bronze dog   *12th Street* (1949)

laughter . . . green   *12th Street* has an additional line: "an empurpled face choked blue with laughter"

a multiformity/ the multiformity   *The Tiger's Eye* (1949)

124–125   Hi Kid . . . So long   KH annotates on UVA typescript "letter to my maid Gladys [Enalls] from her girlfriend [Dolly]," and see Weaver 210. Gladys ran away in 1942, and the letter was among a number found in her room, some of which WCW transcribes in Za188 for possible inclusion in *Paterson*. The original of the letter he finally included, postmarked December 2, 1941, is at UVA.

In the various retypings some changes crept into the idiosyncratic spelling and diction of the original letter. In two cases—"I was a feeling good" and "car slaped on brakes"—I have restored the original because the first edition reproduced it, and the editorial changes ("I was feeling good" and "slapped") were made posthumously with the 1963 printing.

Other verbal differences from the original that occur through various retypings:

only high browns/ only of high browns
stopped facing/ stoped facing
half filled/ half fill
ever since/ every since
supposed to be the father/ suppose to be the father
supposed to be going to have/ suppose to be going to have
to have kids/ to have kid   This change is marked by WCW, Za188.
3rd/ 3th
3 kids/ 3 kid   reads "kid" on KS typescript
your next/ the next
Well here/ Will here

WCW omits a one-sentence paragraph following "everywhere" and before "Bab" in all typescripts: "Well you said you was coming Thankgiven why didn't you come?"

The ellipsis covers one and a half pages in the original that appear on early typescripts but are later cut. The writer details more pregnancies, then names "Boy's trying to go with me," "Boy's I go with," "Boy's I like almost mad *about*," and "Boy's I am trying to get."

129   There is . . . propellers   WCW's own copies of the *Passaic County Historical Society Bulletin* now at Yale include the December 1944 issue, which carried

a piece on "the first successfully operated submarine" now resting "in Westside Park, Paterson, N.J.," designed by John Philip Holland in Paterson in 1881. "His first boat for experimental purposes was tried on the river Passaic and this boat now is . . . housed in the Museum of the City of Paterson."

130   intervenes/ supervenes   *12th Street* (1949)
       sullied/ muddied   *12th Street*
       at the bridge, silent/ silent at the bridge   *12th Street*
       .   O Paradiso!/ to—the history   *12th Street*

132   The remains . . . mourned   KH researched and summarized this material for WCW, which he then revised and shortened. In a note to WCW accompanying her summary, now with Yale Za188, KH notes the titles of her sources. The details and some of the language come from: Lydia A. Jocelyn and Nathan J. Cuffee, *Lords of the Soil* (Boston, 1905) 1–17; Gabriel Furman, *Antiquities of Long Island* (Port Washington, L.I., n.d.) 60; Ralph Duvall, *The History of Shelter Island* (Shelter Island, N.Y., 1932) 14. An earlier version of KH's notes is filed with the UVA typescripts. The two ellipses in the printed version mark WCW's cuts of KH's prose—by a total of thirty-five words.

133–134   About Merselis . . . cattle   In Nelson 269; the first four words of the passage are WCW's summary. In Nelson "Merselis" is also spelled "Merseilles."
    Three of the printed version's verbal differences from Nelson originate with the apparent transcription, filed with Za188:

       confined/ being confined
       that some/ lest some
       to say/ to say that

    The others occur through the various retypings:

       stare/ stare in
       of the whole neighborhood/ not only of herself and her family, but of the
          whole neighborhood
       everybody/ everyone
       he was/ he was commonly
       the witch/ that witch
       would soon be/ were soon to be
       exchange/ interchange
       wife was/ wife had been

135–136   It was . . . bank   WCW's prose. "She" is KH, who annotates on the UVA typescripts "Lester Wadsworth told me of this, he was the orchestra leader c.

1930," and see Weaver 211. In some of the Za188 typescripts the details are in verse. An earlier version identified Wadsworth as the son of Rutherford printer Charlie Wadsworth (see *A* 6).

137　A version of the first three lines appears in WCW's short 1938 poem "At the Bar" (CPI 457), one of a number originally published as "from 'Paterson,'" and part of his earlier concept of the poem.

138　The first two-thirds of a letter sent to WCW by Ezra Pound, October 13 [1948], from St. Elizabeths hospital (Yale uncat.). Through September and October WCW and Pound had corresponded on dramatists.

　　The line　"(re. C.O.E.　　Panda Panda　　)"　is WCW's addition. When Pound received *Paterson III*, Dorothy Pound wrote to WCW, in December 1949: "Ez says many fine things in Paterson iii. . . . E puzzled about a Panda?" (Yale uncat.). WCW replied, "The *Panda Panda*, I'm sorry to say, has no meaning— merely a nonsense value in order not to reveal anything that might identify the work in question. I don't know what put Panda into my head" (December 1949, Lilly Library, Indiana University).

　　In a note on the KS typescript WCW instructs "to occupy a full page, as it stands—facing the page following." The instructions were not followed in NC. WCW incorporated Pound's reaction to this juxtaposition into Book IV, see p. 182.

　　With the posthumous 1963 printing the printed text was altered to bring it closer to the idiosyncratic spelling and spacing of Pound's original, the original having been deposited at Yale. However the first edition arrangement is in the earliest typescripts, and they indicate that WCW was not concerned to check that the original's lineation had been reproduced on the page exactly, or that all of Pound's shorthand had been correctly deciphered. In any case, the spacing in both versions is only an approximation of the original. I have returned to the text as it appeared in the first edition and the NC editions, and record below the verbal differences between the first edition text, the source, and the post-1963 printings:

　　got sake/ gor Zake (source and 1963)
　　exaggerate/ egggzaggerate (source and 1963)

　in the source, written above "! !" is "(my xt)"　Not in any printed version

The spacing and punctuation of the following lines in 1963 more closely approximate the source:

　　　　　　Loeb.—plus Frobenius, plus
　　　　　　Gesell　plus Brooks Adams
　　　　　　ef you ain't read him all.—
　　　　　　Then Golding 'Ovid' is in Everyman lib.

The 1963 version of the last two lines reads:

>   just cause it is mentioned eng
>   passang.   is fraugs. . . .

Below I give these two lines as they appear in the original, and also what follows in
the letter and is omitted from *Paterson*, although included in the earliest drafts:

>   just cause it is mentioned   .   eng
>   then of course there
>   passang   .   is fraugs.   hv. yu
>   read *all* the fraugs fr. Willy to
>   M. Jean? (want "Crucifixion"
>   on loan . ? ? (it aint a ch. service) prob. unobtainable
>   here.
>   (N.B. Nancy has fergave me & no
>   longer thinks I orter be shot fer not
>   assassinatin Franco).
>   & so on yrz
>   Ez

139 SUBSTRATUM . . . found here   The chart and summary are in Nelson
11, although not the title "Substratum."

Four entries, some of them duplications, are in Nelson but omitted in the printed
version. They are included in the earlier drafts, but missing by the KS typescript.

>   540 feet. . . . Soft shale
>   565 feet. . . . Soft shale
>   613 feet. . . . Soft shale
>   1,180 feet. . . . Fine quicksand, reddish

The omitted material marked by the ellipsis reads: "and the character and amount
of the saline impurities giving little hope of success by going deeper." The Nelson
account goes on to describe the analysis of the water's minerals that was subsequently
made.

Two other verbal differences occur through the retypings:

>   the tabular/ a tabular
>   of Europe/ in Europe

2 x 1 x 1/16 in.   I have restored the reading of the original, and of all the
typescripts.

140 *American poetry . . . exist*   Weaver 211 notes the source, "From a review
of a group of American poets by George Barker, 'Fat Lady at the Circus,' *Poetry*

(London) 13 (June–July 1948), 39." See Weaver for further background and a 1966 comment by Barker.

143–44   When an African . . . know   From Sophie Drinker, *Music and Women: The Story of Women in Their Relation to Music* (New York, 1948), 11. Drinker's quoted material slightly misquotes from D. Amaury Talbot, *Woman's Mysteries of a Primitive People* (London, 1915), 208. The ellipsis is Drinker's.

Differences from the original, present by the KS typescript:

slain/ killed
singing songs/ singing sad songs
bough/ boughs
the spirit/ his spirit
fertility/ virility

Until the 1968 fourth printing Ibibio was misspelled Ibidio, probably an error on the galleys, since the spelling is correct on the KS typescript. The error was one listed in Weaver's 1967 note to James Laughlin (see "A Note on the Text").

144   I was thinking . . . him   The speaker is annotated by Thirlwall in his copy of *Paterson*—Betty Stedman, the recipient of the Musty letter, see pp. 53–54. Her friend, Eleanor Musgrove Britton Mark, was shot by husband Noel Thomas Mark on June 24, 1946, in Metairie, Louisiana. The husband told police he mistook his wife for a prowler.

Stanley Stedman writes: "Eleanor was my wife's dearest friend . . . My wife was certain that he murdered her and was upset and bitter for years. Eleanor was also a patient of Dr. Williams. I feel sure that the paragraph in question is a pretty good rendition of what Elizabeth said to Dr. Williams that day. The reference to Clifford occurred because my wife felt that none of this would have happened if Eleanor had married him. I do remember us sending him some off color jokes" (letter to Christopher MacGowan, December 15, 1990).

Shortly afterwards WCW wrote his short story "The Farmers' Daughters," which centers upon the friendship of the two women, but did not publish it until 1957. See *The Farmers' Daughters* (1961), 345–374.

BOOK IV (1951)

Corydon & Phyllis   The two pastoral figures are based, according to WCW's correspondence and evidence in earlier typescripts, on "a distinguished woman, a prominent figure in the New York and international world, living on Sutton Place with a view such as I describe in the poem" (letter to Marianne Moore, June 23, 1951, Rosenbach Library, printed with omissions in SL 305), whose brother was a financier—Thirlwall annotates as "Ann[e] Morgan" in his copy of SL; and on a nurse originally from Paterson whom WCW had known in the late 1920s. The letters in this section are all WCW's inventions.

157   than woman   Harvard typescript reads "than a woman"

160   Via? / Chemistry   Reads "Via/ Chemistry?" in *Wake* (1950)

162   happens me/ happens to me   NC and all subsequent printings. But there is textual evidence that "to" is a deliberate omission. The word is omitted on early typescripts, on one Yale Za189 draft the word is typed in but then typed over as if to be omitted, and it is not on the Harvard typescript. It is on the Dartmouth page proofs, but is then omitted in the first edition.

163   *Voi ch'entrate*   Dante, *Inferno*, Canto III, l. 9.

170   bog/ a bog   *Quarterly Review of Literature* (1951)

170   Norman Douglas . . . die   Weaver notes WCW's amplification of this story in A 207.

171   the air . . . the glow   In *Quarterly Review of Literature* reads "the air above it through the glass room/ having taken up the glow"

171   among/ beside   *Quarterly Review of Literature*
         their talk/ the talk   *Quarterly Review of Literature*

171   Curie (the movie queen)   MGM's *Madame Curie*, starring Greer Garson, was released in 1943.

171   Billy Sunday   Weaver 213 notes the background to the preacher's 1915 visit to Paterson, and his baseball career.

172–74   Dear Doctor . . . A.G.   From Allen Ginsberg, March 30, 1950 (Yale uncat.), the first of three Ginsberg letters included in *Paterson*, see also pp. 193 and 210–211.
Like many of the prose passages in *Paterson*, the text of this letter picked up changes, mostly in small details, through the various retypings and editions of the poem. In the posthumous 1963 printing, with the original letter available at Yale, changes were made in the text in the direction of the original. But not all the

differences were caught, some regularizing of Ginsberg's punctuation and use of lower-case spelling departed even further from the original, and in the case of "dig" and "did" a change initiated by WCW was lost. On the grounds outlined in "A Note on the Text" I have returned the text to the version WCW submitted to the printer in the Harvard typescript (although incorporating the 1963 change in the identifying initials), and note below verbal printed variants and verbal differences from the original:

Doctor   Original reads "Doctor Williams," change marked by WCW on Za189.

once briefly   All printings and typescripts   Original reads "briefly once"

As to my history   WCW omits the five lines that follow in the original, marking the omission on Za189, and adds these four words to the original's next paragraph. The original reads "—my father is Louis Ginsberg, of whom you know. He would send his regards, if he knew I was writing, and also an invitation to come to supper, as we have bought a house in Eastside and are able to entertain for the first time in years. He was remarried last week." WCW's uncatalogued correspondence at Yale indicates that he met Louis Ginsberg in 1931.

schools/ school   1963 and in the original

do there   All typescripts and printings, original reads "do here"

or lyric/ of lyric   1963 and in the original

harking   All printings and typescripts, original reads "harkening"

did   Original and 1963 read "dig," but WCW marked the change on Za189, probably unfamiliar with the usage and thinking "dig" a typing error.

cadences   All printings and typescripts, original reads "cadence"

an old   IST printed "on old," possible uncaught error on the galleys

have real   IST and NC printed "did have real," possible uncaught error on the galleys

bum of a paterson/ bum of Paterson   1963, the original reads "bum of paterson"

A.G.   First edition and NC read "A.P.," original reads "Allen Ginsberg." Although this is a posthumous change, WCW used "A.G." for the Ginsberg letter in Book V, pp. 210–211. The identification of Ginsberg's letters in the first editions runs "A.P," no identification, "A.G." "WCW said 'A.P.' was for 'A Poet,' " letter from Allen Ginsberg to Christopher MacGowan, July 29, 1992.

176   Levy   Weaver 214 identifies as H. Levy, author of *A Philosophy for a Modern Man* (New York, 1938).

176   CASE . . . reprisal   From Joseph Felsen, Alfred J. Weil, and William Wolarsky, "Inapparent Salmonella Infections in Hospitals," in *Journal of the American Medical Association* 143 (29 July 1950), 1136. The passage from the original is cut out and pasted onto a sheet now with Yale Za189. WCW changed the initials, age, and date at a late stage, for the Dartmouth page proofs still read as the original. The original also reads "pediatrics" for "pediatric."

177   On Friday . . . known   From WCW's chapter on Columbus in his 1925 *In the American Grain*, 25–26, which is in turn from Columbus' *Journals*. IAG reads "On shore I sent" and "I had ever seen. . . ." The differences are in the early typescripts.

178   brow/ brows   NC, but in no other printings, and not on any typescripts.

179   *les idées Wilsoniennes nous/ gâtent*   Weaver 214 suggests a reference to *New Democracy*, 1 February 1934, which cited Woodrow Wilson on the control of credit. In his own copy of *Paterson* Thirlwall annotates "Fed. Reserve."

180   Weaver 215 gives the citation, *Money* 15, 4 (June 1950), 1. The original page is pasted in full onto a sheet among the Za189 typescripts, but WCW omits parts of the source in the drafts.
The original carries the headline "DO YOU FAVOR LENIN OR UNCLE SAM?" with a sub-headline "Our Treasury Officials Support A Legally Protected, Dishonest Finance Plan Which Will Accomplish Lenin's Wish to Bankrupt America. There's Still Time to Wreck Lenin's Wish."
WCW omits an introductory paragraph in the original, which reads:

Would you continue to support a strictly dishonest, legally protected finance system if you were convinced the writer has the solution to our financial and economic chaos? Would you continue to oppose a finance system based on the Constitution? Do you know that the Treasury officials are actually assisting the Russians by supporting a finance system which will eventually bankrupt us?

Following "more airplanes" the original adds: "They propose to foist Communism upon the people by force and nothing else."
Between the *Paterson* version's last sentence and "Enforce the Constitution on Money" (which is pasted in separately in Za189) the original has an additional 19 lines, including the assertion that following

the present dishonest, legally protected finance method . . .

1. The airplane would cost 1 million dollars.

2. The National debt would be increased 1 million dollars.
3. Federal taxes would raise to higher levels, so would prices.

WCW moves August Walters' name from a by-line position following the sub-head to the bottom of the page, and omits the full address the advertisement gives. Other differences from the original, all present in the Za189 typescripts:

stronger than they/ stronger than they are
Pay the manufacturer/ Pay the manufacturers
deposits the/ deposits this
his credit/ this credit
Bankers make/ Banker makes
only cost/ actual cost

181   short of/ out of   *Poetry New York* (1950)
      Trade winds . . . drive/ In *Poetry New York* reads "the/ trade wind . . . drives"
      sequestered/ misspent   *Poetry New York*

182   Release the Gamma/ let out the Beta   *Poetry New York*
      out . out/ out of . out   *Poetry New York*
      credit, stalled . . . pen/   *Poetry New York* reads:

            Stalled in money
                              (concealing the generative)
            that kills art   .   or buys it out of
            poverty of wit, to win vicariously
            the blue ribbon   .   for courage   .

            Stalled in money
                        —the Congressional Medal
            for bravery beyond the call of duty and
            end as a bridge-tender
            on government dole

                        Defeat may steel us
            in knowledge; money   :   joke
            to be wiped out at a stroke
                        of thought

182   just . . . NOWHERE   Ezra Pound wrote to WCW on 13 December 1949, concerning the juxtaposition in Book III of the Artesian Well chart against his 13 October 1948 letter (pp. 138–139): "2100 ft.   = thaz v. interestin' page

. but don't prove there aint no water no where" (Yale uncat.). An early Za189 draft paraphrases the letter differently again. Following further comments from WCW, on 30 June 1950 Pound suggested "when artesian at 2055 000 in depth is undrinkable—aqueduct useful" (Yale uncat.). These exchanges on the virtues of aqueducts, and of their effect upon impurities in the water, continued into July. WCW's side of the correspondence is at the Lilly Library, Indiana University.

182 Tolson and . . . Tate   Weaver 215 identifies and annotates the issue of *Poetry* (July 1950) that contains Melvin B. Tolson's "From *Libretto for the Republic of Liberia*" and Allen Tate's commentary.

183 Reuther   United Auto Workers' leader Walter Reuther was wounded in his home April 20, 1948.

184–85 IN . . . cities   From a note sent by Ezra Pound [1950?]. Pound noted in a letter to WCW May 22, 1950, that he had not seen Book II of *Paterson*, and WCW forwarded a copy. Section I of Book II contains a passage on "invention" that resembles the style of Pound's Canto XLV (see p. 50).

In the original "Will you" reads "Will yu" and "cities" reads "italian cities." I have restored Pound's spelling of "splendour," which WCW retained on the typescripts but which was not reproduced on the galleys. WCW omitted a final line in Pound's note: "there is ALso the motto to my Gaudier book/ wunner ef yu evr seen that ?" The two letters are at Yale.

185 cities/ italian cities   *Quarterly Review of Literature*

186 "The past . . . past,"   In a letter to his editor David McDowell, August 22, 1950, WCW writes: "To the Past and those that lived in the Past—which is a direct quotation from my paternal grandmother [Emily Dickenson Wellcome]— or rather a paraphrase of something she once told me, with a dirty look in her eye, in reply to an inquiry I once made of her" (HRC).

186 all but . . . river   "After Newark, the river enters Newark Bay, and merges with salt water," George Zabriskie, "The Geography of Paterson," *Perspective*, 6: 215. Zabriskie's article, pp. 201–16, provides a useful summary of the path of the river and the history and geography of Paterson.

186–87 Jonatan . . . prominence   WCW's notes in Yale Za188 identify the source as Nelson 345.
The first edition's "Jonatan," which I have restored, reproduces a printing error in Nelson, and is present in all typescripts. NC and all subsequent printings

read "Jonathan." The account appears as part of Nelson's genealogy of the Doremus family.

Verbal differences from Nelson: the first occurs on what appears to be the transcription typescript, the other two with subsequent retypings, all filed with Za189:

someone is/ somebody is
bayonetted/ repeatedly bayoneted
attained/ attained to

Gritie (all typescripts and printings) reads "Grietie" in Nelson.

187 an old friend . . . refreshed An early Za189 typescript reads "When Pep West" which WCW revises to the printed version. WCW and Nathanael West edited the short-lived magazine *Contact* together in 1932. West worked at the Kenmore Hotel from 1927 to 1930, and the Sutton from 1930 to 1933, both in New York City. The prose is WCW's.

188 Kill . . . us? Probably WCW's own prose. The passage undergoes revision in a number of the typescripts.

190 The greyhaired . . . secretary A detail of WCW's first air trip in 1941, see A 313–14.

192 The whereabouts . . . buried WCW adapted a note apparently prepared for him by KH (a reference to this passage filed with Za189 reads "see Kitty's note"). An early draft identifies "Peter the Dwarf" as "Peter Van Winkle," although WCW marked the change to "Peter the Dwarf" on a Za189 typescript. Pieter Van Winkle is the figure visited by General Washington (see p. 10) and a relative of the murdered John S. Van Winkle (see p. 197). The genealogy is in NS Volume II 7–8.

192–93 In a deep-set . . . river Adapted, largely verbatim, from prose in scattered pages of Charles P. Longwell, *A Little Story of Old Paterson as Told by an Old Man* (Paterson, 1901). Here from pages 10, 9, 32, 10, 9, 10–11, 12 and 29.

193. A print Weaver reproduces the print opposite page 189.

193 Dear Doc . . . A.G. From Allen Ginsberg, the letter is now at Yale (Yale uncat.). The letter is mistakenly dated by Ginsberg June 6, 1949, but is postmarked 7 June 1950. The second of three letters by Ginsberg in *Paterson*, see pp. 172–174 and 210–211.

As with the other Ginsberg letters, the printed version of this prose was amended in the 1963 and subsequent printings in the direction of reproducing the original more accurately, although the changes are incomplete and inconsistent. Most of the first edition's differences from the original have as their source a retyping of what appears to be a transcription draft, the transcription draft being much closer to the original letter. There is no manuscript evidence that WCW initiated these changes, but in a subsequent draft he cut and pasted a version that contains the differences. He accepted the changes in all subsequent drafts and in both printings that appeared in his lifetime. For the reasons outlined in the "Note on the Text" I have returned to the version WCW submitted to the printer for the first edition, and note below the differences from the original and post-1963 printings.

Doc.   Original reads "Dr. Williams."
which is in/ which in   Original and 1963
neighborhood and/ neighborhood   Original and 1963
the City/ City   Original and 1963
the people   All printings, original has "people."
see in/ see it   Original and 1963
really/ really at   Original and 1963
seen/ known   Original and 1963
day—the look   All printings, original and earliest typescript read "day—that is really my main interest in anything—the look."
A.G.   Added in 1963, see note to pp. 172–174.

WCW omits the final nine paragraphs of the letter, including AG's request for his thoughts on Paterson declaring "a WCW week." "We had Lou Costello week, we had Larry Doby week, why don't we do something princely for a change?"

194   There were . . . days   Adapted, largely verbatim, from the prose in scattered pages of Charles P. Longwell, *A Little Story of Old Paterson as Told by an Old Man* (Paterson, 1901), pp. 29, 23, 11, and 15.

194–95   Paterson . . . skull   From the *New York Herald Tribune*, September 18, 1950, p. 16. September 17 was WCW's birthday.
WCW omits four final paragraphs on the Harvard typescript. The three remaining differences from the printed version are present in the Za189 typescripts:

months/ month
told the police/ told police
Following "county physician" WCW omits "who examined Nancy."

The spelling "Garrett" is in the original and all typescripts and printings.

195–97   There was . . . Falls   Adapted, largely verbatim, from the prose in scattered pages of Charles P. Longwell, *A Little Story of Old Paterson as Told by an Old Man* (Paterson, 1901), pp. 24–25, 32–33, 66–67, 21, 21–22, 47, 51, 52, 53, 59, 49, 33 and 32.

197   Paterson . . . butchery   Taken from a much longer account in *The Prospector*, September 25, 1936, 1 and 4, where it is described as "the first crime of murder, in the County of Passaic." The version in *Paterson* quotes from about a tenth of the source, selecting sentences from throughout the article.

The verbal differences from *The Prospector* appear in Za189 with one exception:

this county/ the county

to find and arrest their man/ to track him, who soon succeeded in finding and arresting him   WCW marks the revision on the Harvard typescript.

knowledge of/ knowledge or

198   Trip . . . was   The Dutch rhyme appears in Nelson 395 and NS 156. All printings have "kocien" for "koeien"—an error on the typescripts.

199   the tame sea/ the time sea   In all printings and on page proof, a possible uncaught error on the galleys. I have restored the reading in all typescripts.

202   John Johnson . . . spectacle   WCW adapted a note researched and prepared for him by KH, now filed with Za189, which reads: "John Johnson from Liverpool was convicted after 20 minutes conference by the Jury. He was hung on April 30th, 1850 in the Jail Yard in full view of thousands who gathered on Garrett Mountain and on the house tops to witness the spectacle." The spelling "Garrett" is in all typescripts and printings.

BOOK V (1958)

WCW originally conceived *Paterson* as having four books, but even while completing Book IV he noted possible themes for a continuation. Subsequently, he published a twenty-four-line poem "Paterson, Book V: The River of Heaven" in 1952, but this poem developed into the long poem "Asphodel, that Greeny Flower." See CP2 238–39, 310–337, and accompanying notes.

For a comment by WCW on *Paterson V* that appeared on the dust jacket of the 1958 text see the "Preface" of this edition.

206   at the end . . . was one   Probably WCW's prose. The material appears as verse in early typescripts filed with an uncatalogued box at Yale.

206   The Unicorn   Within sections I and III of Book V WCW makes a number of references to details in the 15th–16th-century Hunt of the Unicorn tapestries in the collection of the Cloisters Museum, Metropolitan Museum of Art, New York. The six tapestries, and the fragments of another, all have rich floral backgrounds. The first tapestry depicts the hunters and dogs setting out, the second the surrounded unicorn at a fountain, and the third its attempted escape. In the fourth the unicorn gores a greyhound, in the fifth, the fragment, the virgin/maiden fondles the neck of the unicorn while the huntsmen gather, and in the sixth the slain unicorn is brought before the castle. In the seventh tapestry the gored but alive unicorn is alone within a low, circular wooden enclosure, and the image has been discussed as a symbol of the risen Christ, of the Blessed Virgin and the Incarnation, and as the consummation of marriage.

207   the Dadaist novel   WCW's translation of Soupault's novel was published in 1929.

208   Dear Bill . . . Josie   From a letter to WCW from Josephine Herbst, Monday May 14 [1956] (Yale uncat.).
As with the prose based on some other letters that are now at Yale, this passage was amended with the posthumous 1963 printing to bring it closer to the original, but inconsistently and—in this case—with the introduction of two new printing errors. In keeping with the principles for Book V laid out in "A Note on the Text," I have generally followed WCW's probable transcription typescript, filed with Za190, and note below the verbal differences from the original, the first edition and the post-1963 printings. Most of the changes from the original are introduced in one of the later Za190 drafts. For this particular passage, however, WCW or his typist apparently went back to the original after a number of retypings and picked up some dropped material. I have incorporated these changes from the transcription typescript into the text.

F.   Original reads Florence [Mrs. Williams]
The farm . . . saw them.   I have restored this sentence, which appears on the transcription typescript, but is dropped on the retyped draft that introduces most of the differences from the original. The next sentence begins directly under this sentence's opening "The" on the transcription, and with the same word, and thus the omission is quite possibly a typing error. The 1963 text added an ellipsis. See A 269–271, where WCW describes the farm at Erwinna, Pa.

D.E.   Dick Eberhart
one D.E. envied when he saw it and/ and D.E. envied it when he saw it   IST
writing   Omitted in IST
barn/ farm   IST
who   Omitted in transcription, but appears in later drafts
in space/ for space   IST
E's/   E. in IST, "Eberharts" in original
E's will / E'll   IST and 1963, "Eberharts will" on original. I follow the
  transcription typescript.
H./ Hanover   Sentence omitted in transcription, but appears in later drafts
J.G./ Jean Garrigue
of memories/ of them   IST
Hepatica/ Hepaticas   IST
trees/ the trees   IST
warblers . . . warbler/ warbler . . . warblers   IST and 1963. I follow the tran-
  scription, which is as on the original.
confused   1963 and original have confounded
lined with sheepskin/ lines with shipskin   1963   Error originates with 1963
  printing.
Best/ Warmest   IST
everyone/ everybody   IST
Josie   Original and Yale typescripts read Jo; change occurs on Harvard printer's
  typescript.

209   wounded wounded   Treated as an error and amended to "wounded" in
the 1963 printing. As 1963 on one of the Za190 typescripts and as first edition on
a number of others and the Harvard typescripts. When consulted during prepara-
tions for the 1963 printing, Thirlwall listed this among a number of suggested
changes in a note to James Laughlin, adding "sounds a bit mushy for WCW" (ND
Archives). Since WCW let the repetition pass on a number of the late typescripts
and in the first edition I have restored it.

210–211   Dear Dr. . . . A.G.   The third letter from Allen Ginsberg included
in *Paterson*, see also pp. 172–174 and 193. (May 20, 1956, Yale uncat.). The text
was amended with the posthumous 1963 printing to bring it closer to the original,
but inconsistently. In keeping with the principles for Book V laid out in "A Note
on the Text," I have generally followed WCW's probable transcription typescript,
filed with Za190, and note below the verbal differences with the original, the first
edition and the post-1963 printings. Most of the changes from the original are
introduced on one of the later Za190 drafts.

your introduction   WCW's introduction "Howl for Carl Solomon" to Gins-
   berg's *Howl and Other Poems* (1956).
the point/ to the point   IST
though/ thought   IST
on a ship/ in a ship   IST
family on my/ family on way to a   Original and 1963. I follow the transcrip-
   tion and IST.
have a whitmanesque/ do have a whitmanic   Original and 1963. I follow the
   transcription and IST.
&/ and   IST
image/ images   Original and 1963. I follow the transcription and IST.
poppa/ papa   IST
any case/ my case   IST
struggle/ trouble   IST
the stones/ stones   IST
to the mind   All printings and transcription, original has "of the mind"
mind/ mind too   Original, transcription and 1963, change occurs when original
   cut later.
magazine will be put out/ magazeen will be out   IST
ANY TIME   All printings and transcription, original has TIME
SUNFLOWER SUTRA   Omitted in IST. The poem appears in *Howl and
   Other Poems*

WCW omits following "contain":
   3 shorter poems too, written subsequent to howl:

            Supermarket in California—a homage to whitman
            Sunflower sutra—declaration of the experience of
                        happy real mercy
            America—make of it what you can.

WCW omits eleven lines of the letter following "times" that discuss the literary
   and travel activities of Jack Kerouac, William Burroughs, Robert Creeley, and
   Richard Eberhart.
Following "weeks" WCW omits "if the FBI doesn't get me first. Shipping out
   for Govt Military Sea Transport to refurbish the DEW (defense radar arctic
   paranoia installactions)."
compassion   The two dots are in AG's original.
Following "find" WCW omits "not that hard. I mean to indicate next move,
   next step ahead, jump of the imagination, Whitman had enormous sense of
   humor and Freedom"; and following "shut up" WCW omits "here's some
   more poems which will be going in the book."

etc etc   In all printings, but not in the original, which has a period following "too," the only word omitted here from the original.

out . . . etc.   WCW omits the final fourteen lines of the letter, which concern details of the magazine, *Moby*, and of possible contributors.

A.G.   Original reads Allen Ginsberg, is signed Allen, and adds a c/o address.

212   . . . The whores . . . G.S.   Taken from a four-page typescript titled "Bordertown" now with Yale Za190, sent to WCW by Gilbert Sorrentino. An accompanying letter, dated 9 January, 1956 (Yale uncat.), begins:

> I have just finished reading your book *The Desert Music*, and I'd like to tell you that I haven't read poems of such beauty in months or even years. What interested me especially was the last (title) poem, 'The Desert Music,' since, about four years ago, when I was in the Army, I wrote a narration in prose, I suppose you could call it, called *Bordertown*, which deals with a town like the Juarez of your poem . . . this being Nuevo Laredo.
>   I'm taking the liberty of sending you the writing, even though it needs revision. . . .

WCW replied on January 12, "Your story is a knockout and one of the best written accounts of the sort that I remember ever to have read." And a week later: "The story is a rough one but exceptionally well written and must not be lost sight of—and I don't intend to lose sight of it as you'll see when the occasion shall arrive. . . . an unusual success in a young writer. More power to you" (Univ. of Delaware). And see Weaver 217. The sketch has not been published elsewhere.

On 6 April 1962 Sorrentino wrote to WCW: "When you praised that short sketch of mine (the one that you later used pieces of in Paterson 5) it was one of the great things to ever happen to me, both as a writer, *perse*, and as a man. At the time, I was broke, miserable, had a huge body of poems and prose that no one had any interest in, and worst of all, I didn't know a single writer to whom I could show any of the work, for 'professional' criticism. You gave me the confidence and the strength to feel my own slowly-ebbing confidence and strength fully. . . . I am deeply and permanently grateful to you" (Yale uncat.).

A number of changes were made to the passage in the 1964 second printing of the 1963 text (referred to below as 1964), in part through a note to James Laughlin from Hugh Kenner reporting "indirectly" on nine suggested corrections by Gilbert Sorrentino (Sept. 1, 1963, ND Archives), and also by the original typescript's arrival at Yale. Nine of the ten changes are those communicated by Professor Kenner. While some of the changes return to the original, others create a further version. In keeping with the principles for Book V laid out in "A Note on the Text," I have generally followed WCW's probable transcription typescript, filed with Za190 (which in this case returns the text closer to the original than either previous printing), and note below the verbal differences with the original, the first edition and the 1964 text. Most of the changes from the original were introduced on one of the later Za190 drafts.

pleading/ bleeding   IST

A real house, a real house   I follow the transcription and IST; original reads "A real house, a reel house," 1964 reads "A reel house, a real house," following the Kenner/ Sorrentino correction.

vulgar assailing/ vulgarassailing   IST and on transcription

against the dancers/ against the door   In all printings. I follow the original and the transcription.

your ear/ your ear dances   IST, your ear dancers 1964 following the Kenner/ Sorrentino correction. I follow the original and the transcription.

you argue/ argue   IST, and you argue 1964, following the Kenner/ Sorrentino correction. I follow the original and the transcription.

laughs noise/ laughs nose   All printings, I follow the original and the transcription.

four cuatro . . . cuatro dolares/ four quarto . . . quatro dollars   IST/ four quatro . . . quatro dolares 1964, following the Kenner/ Sorrentino correction. I follow the original and the transcription (although the latter reads "dolars").

friend's voice/ friends   IST, friends' voices 1964 following the Kenner/ Sorrentino correction. I follow the original, the transcription reads "friend's" but omits "voice."

his face/ the face   1964 following the Kenner/ Sorrentino correction. I follow the original, the transcription and IST.

her fingers fragile touches/ fingers fragile touch   1963, original has "fingers fragile touches"; I follow transcription and IST.

of whorehouses/ of the whorehouses   1964, following the Kenner/Sorrentino correction. I follow IST and transcription, original has "of the whorehouse."

G.S.   not in the original—which also ends here.

WCW omits all but two lines of the first two pages. Other differences between the original and the *Paterson* text of this edition (almost all with their source in the transcription):

dolla, two dolla/ dollah, two dollah

shit/ sh—

fills . . . the . . . guitar soaked night air/ fills the dust of air and corners, fills the dust and guitar-soaked air of night. WCW marks the omissions and changes. He also omits the next, two-line, paragraph, and following "the house" omits fourteen lines in which the narrator takes in "the wild incredulous scene," and sits down with a beer.

against a door/ against the door

all white/ all in white

white ... bride ...   Both ellipses are in Sorrentino's original

and find her/ and you find her

and smile/ and smilesmile   Revised by WCW, Za190.

a buttock/ buttock

please and/ please

Between "twice" and "I go twice" WCW omits ". . . you go twice? And smile yes yes twice"

213   the birds ... also   Possibly WCW's prose. The description is of the second of the unicorn tapestries, see note to p. 206.

214   One warm . . . away   Probably WCW's prose. In earlier typescripts "Willow Point" reads "Santiago Grove" and "San Diego Grove" (in Rutherford), while the initials G.B. and L.M. are late substitutions for the initials of the actual persons. A staff memorandum in the New Directions files dated 3/3/58 reads "Wittenberg thought long about the short passage in PAT V . . . and suggested that I talk again with W.C.W. about the presumed death of the lady. He also suggested that we change some of the details, but we both thought that 'Sandy Bottom' should not be molested. I called W.C.W. this morning. . . . and Bill said to change the initials . . . and we agreed to change 'San Diego Grove' to 'Willow Point.' We also changed the initials of the young sailor. Bill said, by the way, that the lady and all her family had been dead for 30 years."

214   "Loose your love to flow"   From WCW's poem "The Wind Increases" (CP1 339).

215   "I am ... A.P.   A.P. is Levi Arnold Post (1889–1971), then Emeritus Professor of Greek at Haverford College. WCW told his friend Charles Abbott, the librarian at the University of Buffalo, on November 3, 1956, that he had received the letter Post had written to Abbott, and "his opinion of the writings of Sappho, that which makes her verse distinctive in quality, fascinates me, it is just what I wanted to find out" (Buff F 985). WCW and Post exchanged correspondence in 1957 and 1958, and WCW told Abbott on Jan 1, 1958, that in *Paterson* he was quoting from Post's "letter to me which I can no longer find" (Buffalo F989). But these lines are not in the two Post letters to WCW filed among WCW's uncatalogued correspondence at Yale, and may be from Post's letter to Abbott.

WCW and Post met briefly at the wedding of Abbott's son David, and when **WCW** read at Haverford. Post was editor of the Loeb Classical Library. See also Weaver 217–18.

215 Peer of . . . dying A translation of Sappho's Fragment 31. In 1957 WCW published a slightly different version as a separate poem, see CP2 348 and accompanying note.

215–216 13 Nv . . . ?????? A 1956 letter from Ezra Pound to WCW (Yale uncat.). In a letter to New Directions on 25 February 1958 Pound expressed concern about the letter's planned inclusion in *Paterson* in the light of efforts to have him released from St. Elizabeths (which happened in May 1958): "it may be o.k. or it may be MOST untimely to release it/ no need to protrude my blasted nekk any FURTHER at this time. . . . Bill dun't mean no harm, but I am gittin tired of incarceration. gap cd/ be left for later edition/ soz not to afflict his artistik cawnscience" (ND Archives). And Pound wrote to WCW on 27 February 1958, "I dunno that I can afford to be quoted at this time. especially as yu indicate the expressed emotion has not been Wordsworth'd in tranquility" (Yale uncat.). Somewhat irritated, WCW was ready to cut the entire letter out, but Pound subsequently made some cuts and revisions—noted below—and WCW accepted the emendations for the first edition. And see Mariani 713–14.

The cuts were restored in the 1963 printing, when some further changes were made to bring the text closer to the original letter, although some differences remained. In keeping with the principles for Book V laid out in "A Note on the Text," I have generally followed WCW's probable transcription typescript, filed with Za190, and note below the verbal differences with the original, the first edition and the post-1963 printings. Where the transcription reflects a probable misreading of EP's handwriting, I have followed the original. Most of the changes are introduced through the various retypings, including the copy prepared for Pound that carries his revisions.

my BilBill/ by BilBil IST, change occurs in draft for EP
vide/ Vid IST and transcription—misreading of EP's script, I follow the original
makes/ make IST, change occurs in draft for EP
they offered/ was offered IST and transcription, misreading of EP's script, I follow the original
economics/ econ 1963 and original, I follow the transcription
dunghill FDR Omitted IST, one of EP's deletions. In the 1963 printing although the material was restored, the ellipsis periods were retained in error.

and the stink that elevated him   Omitted IST, not on draft sent to EP
to Rapallo   Omitted IST, one of EP's deletions
still want/ want   1963 and original, I follow the transcription
the book/ his book   1963 and original, I follow the transcription
educ/ educate   IST, I follow the original and the transcription
buzzards/ old buzzards   IST, added in draft for EP, I follow the original and
    transcription
shittahd aaabull   I follow the original and transcription. IST has shitta daaabull,
    an EP revision, 1963 has shittad aaabull

Some additional verbal differences from the original remain:

for SIX/ or SIX   Transcription has "(f)or"; EP amends
don't/ dont   Difference is on transcription
re Beum/ re . . .   All printings. EP removes the name. Robert Lawrence Beum
    was editor of the magazine *The Golden Goose.*
I found/ I have found   Difference is on transcription

217   us of/ of   *Spectrum* (1958)

219   Knocking around . . . eat   From Milton "Mezz" Mezzrow and Bernard
Wolfe, *Really the Blues* (New York, 1946), p. 53.
    The text was changed with the 1963 printing to read as the source, although
two minor punctuation differences remained. In keeping with the principles for
Book V laid out in "A Note on the Text," I have generally followed WCW's
probable transcription typescript, filed with Za190, and note below the verbal dif-
ferences with the original, the first edition and the post-1963 printings. Most of
the changes from the original are introduced in one of the later Za190 drafts.
WCW's transcription accurately recorded the two minor punctuation differences
not restored in 1963.

Rapp/ the Rapp   IST
be/ begin   IST
know that/ know why   IST
mournful/ moanful   Original and 1963, I follow the transcription.
patterns/ patters   IST
even/ not even   Original and 1963, I follow the transcription.

219–221   Satyrs dance . . . beasts   These lines appear as part of WCW's
1955 poem "Tribute to the Painters," see CP2 296–98 and accompanying note.

220   abstraction/ abstractions   *New World Writing* (1955)

was aware   WCW's typescripts read "was ware," as do all non-*Paterson* printed
versions of these lines. The change is made by an editor on the Harvard
printer's typescript, possibly with WCW's approval.
prey on/ prey upon   *New World Writing*
A letter/ the letter   *New World Writing*

221   a Minotaur/ the Minotaur   *New World Writing*
   Fifth/ 9th   *New World Writing.* WCW realized he had the wrong
      symphony, see note on CP2 494.
   tail/ back   *New World Writing*
   had not/ has not   *New World Writing*
   The *New World Writing* version omits "comforting/ his companions."

221–222   (Q. Mr. . . . difficulty   The first two-thirds of an interview with
Mike Wallace as printed in "Mike Wallace asks William Carlos Williams Is
Poetry a Dead Duck?" in the *New York Post*, October 18, 1957, p. 46. Thirlwall's
note on a typescript at Yale identifies this as an interview carried on the tele-
vision program *Night Beat*, and the annotation has misled some commentators.
But a recording of the program now at the Rutherford Public Library does not
include these exchanges, and WCW is not interviewed there by Wallace. Mike
Wallace confirms, letter to Christopher MacGowan, April 30, 1991, "The *New
York Post* piece with William Carlos Williams was done *only* for print, and *only*
for the *New York Post* and the syndicated papers that carried it."

"2 partridges . . . Denmark . . ."   From WCW's poem "Two Pendants: For the
Ears" see CP2 208.

Robert MacGregor, vice-president of New Directions, in telling WCW on
March 13, 1958, that E.E. Cummings wanted $25 for use of his poem in *Paterson*,
also reported a visit to Cummings to check the manuscript's version with him. "He
said it was not right at all and took it upstairs and then came back with it retyped
somewhat differently. . . . He . . . evidently had seen the interview as reported in
the *New York Post*. He said that what you should have replied was that this was
not a poem at all, 'and it isn't.' I told him that this is all very well for the author
to say, but that you, as a defender of modern poetry, had to defend it, no matter
if you didn't see much sense in it. He wants to see proof, too." This letter, and
Cummings' typescript, are in the New Directions files. Cummings adds an "l" to
the Post's "FalleA" and adds the stanza breaks. In Cummings' *Collected Poems*
(1968) the poem has another six lines.
   Verbal differences from the *New York Post*, all present on early typescripts:

   here's part/ here's a part
   that it is/ that it's

of poetry and the sense / between the essence of poetry and the sense
ignore sense / ignore the sense

I have retained the *Paterson* punctuation. All ellipses are in the source except the final one.

223   a Nativity /   *The Adoration of the Kings*, 1564, in the National Gallery, London.

223   got to / get to   *The Nation* (1958)

225   we have come / have come   All printings. A possible uncaught error on the galleys, I have restored the reading of all typescripts, including the Harvard printer's typescript.

226   The Gospel . . . heart   With the 1963 printing the passage was changed to bring it closer to the King James version, although "Miriam" and two other differences ("to him" for "unto him" and "just man" for "just *man*") were allowed to remain. A footnote added in the 1963 printing and keyed to "Miriam" reads: "The King James version, of course, reads 'Mary,' but it is recalled that Dr. Williams often referred to the mother of Jesus as Miriam. Cf. the Hebrew Miryām as root for both names.—ED."

In keeping with the principles for Book V laid out in "A Note on the Text," I have followed WCW's probable transcription typescript, filed with Yale Za190, and note below the verbal differences with the first edition and the post-1963 printings.

> found / found to be   IST
> public / publick   1963
> privately / privily   1963
> And Mary / But Mary   1963
> sayings, pondering / things, and pondered   1963. The transcription typescript
>   has no comma, added later.
>
> Luke   From St. Luke 2:19

226–227   Dear Bill . . . Edward   From a letter to WCW from Edward Dahlberg, September 20, 1957 (Yale uncat.), the second of two letters from Dahlberg in *Paterson*, see note to p. 28. WCW omits the first page and the final page and a half of the letter. This first page, which asks whether any of WCW's letters to Dahlberg were included in WCW's *Selected Letters* (1957)—none were—is also omitted by Dahlberg in his *Epitaphs of Our Times: the Letters of Edward Dahl-*

berg (New York, 1967) 182–85, although he does include most of the final page and a half omitted in *Paterson*.

The text of this prose was checked against the original letter by the New Directions staff in February 1958, anticipating possible concerns of Dahlberg's, and with WCW's approval; however, some differences remain between the quoted text and its source, as noted below. The origin of the differences is WCW's apparent transcription typescript filed with Za190, unless otherwise noted. There are no verbal differences between the first edition and the 1963 printing.

G.D./ Georges Duthuit
had returned/ had to return
enclose/ inclose
influenced/ could influence

Following "is cheap" WCW added "(in Majorka)" but this is cut on the Harvard printer's typescript.

Dahlberg continued to be no fan of *Paterson*, telling Josephine Herbst of Book V that he "could not refrain from feeling that the only good thing in Williams' last poem is your letter, and all those winged and almost bird-like delights in the honey of flowers," *Epitaphs of Our Times* 158.

227 ". the unicorn . . . background,." The seventh tapestry of the Unicorn series, see note to p. 206.

227 There's . . . to talk to Recorded as WCW's prose by an editorial note on a Harvard typescript.

gets courage/ get courage IST, *Poetry* (1958) Typing error in later typescripts

228 "That slepen . . . yë" Line 10 of the "General Prologue" of *The Canterbury Tales*.

228 beside the purple . . . threads besides/ besides the purple . . . threads besides IST, *Poetry*/ beside the purple . . . threads beside 1963. Possible error on the galleys. I follow the Harvard and earlier typescripts.

229 Godwin WCW's uncle Godwin Wellcome, see A 7.

229 "the river . . . me" WCW paraphrases and directly quotes from his early poem "The Wanderer," see CP1 35, 116.

232 a French/ French *Art News* (1958)

234–235   She did . . . past   WCW's paternal grandmother Emily Dickenson Wellcome, see note to p. 186, and A167–168.

235   Osamu/ Dazai and his saintly sister   As Weaver 218 notes, a reference to the last chapter of Osamu Dazai, *The Setting Sun* (Norfolk CT, 1947).

235   "unless . . . anew"   The end of WCW's 1955 poem "Shadows" (CP2 310) reads:

unless—unless
things the imagination feeds upon,
the scent of the rose,
startle us anew.

BOOK VI (c. 1961)

WCW told James Laughlin on September 23, 1958, that there might be a *Paterson VI* (WCW/JL 226), but these four preliminary typescripts were all that he completed of the project, and they were found among his papers at his death. A corrected version of the four pages was published with the 1963 and subsequent printings of the poem as an appendix. The typescripts themselves are reproduced here to illustrate the extreme difficulties WCW labored under in these last years in trying to compose. As a result of a series of strokes, his vision was poor, and problems of physical coordination frustrated his efforts to hit the intended typewriter keys.

The first typescript is reproduced from a private collection, the next two from copies in the ND Archives, and the fourth—which Mariani (847) suggests dates from July 1961—from a copy filed with Yale Za 191.

Lucy   "The 'Lucy' poem, what memories *that* brings up! What a gal—a heart of gold—common as dirt she was—but Bill and I were very fond of her," Florence Williams to James Laughlin, August 6, 1963 (ND Archives).

Mrs. Blackinger   The name was changed to "Mrs. Carmody" for the printed version at the request of Mrs. Williams.

Acknowledgments

———————— ◆•◆ ————————

In preparing this new edition of *Paterson*, I have been helped by the generosity of many individuals and institutions. At New Directions, Peggy Fox continued the sensitive, invaluable editorial advice that she contributed to the two volumes of Williams' *Collected Poems*. James Laughlin very kindly allowed me to study the New Directions Archive in Norfolk, and his warm hospitality, and that of Mrs. Laughlin, will be a pleasure always remembered. I also thank Norman MacAfee for his careful and informed reading of the proofs and Hermann Strohbach, who is responsible for the elegant look of the *Collected Poems*, for so carefully adapting the design of the original volumes of *Paterson* to the present edition. I continued to draw on the experience and wisdom of my co-editor on Volume I of the *Collected Poems*, A. Walton Litz, and am deeply appreciative of his contributions.

My resources for preparing the edition were greatly increased by the kindness of individuals who allowed me to study and quote from material in private hands. William Eric and Paul Williams provided helpful information on their father, and were very generous in allowing me access to material. Priscilla and John Costello allowed me to study the papers of Kathleen Hoagland, and Elizabeth O'Neil the papers of Marcia Nardi. Thomas Thirlwall again allowed me access to his father's records of his friendship with Williams, including a very helpful annotated copy of *Paterson*. Mike Weaver went to considerable trouble to send me his correspondence with Herbert Fisher. Gilbert Sorrentino and Stanley Stedman were kind enough to write informative letters in answer to my queries, as were Professor John Dollar, Mike Wallace, Allen Ginsberg, Patricia Willis, Miriam Sawyer, Robert Bertholf, Richard Swigg, Terry Halladay, J. Howard Woolmer, Andreas Brown, John Sitnik, Terry Thibodeaux, Paul Mariani, Deborah

Morse, Barry Magid, W. Scott Peterson, Theodora Graham, Howard A. Levin, Pamela McCorduck, Linda Wagner-Martin, Jim Lowell, Albert J. Monack, Mrs. L. A. Post, and Thomas Sweetin. I would like to thank all of these correspondents for their time, their information, and for allowing me to quote from their letters, as needed, in the notes.

The notes to this edition demonstrate something of my indebtedness to scholars who have worked on Williams, and particularly on *Paterson*. Every Williams scholar knows the importance of Emily Wallace's *A Bibliography of William Carlos Williams*. The catalogue of the SUNY Buffalo Williams collection compiled by Neil Baldwin and Stephen L. Meyers was very helpful, as was Paul Mariani's biography of the poet. I came to appreciate anew the ground-breaking work of Mike Weaver, Benjamin Sankey, Joel Connaroe, Ralph Nash, George Zabriskie, Margaret Lloyd, and W. Scott Peterson.

I owe a debt of gratitude to the staffs of many libraries, including: the Yale Collection of American Poetry, Beinecke Rare Book and Manuscript Library, Yale University; the Poetry/Rare Books Collection, SUNY Buffalo; the Houghton Library, Harvard University; the Harry Ransom Research Center, University of Texas at Austin; Kent State University Library; the Lilly Library, Indiana University; the Alderman Library, University of Virginia; the Rosenbach Museum and Library; Special Collections, the Morris Library, Southern Illinois University at Carbondale; Special Collections, University of Delaware Library; I am also grateful to these libraries for granting permission to quote from materials in their possession.

I am also indebted to the resources and staffs of the New York Public Library; the Rutherford Free Public Library; the New Jersey Historical Society Library, Newark; The Bloomfield Public Library; the Paterson Free Public Library, with special thanks to Linda Brown; and the Passaic County Historical Society Library at Lambert Castle. My preparation of the edition was also helped by the following libraries: the Starr Library of Middlebury College; the John Hay Library, Brown University; the Rare Book and Manuscript Library, Columbia University; Fairleigh Dickinson University Library; the Dartmouth College Library; Special Collections, Van Pelt Library, University of Pennsylvania. At the Swem Library, College of William and Mary, Carol Linton of inter-library loan services continued to be a tremendous help, as was my graduate assistant Susan Becker-Welts.

Grateful acknowledgment is made for the following quotations: from *Really The Blues* by Mezz Mezzrow and Bernard Wolfe; copyright 1946 by Milton Mezzrow and Bernard Wolfe; reprinted by permission of Random House, Inc.; and from *Poems 1923–1954* by E. E. Cummings, copyright © 1950 by E. E. Cummings, published by Harcourt, Brace and Co.

An award from the National Endowment for the Humanities allowed me time to prepare this edition, and I am very grateful for their interest and support and for the additional research funds provided by the College of William and Mary.

Additional acknowledgments with the paper edition, 1995: I would like to thank Professor Louis Martz, and Professor Hugh Witemeyer, for drawing my attention to errors of detail in the notes to pages 15 and 184 of the poem, which this printing has given me the opportunity to correct. I have also added a bibliographical detail to the note for pages 87–91, and a version of Williams' "Author's Note" to the prefatory matter on p. xiv, both at the suggestion of Professor Martz.